The Transformative Flow

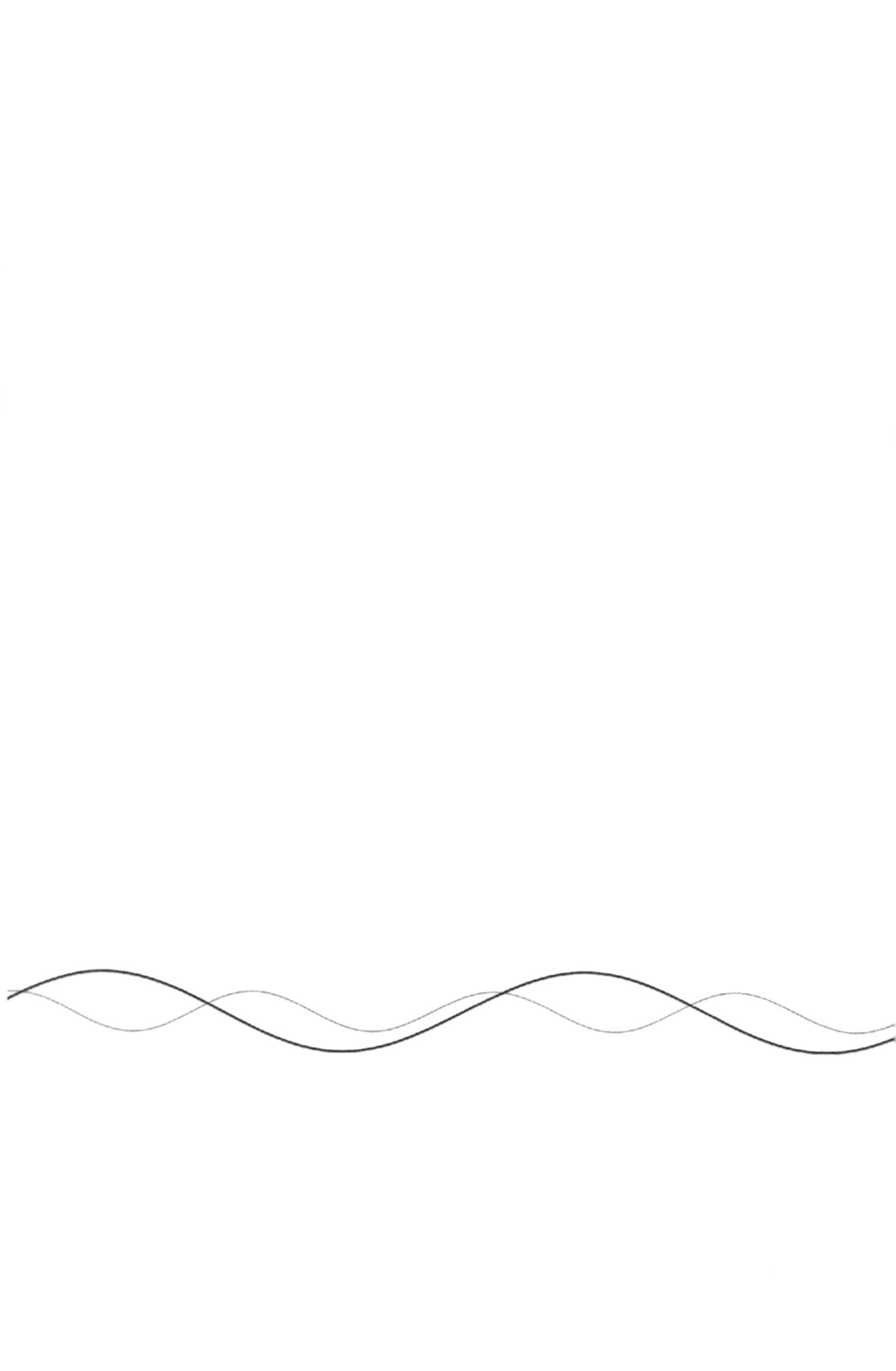

The Transformative Flow

Rhythm as Medicine

Ancient Wisdom to Unlock Creativity, Peak Performance, and Deep Recovery

Carolyn Bentley Wells

IF SO
INCLINED
PRESS

An Imprint of OurGreenMoment

THE TRANSFORMATIVE FLOW

Copyright © 2025 Carolyn Bentley Wells

Published by If So Inclined Press
An imprint of Our Green Moment LLC

ISBN 979-8-9989157-3-4 (Jacketed Hardcover)
ISBN 979-8-9989157-0-3 (Hardcover)
ISBN 979-8-9989157-2-7 (Paperback)
ISBN 979-8-9989157-1-0 (Ebook)
Library of Congress Control Number: 2025910753

First Edition (Hardcover and Paperback)
First Edition (Ebook)

Cover, design, and illustrations by Carolyn Bentley Wells / If So Inclined Press

Disclaimer: This book is intended for informational and inspirational purposes only. It is not a substitute for medical advice, diagnosis, or treatment. Always consult a qualified healthcare provider before beginning any exercise or nutritional program. The author and publisher disclaim liability for any injury or adverse effects resulting from the use or misuse of the information contained herein.

Printed in the United States of America 10 9 8 7 6 5 4 3 2 1

For my daughters, Sasha and Maya

Advance Praise
for The Transformative Flow

"Integrating ancient wisdom and modern science, Carolyn Bentley Wells provides a clear path for the reader to achieve a life of harmonic flow."

–Dr. Irene M. Pepperberg
Harvard-trained cognitive scientist & New York Times *bestselling author of* Alex & Me, *President of The Alex Foundation*

———————

"In luxury events, every detail matters and every decision counts. Carolyn's book offers a framework for sustaining creativity and calm in exactly those moments."

–Sonal J. Shah
Founder & CEO, SJS Events

———————

Contents

Why This Book Matters

We're living through a crisis of rhythm. Burnout is normalized. Focus is fractured. Presence is rare.[1] The Transformative Flow offers a new way forward—one rooted not in productivity hacks, but in resonance. This book bridges science and story, practice and poetry, to help you reclaim your natural state of deep engagement. Whether you're a creative professional, a high-performing leader, or someone simply craving more ease and alignment, this book will guide you to:

- Recognize the hidden cost of hustle and rediscover the power of rhythm
- Understand the neuroscience behind flow and how to cultivate it
- Implement personal rituals and tools for clarity, creativity, and calm

This is not a book to race through. It's a rhythm to return to—a companion for those ready to stop forcing and start flowing.

Author's Note

Dear Reader,

Welcome to The Transformative Flow.

This is not just a book. It's a rhythm. A remembering. A return.

This manuscript was written for seekers, creators, leaders, and feelers. For those who've tasted moments of deep alignment—and are ready to live from that place more often.

It's about flow, yes.

But it's also about energy. Resonance. Green Moments.

And what it means to build a life where clarity, creativity, and calm are not rare—but repeatable.

As you read, I invite you to:

- Pause where something stirs you.
- Highlight what resonates.
- Circle back to the reflections at your own pace.
- Track your own Green Moments.
- Let this book meet you where you are—and move with you toward who you're becoming.

If something makes you feel more whole, more heard, or more energized— I'd love to know. If a sentence stays with you, or a chapter shifts something, please feel free to share.

This book is part of something bigger: A movement of conscious creation, daily alignment, and sustainable personal power. I'm so honored to walk this path with you.

InJoy,
Carolyn Bentley Wells

INTRODUCTION.

The Return to Rhythm

"We don't need to force clarity. We just need to remove what's in the way."

~ / ~

I was sprinting down a field in Norway, thirteen years old, the tall green grass slick beneath my cleats.

Nothing like the hard dirt fields back home in Arizona. Every stride demanded more focus to stay upright, to keep the ball moving forward. The world blurred at the edges, but I could feel everything with piercing clarity—the tension in my legs, the rhythm of my breath, the electric hum of focus that let me see the whole field in one glance.

Then time slowed.

I sensed my teammates' positions without looking. Felt the defender's hesitation before she committed. Visualized exactly where the ball needed to go before my foot connected.

In that space between heartbeats, I wasn't thinking about the game anymore. The game was playing through me.

We were at the Norway Cup—the world's largest international youth soccer tournament—and our Arizona Sunbirds team was representing the USA. We'd finish undefeated, taking home all three cups across Norway, Sweden, and Denmark. But in that moment, the tournament didn't matter. What mattered was the feeling: complete absorption, perfect alignment of challenge and skill, body and mind moving as one.

I didn't have words for it then. I would later learn to call it flow. But on that Norwegian field, I just knew I had touched something real. Something I wanted to find again.

This is a Green Moment.

I found that same feeling behind the lens of a camera, which, notably, began on that same trip to Europe. Years later, as a professional photographer, I became highly aware that capturing decisive moments at high-stakes, once-in-a-lifetime wedding events required the same quality of presence I had known on that Norwegian field. When photographing subjects, especially in uncontrolled environments, I couldn't force the perfect shot. But when I dropped into flow—when I stopped trying to control the outcome and instead became fully present to what was unfolding—something magical happened. My technical skills merged with intuitive timing. I could anticipate moments before they occurred, reading subtle shifts in emotion and light that signaled when to press the shutter.

Whether on a soccer field or behind a camera, these moments shared a common quality—a sense of effortless attention, where action and awareness merged. I didn't yet have words for this state, but I would come to recognize it as a compass, a way of being, and eventually, a path back to myself.

This is what I call a Green Moment—that rare, resonant point when everything aligns. When your breath moves without effort. When thought and action become one. When something inside you softens—and simultaneously sharpens. It's fresh, alive, like the color green, which happens to be the color of the heart chakra where gratitude resides. You arrive fully.

What Is Flow?

Flow is a peak state of consciousness where your mind, body, and energy align in seamless, effortless action. First coined by psychologist Mihaly Csikszentmihalyi, flow is often described as being "in the zone."[2] It's marked by deep focus, a loss of time awareness, decreased inner chatter, and an elevated sense of connection or purpose.

The science behind this state is fascinating. Neurochemically, your brain releases a cocktail of feel-good signals—dopamine, serotonin, endorphins, even anandamide (nicknamed the bliss molecule).[3],[4] These aren't just for pleasure— they heighten learning, enhance pattern recognition, and create deep emotional memory.

But more importantly, they make us feel connected to something real.

Flow states are the architecture of peak performance.[2] Green Moments are the emotional and energetic memory of flow—they're what keep us coming back to the practice.

Flow feels good because it is good. It's not just an optimal state for performance; it's an optimal state for being human.

The Flow Crisis

We're living through a crisis of rhythm—one that's largely invisible because we've normalized its symptoms.

Consider what we're up against:

The average time spent on a single screen before switching tasks is 47 seconds—down from 2.5 minutes just twenty years ago. [7],[8],[9],[10] Office workers manage only 3 minutes of focused work before being interrupted. [5],[6] And 77% of U.S. workers now report experiencing burnout. [11],[12],[13]

Globally, an estimated 301 million people live with an anxiety disorder as of 2025, reflecting a 27.9% jump in global prevalence from 2019–2020 due to the COVID-19 pandemic. Rates have remained historically high since.[14],[15],[16],[17]

This isn't a personal failing. It's an environmental crisis of attention.

As a photographer, I witnessed this inner crisis state firsthand—both in myself and in the subjects I photographed. I would see clients arrive for portrait sessions tense and distracted, checking phones between shots, struggling to be present even for moments meant to capture their essence. At weddings, I watched guests experience pivotal moments through their screens rather than their senses.

In my own creative work, I noticed how fragmentation crept in. The early days of losing myself for hours in the darkroom gave way to a fractured attention economy—editing sessions on a computer interrupted by notifications, creative vision diluted by constant comparison to others' work online, the pressure to produce content rather than create with presence.

These aren't just professional challenges—they represent a fundamental shift in our relationship with attention, energy, and time. We've been told this is the price of modern life. That distraction is inevitable. That burnout is the cost of success. That rhythm is a luxury.

I'm here to tell you that's simply not true.

Flow—that state of effortless attention where you're fully absorbed in what you're doing—isn't something exotic or reserved for elite athletes and artists. It's your natural state. It's what happens when you remove the obstacles to rhythm, not when you add another productivity technique or forcing mechanism.

The crisis isn't that we've lost our capacity for flow. It's that we've forgotten how to listen for it.

My Journey: From Burnout to Flow

I didn't quite set out to become an expert on flow states. My deep and persistent curiosity about them turned into a lifeline when my life collapsed under the weight of perpetual fragmentation.

In my photography career, I had the privilege of learning from extraordinary mentors who understood the power of flow intuitively, even if they didn't always call it that. Phyllis Lane, a former teen magazine cover model turned celebrity photographer, taught me how to create an environment where authentic moments could emerge naturally. Jesh de Rox introduced a group of us to living life as an artform and sparked a movement among photographers, teaching us how to consistently guide couples into states of genuine connection and presence. Tamara Lackey revealed the secrets of capturing children's spirits in their most unguarded moments. Claudio Basso, who had photographed supermodels like Cindy Crawford, demonstrated with such fluidity that subjects forgot they were being photographed. Rassouli specifically taught creative flow through his fusionart painting workshops.

Through their guidance, I further developed and consciously refined a valuable professional skill—the ability to create conditions where others could drop into flow, allowing me to capture moments of authentic emotion and connection, including my own when in full photojournalistic mode. This skill became the foundation of my success as a photographer.

After years building my photography business, I was by all external measures successful—shooting high-profile events, building a reputation for capturing authentic moments, publishing work that connected with audiences. What no one saw was that I was also experiencing chronic fatigue, cognitive fog, and a profound sense of disconnection from work that had once energized me.

One morning, after shooting back-to-back weddings on a weekend, I found myself staring at my memory cards, unable to remember what I had actually captured. It wasn't just fatigue—I couldn't access the emotional memory of moments I had physically witnessed hours earlier. Something in my brain had stopped recording the present moment.

Most people call it burnout. I call it rhythm bankruptcy—the state where you've depleted your capacity for presence so thoroughly that your system begins to shut down.

The conventional advice was clear: take time off, meditate, exercise, get more sleep.

I did all of that. It helped, but only temporarily. The moment I returned to my normal life, the same patterns reemerged.

What I didn't understand then was that burnout isn't just about doing too much—it's about living in a way that systematically blocks access to your natural state of flow. Recovery doesn't just require rest. It requires rhythm.

My healing began when I stopped trying to fix myself and started studying how flow actually works—not just as a peak experience, but as a biological reality that can be cultivated through specific practices.

I observed, researched, and gathered information from hundreds of people who maintained flow despite demanding lives—surgeons who performed 12-hour operations with complete presence, parents who found deep states of flow amid family chaos, executives who made decisions affecting thousands without becoming fragmented. I also revisited what had created those perfect flow states during my soccer days—the physical training, the team synchronicity, the complete immersion in the present moment when everything else fell away.

What I discovered changed everything. These people weren't superhuman. They weren't immune to pressure. They simply understood rhythm—the natural oscillation between focus and release, challenge and recovery, depth and integration.

They had developed what I now call Flow Intelligence—the ability to recognize, access, and sustain states of optimal experience regardless of external conditions.

This book distills what I've learned from these flow masters, combined with cutting-edge research from neuroscience, psychology, and performance studies.[2,3,19,20] It's the guide I wish I had during my own burnout.

The Promise of This Book

This book makes a simple but profound promise: You can reclaim your natural state of flow, even in a world designed to disrupt it.

Not occasionally. Not just during retreats or vacations. But as your baseline way of working and living.

You'll learn:

▸ **The Flow Gateway Protocol**: A step-by-step method for entering flow states on demand, even when you feel blocked or distracted

▸ **The CLEAR Method**: A five-step process for moving through resistance and returning to rhythm when you feel stuck

▸ **The Flow Cycle Framework**: How to honor all four phases of the flow experience for sustainable performance without burnout

▸ **The Flow Manifestation Method**: A powerful approach to creating alignment between your vision, energy, and actions

▸ **The RHYTHM System**: A comprehensive lifestyle design that supports flow across all domains of life

▸ **The CREATES Method**: A seven-step process for accessing creative flow by combining clarity, rhythm, embodiment, and expression. Designed to unlock your full creative potential and help you bring meaningful work into the world.

But this isn't just a collection of techniques. It's an invitation to a fundamentally different relationship with your attention, energy, and purpose.

By the end of this book, you'll understand:

- Why willpower and discipline often fail, while rhythm and resonance succeed
- How to design environments that naturally support flow rather than disrupt it
- Which specific triggers help you personally access flow states most readily
- How to build recovery into your life as a non-negotiable foundation for peak performance
- What it takes to create not just individual flow, but collective flow in teams and relationships

Most importantly, you'll have a personalized roadmap for building a flow-based life—one where you don't just survive your days, but thrive within them.

How to Use This Book

This book is designed to be both read and experienced. Each chapter includes:

▸ **Concepts**: The science and theory behind each aspect of flow
▸ **Stories**: Real-world examples of flow principles in action
▸ **Practices**: Specific techniques you can implement immediately
▸ **Reflection Prompts**: Questions to deepen your understanding and personalize the content
▸ **Callout Quotes**: Core insights to remember and return to

While you can read from beginning to end, the book is structured in four parts and two guides that can be approached based on your needs:

▸ **Part I: Foundations** – The essential concepts and self-assessment that ground everything else
▸ **Part II: Applications** – How flow operates in specific domains like work, creativity, sports, and relationships
▸ **Part III: Mechanisms** – The deeper tools and techniques for accessing and sustaining flow
▸ **Part IV: Integration** – How to build a comprehensive lifestyle that supports ongoing flow
▸ **Integration Guide I: The RHYTHM Framework**
▸ **Integration Guide II: The Seasonal Flow – 108 Practice Guide**

For the most transformative experience, I recommend:

▸ **Read actively**, not passively—try the practices as you encounter them
▸ **Complete the Flow Profile Assessment** in Chapter 3 before proceeding further
▸ **Choose one practice from each chapter** to implement before moving to the next
▸ **Return to sections** that resonate most strongly for deeper implementation

This isn't a book to rush through. It's a relationship with rhythm that unfolds over time. Some concepts will make immediate sense; others may challenge your existing patterns. Both are valuable.

Who This Book Is For

This book is for you if:

▸ **You're high-functioning but fragmented** – accomplishing much but feeling scattered and depleted
▸ **You remember what flow feels like** but find it increasingly elusive
▸ **You're tired of productivity systems** that treat you like a machine rather than a human
▸ **You sense there's a deeper way to work and live** but haven't found practical guidance to access it
▸ **You're ready to move beyond** burnout culture, hustle mentality, and fragmented attention

Whether you're:

▸ A **creative professional** seeking deeper access to inspiration
▸ An **executive** balancing high performance with sustainability
▸ An **athlete** looking to translate physical flow to other areas of life
▸ A **parent** trying to find presence amid constant demands
▸ A **teacher, coach, or leader** hoping to cultivate flow in others

This book offers a framework that adapts to your unique circumstances while addressing the universal principles that govern flow.

This is not for those seeking quick fixes or surface-level productivity hacks.

Flow isn't a shortcut—it's a fundamental realignment that requires commitment and practice. But unlike approaches based on willpower and discipline, flow-based living becomes self-sustaining once established because it works with your nature rather than against it.

A note for those who've experienced something more in flow—moments that seem to transcend ordinary explanation: you'll find acknowledgment of that territory in the Afterword. For now, let's build the foundation.

The Green Moment: Your First Taste

Before we dive into the science and strategies, I'd like to invite you into an experience—a taste of what we're working toward.

Think back to a moment when you were completely absorbed in what you were doing. Perhaps it was while creating something, solving a problem, engaged in movement, or deeply connected with another person.

Remember how time seemed to shift—either slowing down or speeding up. How self-consciousness faded. How effort gave way to ease, even if the activity was challenging.

That was a Green Moment—a point of perfect alignment between your attention, your energy, and your activity.

These moments aren't accidents. They're glimpses of your natural state when the obstacles to presence are temporarily removed.

The practices in this book are designed to help you:

- **Recognize** your Green Moments when they occur
- **Understand** the specific conditions that create them for you
- **Replicate** those conditions intentionally and consistently
- **Extend** the duration and frequency of these states
- **Integrate** the flow experience into your everyday life

The journey begins not with adding something new, but with remembering something ancient—your innate capacity for complete presence.

Let's begin.

PART I.

FOUNDATIONS

~ / ~

"Every rhythm is a doorway to flow."

CHAPTER ONE.

Entering the Flow

"Flow isn't something you force. It's something you allow."

~ / ~

Γhe wedding was meant to be a photographer's nightmare. Rain poured relentlessly across Central Park, turning manicured paths into puddles. The bride's intricate henna patterns needed protection. The groom's family arrived late. The ceremony was relocated – twice.

Yet standing there, raindrops sliding off my camera, I felt strangely calm.

As I framed the shot of the couple under a sheltering elm tree, something shifted. The rain became an asset rather than an obstacle—creating a glistening backdrop and soft, diffused light. I stopped fighting against the conditions and instead moved with them. Time slowed. My awareness expanded to include everything: the droplets catching on the bride's eyelashes, the way her crimson sari contrasted against the green foliage, the subtle shift in the groom's expression as he looked at her.

I wasn't thinking about settings or composition. My technical knowledge had become automatic, seamlessly integrated with intuition. I was simply there, completely present, capturing moments that told a story beyond what I could have planned.

This wasn't just focus—it was flow.

What Is Flow?

Flow is a specific psychological state where we become fully immersed in what we're doing.[1] Time bends. Self-consciousness dissolves. Action and awareness merge.[2]

First identified and named by psychologist Mihaly Csikszentmihalyi after interviewing thousands of people across cultures and professions, flow represents a universal human experience. Chess players, surgeons, artists, athletes, writers, and business leaders all described remarkably similar experiences of optimal performance and profound enjoyment.[3]

As Csikszentmihalyi discovered, flow isn't just a pleasant state—it's where we find our deepest fulfillment and perform at our highest level. In his words: "The best moments in our lives are not the passive, receptive, relaxing times... The best moments usually occur when a person's body or mind is stretched to its limits in a voluntary effort to accomplish something difficult and worthwhile."[4]

Flow isn't just about getting things done. It's about the quality of your experience while doing them. It's about being fully alive in the present moment.[5]

The Core Characteristics of Flow

Through decades of research, scientists have identified several defining features of the flow state:[6]

Complete Concentration

In flow, your attention is entirely in the present. Not split between multiple tasks or hijacked by worries about the past or future. This full engagement creates a clarity of focus that feels both intense and effortless.[7]

The Merging of Action and Awareness

Ordinarily, there's a separation between the doer and the doing—you're aware of yourself performing an action. In flow, this separation dissolves. You become the activity. A dancer becomes the dance. A writer becomes the writing. A photographer becomes the seeing.[8]

Loss of Self-Consciousness

The voice of self-criticism and self-monitoring fades away. You're not worried about how you look, what others think, or whether you're doing it "right." This doesn't mean you lose awareness of your body or surroundings— in fact, your sensory perception often sharpens—but concern about the self temporarily drops away.[9]

Distorted Sense of Time

Time either expands or contracts. A rock climber might experience seconds as minutes during a crucial move, while a surgeon might find that hours pass like moments during a complex procedure. This time dilation relates to how completely your attention is absorbed in the present moment.[10]

Autotelic Experience

The activity becomes intrinsically rewarding—worth doing for its own sake. Even when pursued for external goals (like competition or payment), the experience itself becomes the primary reward. There's a sense of rightness about the activity, a feeling that this is what you were meant to do.[11]

Balance Between Challenge and Skill

Flow emerges in the sweet spot where the challenge at hand stretches your abilities without overwhelming them. Too easy, and you fall into boredom. Too difficult, and you tip into anxiety. The flow channel represents that optimal middle ground where you're operating at the edge of your capabilities.[12]

Clear Goals and Immediate Feedback

In flow states, you have clarity about what you're trying to accomplish, and you receive continuous information about how you're doing. This doesn't require external validation—you can sense when your actions are aligned with your intentions, creating a tight feedback loop that guides adjustments.[13]

Sense of Control

Not rigid control over outcomes, but a sense of agency and capability. You feel equipped to respond to whatever arises. Paradoxically, true flow often involves surrendering control in order to gain it—letting go of forcing a particular result in order to move with what's actually happening.[14]

Flow vs. The Hustle Myth

Our culture often glorifies hustle—pushing harder, moving faster, doing more. We're told that peak performance requires grinding, suffering, and sacrifice. While effort certainly matters, pure hustle without flow is a recipe for burnout and diminishing returns.[15]

The key difference is this: Hustle is about forcing. Flow is about aligning.

In hustle mode, you're working against resistance. In flow, you're working with momentum. Hustle depletes. Flow energizes. Hustle narrows possibilities. Flow expands them.[16]

Consider these contrasts:

HUSTLE MENTALITY VS. FLOW APPROACH

"No pain, no gain"	vs.	*"Right effort, right time"*
Force through resistance	vs.	*Move around blocks*
Focused on outcome	vs.	*Engaged in process*
Urgency and pressure	vs.	*Intensity with ease*
External validation	vs.	*Intrinsic satisfaction*
Linear productivity	vs.	*Cyclical creativity*
Time as enemy	vs.	*Time as dimension*

This isn't to say that flow states are always comfortable. They often involve intense concentration and pushing beyond comfort zones. The difference is that the challenge feels aligned, meaningful, and energizing rather than depleting.

Flow isn't the absence of effort—it's effort applied with precision.[17]

The Science of Green Moments

Remember the Green Moments I mentioned in the introduction? Those instances of perfect alignment that signal flow? There's fascinating science behind why they feel so distinctive and memorable.

When you enter a flow state, your neurochemistry changes dramatically. Your brain releases a powerful cocktail of performance-enhancing and mood-elevating chemicals:

- **Dopamine** sharpens your focus, pattern recognition, and motivation
- **Norepinephrine** increases arousal, attention, and neural efficiency
- **Endorphins** elevate mood and decrease pain perception
- **Anandamide** (the "bliss molecule") enhances lateral thinking and mood
- **Serotonin** creates the afterglow of satisfaction following flow[18]

This neurochemical "cocktail" doesn't just feel good—it creates optimal conditions for learning, performance, and memory formation. That's why Green Moments often become deeply encoded in our memory and serve as reference points we return to again and again.[19]

Simultaneously, your brainwave activity shifts. From the fast-paced beta waves of normal waking consciousness, you move into the alpha-theta borderline—a state of relaxed alertness that enhances creativity and intuition while maintaining focus. This is the same brainwave pattern observed in experienced meditators, suggesting that flow and meditation may be different paths to a similar neural state.[20]

Perhaps most fascinating is what happens in your prefrontal cortex—the brain region responsible for self-monitoring, time tracking, and critical analysis. During flow, activity in this region temporarily decreases, a phenomenon scientists call "transient hypofrontality."[21] Your inner critic literally goes quiet, allowing you to act from intuition rather than analysis.

This is why Green Moments feel so liberating. You're temporarily freed from the voice of doubt, hesitation, and self-consciousness that normally narrates your experience.

The goal isn't to chase that state. It's to train your nervous system to find its way back. Over time, return becomes less accidental and more intentional.

Flow Across Cultures and Traditions

While the science of flow is relatively recent, the experience itself is ancient and universal. Different cultures and wisdom traditions have recognized and cultivated these optimal states for millennia, albeit using different language:

▸ In Japan, this state is called *"mushin"* or "no-mind"—a mental state of complete presence without attachment to outcome.[22]

▸ Taoist philosophy refers to *"wu-wei"*, the paradoxical "action of non-action" or effortless effort.[23]

▸ In Islamic Sufism, the state of *"fana"* describes absorption in the present moment.[24]

▸ Many indigenous traditions reference states of harmony where the boundary between self and environment dissolves.[25]

- In classical Yoga, Patañjali's concept of "*samādhi*" describes total absorption in which the fluctuations of the mind still and the sense of separateness dissolves.[26]
- Paramahansa Yogananda's 20th-century Kriya Yoga teaches rhythmic breath as a swift path to the same *samādhi*—what he called "the airplane route to God."[27]
- Even the Greek concept of "*kairos*"—qualitative time rather than chronological time—reflects the flow experience of time distortion.[28]

These cross-cultural parallels suggest that flow isn't just a psychological construct but a fundamental human capacity—one we've been exploring and refining throughout history.[29]

Why Flow Matters Now More Than Ever

We're living in an age of unprecedented fragmentation. The average smartphone user touches their phone 2,617 times per day.[30] Office workers typically manage only 3 minutes of focused work before being interrupted.[31] Our attention has become our most precious and endangered resource.

This constant switching and splitting of attention extracts a heavy cognitive toll. Each time you shift focus, you leave behind what neuroscientists call "attention residue"—part of your mental processing remains stuck on the previous task.[32] The result isn't just inefficiency; it's a fundamental inability to be fully present anywhere.

The cost extends beyond productivity. When we can't access states of deep engagement, we lose:

- **Meaning and purpose**: Flow experiences create a sense of significance and connection to something larger
- **Learning and growth**: Our most profound development happens in states of focused challenge[33]
- **Joy and well-being**: Flow consistently ranks among the most positive human experiences[34]
- **Creative insight**: Breakthrough ideas emerge when the mind can fully explore a problem space[35]

▸ **Authentic connection**: Our relationships deepen through moments of undivided presence[36]

Flow isn't just a performance enhancer—it's an antidote to the modern crisis of distraction and disconnection.[37] It restores our capacity for depth in a world engineered for shallowness.

The Flow Mindset: From Doing to Being

Accessing flow requires a fundamental shift in how we approach activities. This shift isn't about doing different things—it's about bringing a different quality of attention to whatever we're doing.[38]

The flow mindset involves three key perspectives:

1 - Process Over Outcome

When we fixate on results, we activate the evaluative, self-conscious parts of our brain that inhibit flow. Shifting attention to the process itself—the moment-to-moment experience of the activity—creates the conditions for immersion.[39]

This doesn't mean abandoning goals. Rather, it means holding them lightly while engaging fully with each step of the journey. A mountain climber certainly wants to reach the summit, but flow emerges when attention shifts to the immediate experience of the climb itself—the next handhold, the texture of the rock, the rhythm of breath.

2 - Challenge as Opportunity

Flow thrives on optimal challenge—situations that stretch but don't overwhelm our capabilities. This requires reframing challenges from threats to opportunities for growth and engagement.[40]

When I photographed that rainy wedding in Central Park, the moment flow emerged was precisely when I stopped seeing the weather as an obstacle and began viewing it as a creative opportunity. The mindset shift was subtle but transformative: from resisting what was happening to exploring what it made possible.

3 - Presence Over Perfection

Perfectionism keeps us oscillating between past and future—comparing the present moment against an imagined ideal, analyzing what we've done wrong, worrying about potential mistakes. Flow requires presence—complete attention to what's actually happening now.[41]

This presence isn't passive; it's a dynamic, responsive engagement with the current moment. It's about creating from where you are rather than where you think you should be.

Recognizing Your Flow Signals

While the general characteristics of flow are universal, how you personally experience this state may be unique. Each person has specific physical, mental, and emotional signals that indicate when they're entering, maintaining, or exiting flow.[42]

Learning to recognize our personal flow signatures is the first step toward accessing this state more consistently. Consider:

Physical Signals

- How does your breathing change during flow?
- Do you notice changes in posture, muscle tension, or physical energy?
- Is there a characteristic feeling in your body that accompanies flow?
- How do your gestures or movements shift?

Mental Signals

- What happens to your inner dialogue?
- How does your sense of time change?
- What quality of focus or attention do you notice?
- How does your decision-making feel different?

Emotional Signals

- What emotions typically accompany your flow states?
- Is there a particular feeling tone that signals you're in flow?
- How does your emotional relationship to challenges shift?
- What do you feel after experiencing a flow state?

By becoming more aware of these personal indicators, you create a feedback system that helps you recognize flow as it emerges and identify the conditions that support it.

The First Gateway: Intentional Attention

If flow is fundamentally about where and how we place our attention, then the first gateway to entering this state is developing greater control over our focus.[43]

Here's a simple practice to begin cultivating the quality of attention that supports flow:

~ § ~

THE 3-MINUTE ATTENTION RESET

This practice can be used before any activity where you want to access flow, or whenever you notice your attention has become fragmented:

- **Settle** your body in a comfortable position

- **Close** your eyes or soften your gaze

- **Breathe** deeply for 3-5 cycles, extending your exhale

- **Notice** any physical sensations without trying to change them

- **Choose** one specific point of focus related to your upcoming activity

- **Commit** to giving this focus your complete attention for the next period

- **Open** your eyes and begin with full presence

This practice helps prepare your grounding for flow to emerge.

~ § ~

This brief reset helps transition your nervous system from scattered to centered, preparing, grounding, for flow to emerge. It's not about forcing a particular state, but about removing the obstacles that prevent your natural capacity for immersion.

The Four Doorways to Flow

While flow can emerge in countless contexts, most flow experiences fall into one of four primary categories or "doorways." Understanding which doorways you naturally gravitate toward can help you identify your most accessible entry points to flow:[44]

CREATIVE FLOW
Activities where you're creating something new

KINESTHETIC FLOW
Physical movement and bodily awareness

COGNITIVE FLOW
Intellectual challenges requiring deep focus

CONNECTIVE FLOW
Deep engagement with others

Creative Flow

This doorway involves activities where you're creating something new—writing, designing, problem-solving, improvising music, cooking without a recipe, or developing innovative solutions.

Key Characteristic: Navigating open-ended possibilities with a balance of structure and freedom.

Example: A writer finding that the characters in their novel begin taking actions the writer hadn't consciously planned, or a designer experiencing a solution emerging organically through deep engagement with a problem.

Kinesthetic Flow

This doorway involves physical movement and bodily awareness—sports, dance, yoga, rock climbing, martial arts, or even activities like gardening or crafting that engage the body in skilled movement.

Key Characteristic: The intelligence of the body leading while the analytical mind steps back.

Example: A soccer player instinctively knowing exactly where to position themselves on the field, or a dancer finding that their body knows the next move before their mind does.

Cognitive Flow

This doorway involves intellectual challenges that require deep focus and analytical thinking—strategic planning, coding, mathematics, chess, research, or complex problem-solving.

Key Characteristic: Complete absorption in mental models, patterns, and logical sequences.

Example: A programmer losing track of time while solving a complex coding problem, or a researcher following a chain of ideas that leads to an unexpected connection.

Connective Flow

This doorway involves deep engagement with others—meaningful conversation, collaborative creation, teaching and learning exchanges, or powerful shared experiences.

Key Characteristic: The boundaries between self and other becoming more permeable, creating a sense of shared consciousness.

Example: A profound conversation where ideas build effortlessly between people, or musicians improvising together in perfect synchronicity.

Most people have natural affinities for one or two of these doorways, but all are available to everyone. By recognizing your preferred pathways, you can more intentionally design flow experiences that align with your natural tendencies while also exploring less familiar territories.

~ § ~

REFLECTION: MAPPING YOUR FLOW HISTORY

Before moving into specific techniques for accessing flow, let's take a moment to reflect on your personal history with this state. This reflection will help you recognize patterns and preferences that can inform your approach going forward.[45]

Take a few minutes to consider:

• **Recall a memorable flow experience from your past.** Where were you? What were you doing? Who else was present, if anyone?

• **What conditions helped create that experience?** Consider time of day, environment, challenge level, preparation, physical state, and mindset.

• **How did you know you were in flow?** What specific sensations, thoughts, or feelings signaled this state?

• **Which of the four flow doorways was primary in this experience?** Was it primarily creative, kinesthetic, cognitive, or connective?

• **What has made accessing similar states difficult since then?** What obstacles or patterns might be blocking your natural flow capacity?

This practice provides you with valuable data about your personal relationship with flow.

~ § ~

The insights from this reflection aren't just interesting—they're valuable data about your personal relationship with flow. Your history with these states contains important clues about what conditions, activities, and approaches will be most effective for you going forward.

The Green Moment Practice

As we conclude this chapter, I'd like to offer a simple daily practice that can help you begin recognizing and cultivating flow in your everyday life.

~ § ~

DAILY GREEN MOMENT TRACKING

• **Set an intention** each morning to notice at least one Green Moment during your day—a moment of complete presence, absorption, or flow, however brief

• **Create a physical reminder** of this intention—a green dot on your wrist, a small stone in your pocket, or an image on your phone or desktop

• **When you notice a Green Moment occurring,** take a mental snapshot of what helped create it

• **At day's end, record** a brief note about any Green Moments you experienced, including:

> • The activity or context
>
> • The approximate duration
>
> • What preceded or triggered the state
>
> • How you knew you were in a different state
>
> • How you felt afterward

This practice trains your attention, builds your personal flow database, and makes flow states more accessible.

~ § ~

Over time, this simple practice accomplishes three important things:

▸ It trains your attention to recognize flow states as they occur
▸ It builds a personalized database of your flow triggers and patterns

▸ It reinforces the neural pathways associated with flow, making these states more accessible

Remember: Flow isn't something you achieve through force of will. It's a natural capacity you allow to emerge by creating the right conditions and removing obstacles. The practices in this book are not about adding something new to your life, but about remembering and returning to your innate ability to be fully present.[46]

In the next chapter, we'll explore the fascinating science behind flow states—how they change your brain, enhance performance, and even alter your perception of reality. This understanding will provide the foundation for the practical applications and techniques that follow.

You've experienced the zone. Now we'll build your access point.

~ § ~

REFLECTION PROMPT

• When was the last time you felt completely absorbed in what you were doing?

• What allowed that experiment to unfold naturally, without force?

How might you invite that same sense of effortless attention into your daily rhythm?

~ § ~

"Flow begins not with control, but with surrender to what is already moving through you."

Yoga Connection: *In the Yoga Sutras, sraddha speaks of deep inner trust—a quiet confidence your path is unfolding as it should. Flow depends on this same faith. When you release tension and begin trusting the rhythm of life, focus expands and creative energy moves freely. Sraddha reminds us that flow is not achieved through effort alone but through devotion to the process itself.*

Chapter Two.

The Science of Flow

"Flow feels magical–but it's not a mystery. It's a measurable, trainable, and deeply human neurobiological state."

~ / ~

As a thirteen-year-old on that slippery grassy field in Norway that kept untying my shoelaces, I experienced something that felt almost supernatural.

Playing in the Norway Cup—the world's largest international youth soccer tournament—representing the USA with my Arizona Sunbirds teammates, something shifted during a crucial match. Time seemed to slow down. The tall, vibrant green grass appeared to part before me. I could sense my teammates' positions without looking, feel the opposing defender's hesitation before she committed, and visualize exactly where the ball needed to go.

In that moment, I wasn't thinking about technique or strategy. My years of training—the countless daily two-hour practices leading up to the overseas tournaments, the scrimmages against boys' teams, the indoor arena sessions—had integrated into something beyond conscious thought. I was simply responding with perfect timing and precision, as if the game was playing through me rather than me playing the game.

After the match (another victory in what would become an undefeated 21-game run through tournaments in Norway, Sweden, and Denmark), I couldn't fully explain what had happened. I just knew I had accessed a different quality of awareness and performance—something beyond my normal capabilities.

Years later, as a photographer capturing decisive moments, I found myself experiencing that same quality of awareness. During a particularly challenging shoot in low light conditions, tracking unpredictable movements at a celebration, something shifted. My technical knowledge moved to the background. My awareness expanded. I wasn't thinking about shutter speeds or composition rules—I was simply responding in perfect synchronicity with what was unfolding before me.

These experiences weren't magical, though they felt that way. They were the result of specific changes in brain function, neurochemistry, and perception—changes that scientists have now mapped with remarkable precision.

In this chapter, we'll explore what actually happens in your brain and body during flow. Understanding these mechanisms doesn't diminish the wonder of flow—it gives you the knowledge to access these states more reliably.

What Happens in the Brain During Flow?

Flow feels distinctive because it is distinctive—not just subjectively, but in the objective functioning of your nervous system. When you enter flow, your brain undergoes several significant shifts:

Transient Hypofrontality: The Quieting of Self-Consciousness

One of the most important neural changes during flow is a temporary downregulation of the prefrontal cortex—particularly the dorsolateral prefrontal cortex. This brain region is responsible for self-monitoring, self-criticism, and analytical thinking. When activity in this area decreases, several things happen:

- Your inner critic goes quiet
- Self-consciousness diminishes
- Time perception alters
- Action and awareness merge

Neuroscientist Arne Dietrich, who first identified this mechanism, named it "transient hypofrontality"—a temporary ("transient") reduction ("hypo") in prefrontal cortex activity ("frontality").[1] It's important to note that your prefrontal cortex doesn't shut down entirely—it simply steps back from its usual dominant position, allowing other neural networks to take the lead.

This is why flow feels like freedom. The constant self-evaluation that normally runs in the background of consciousness—Am I doing this right? What will people think? What should I do next?—temporarily subsides.

Without this inner narration, you're able to engage directly with experience rather than your thoughts about the experience.

Neural Synchronization: The Harmony of Brain Activity

Another key characteristic of the flow state is increased synchronization across brain regions. Using EEG (electroencephalography) to measure electrical activity in the brain, researchers have observed that during flow, neural oscillations become more coherent—different areas of the brain begin firing together in harmony.[2]

This synchronization creates more efficient information processing. Rather than different brain regions competing for attention and energy, they work together in a coordinated system. The result is a sense of integration and coherence—both in neural activity and in subjective experience.

In practical terms, this means:

- Faster reaction times
- More intuitive decision-making
- Enhanced pattern recognition
- Smoother execution of complex skills

This is why a basketball player in flow can perceive, decide, and act almost simultaneously, or why a photographer can anticipate and capture fleeting moments that would normally be missed.

Brainwave Shifts: From Beta to the Alpha-Theta Border

Your brain constantly generates electrical rhythms that can be measured as brainwaves. Different states of consciousness correspond to different brainwave patterns:

▸ **Beta waves (13-30 Hz)** characterize normal waking consciousness, active thinking, and problem-solving

▸ **Alpha waves (8-12 Hz)** emerge during relaxed awareness, light meditation, or when you close your eyes

▸ **Theta waves (4-7 Hz)** typically occur during deep meditation, drowsiness, or REM sleep

▸ **Delta waves (0.5-4 Hz)** predominate during deep, dreamless sleep

During flow, research shows a characteristic shift from predominantly beta waves to the border between alpha and theta waves—a pattern associated with heightened creativity, intuition, and receptivity while maintaining alertness.

This alpha-theta border state is significant because it combines the relaxed receptivity of alpha with the creative access to subconscious material of theta. It's the same brainwave pattern observed during "Eureka!" moments of insight and in experienced meditators during deep practice.

Interestingly, this shift helps explain why flow often feels simultaneously energizing and relaxing. You're alert and engaged, but without the mental tension that accompanies normal beta-dominant thinking.

The Neurochemistry of Flow: Your Brain on Flow

Beyond electrical activity, flow involves a complex cascade of neurochemicals—what Steven Kotler calls the "flow cocktail." This potent mixture includes:

Dopamine: The Motivation and Focus Molecule

During flow, your brain releases dopamine—a neurotransmitter associated with pleasure, motivation, and learning. Dopamine:

- Narrows your attention to the task at hand
- Enhances pattern recognition
- Creates a sense of enjoyment in the activity itself
- Strengthens neural connections, facilitating learning

This dopamine release helps explain the intrinsic motivation aspect of flow—why activities become rewarding for their own sake rather than for external rewards.

Norepinephrine: The Performance Enhancer

This excitatory neurotransmitter increases during flow, creating:

- Heightened alertness and arousal
- Faster processing speed
- Enhanced emotional control
- Increased pain tolerance

The careful balance of norepinephrine contributes to the sense of being "in the zone"—alert and energized but not anxious or overwhelmed.

Endorphins: The Natural Euphoria

Particularly in flow states involving physical activity, your brain releases endorphins—natural opioids that:

- Reduce pain perception
- Create feelings of euphoria
- Dampen stress responses
- Enhance pleasure

This is why athletes sometimes report pushing through pain without noticing it during flow, or why hours of demanding creative work can feel pleasurable rather than exhausting.

Anandamide: The Bliss Molecule

Named after the Sanskrit word "ananda" (bliss), this endocannabinoid:

- Elevates mood

- Enhances lateral thinking and creativity
- Increases pattern recognition
- Promotes feelings of unity and connection

Anandamide helps explain the boundless creativity and novel connections that often emerge during flow.

Serotonin: The Satisfaction Neurotransmitter

While serotonin's role during flow is more complex, it appears to contribute to the afterglow of flow experiences, creating:

- Feelings of accomplishment and wellbeing
- Reduced anxiety
- Improved mood stability
- Enhanced social connection

This neurochemical cocktail doesn't just feel good—it creates optimal conditions for performance, learning, and creativity. It's a state your brain evolved to enter when complete focus and optimal functioning were necessary for survival or advancement.

Time Distortion and Identity Dissolution

Two of the most fascinating aspects of flow are how it changes your perception of time and self. These phenomena are directly linked to the neural mechanisms we've discussed.

The Warping of Time

Almost everyone who experiences flow reports some alteration in time perception—either time seeming to slow down, speed up, or simply drop away from awareness altogether. This isn't merely a subjective illusion; it reflects actual changes in how your brain processes temporal information.

Time perception is primarily managed by the prefrontal cortex— specifically the dorsolateral prefrontal cortex. When this region becomes less active during transient hypofrontality, your normal time-keeping mechanisms are disrupted.

This explains why:

- A rock climber might experience seconds stretching into minutes during a critical move
- A surgeon might perform a four-hour operation that subjectively feels like just one hour
- A writer might look up after what feels like minutes to discover hours have passed

These time distortions aren't random—they typically enhance performance in context-specific ways. When rapid decisions are needed (as in sports or emergency situations), time often seems to slow, allowing for more detailed perception and response. When sustained creative work benefits from uninterrupted focus (as in writing or problem-solving), time often seems to compress, allowing for extended periods of engagement.

The Hard Problem: Time in Flow

Neuroscience can explain altered time perception in flow—reduced prefrontal cortex activity disrupts normal time-keeping mechanisms. But this raises philosopher David Chalmers' "hard problem of consciousness": how do physical processes create subjective experience?

When time feels non-linear in flow—not just faster or slower, but somehow simultaneous or accessible in unusual ways—are you misperceiving due to brain changes? Or briefly accessing time as it actually is beyond our normal perceptual filters?

Yogananda described the "eternal now" where all moments exist simultaneously. Modern physics acknowledges time's malleability, especially at quantum scales. Whether flow reveals reality more accurately or distorts it remains genuinely unknown.

The practices work either way. The mystery invites investigation.

The Dissolution of Self

The second profound perceptual shift involves your sense of self. In everyday consciousness, you maintain a clear boundary between "self" and "other"—between the subject having an experience and the object being experienced. In flow, this boundary becomes more permeable.

This shift relates to reduced activity in the Default Mode Network (DMN)—a brain network active when you're thinking about yourself, remembering the past, or imagining the future. When the DMN quiets down during flow, your normal self-referential processing diminishes.

The result isn't the complete loss of self, but rather a transformation in how you experience selfhood:

▸   Self-consciousness is replaced by expanded awareness
▸   The sense of doing is replaced by a sense of happening
▸   The feeling of effort gives way to a feeling of effortlessness

Athletes describe this as "becoming one with the mountain" or "letting the game play through you." Musicians talk about becoming the music.

This shift in self-experience isn't mystical—it's a natural capacity of your nervous system under specific conditions. When the brain regions responsible for maintaining rigid self-boundaries become less dominant, you experience a more fluid, connected relationship with your activity and environment.

Why Flow Enhances Learning and Performance

Beyond the subjective experience, flow creates ideal conditions for both peak performance and accelerated learning. This happens through several mechanisms:

1. Attention Density

In flow, your complete focus creates what neuroscientists call high "attention density"—intense concentration on a limited stimulus field. This concentrated attention literally changes the physical structure of your brain through neuroplasticity.[7]

When neurons fire together repeatedly (as they do during focused attention), the connections between them strengthen. This is often summarized as "neurons that fire together, wire together"—a principle known as Hebbian learning.

The intense focus characteristic of flow creates ideal conditions for this neural strengthening, which is why skills often improve rapidly during flow sessions.

2. Implicit Learning Systems

Your brain has two primary learning systems:

▸ **Explicit learning**: Conscious, analytical, verbal, and effortful—mediated by the prefrontal cortex
▸ **Implicit learning**: Unconscious, intuitive, non-verbal, and effortless—mediated by deeper brain structures including the basal ganglia and cerebellum

Flow shifts activity from explicit to implicit systems, activating what is sometimes called "muscle memory" or "embodied knowledge."[8] This shift allows you to perform complex skills without conscious deliberation—like driving a car without thinking about every movement, or a musician playing difficult passages automatically.

The reduced activity in the prefrontal cortex during flow essentially gets the analytical mind out of the way, allowing these more efficient implicit systems to take over.

3. Optimal Arousal for Performance

Performance in any domain follows an inverted U-shaped curve in relation to arousal level:

▸ Too little arousal leads to disengagement and boredom
▸ Too much arousal leads to anxiety and impaired function
▸ The "just right" middle represents optimal performance conditions

The neurochemical profile of flow—with balanced dopamine and norepinephrine, along with stress-reducing endorphins and anandamide— creates this optimal arousal state. You're alert and energized without being anxious or overthinking.

4. Enhanced Pattern Recognition

The neurochemical and brainwave changes during flow enhance your ability to recognize patterns and make novel connections. Dopamine increases pattern recognition, while the alpha-theta brainwave state facilitates connections between previously unrelated ideas.

This is why creative insights and elegant solutions often emerge during flow—your brain is literally processing information differently, seeing connections that might be missed in normal consciousness.

5. Motivation-Learning Feedback Loop

Finally, flow creates a positive feedback loop between motivation and learning:

- The intrinsic reward of the flow state (via dopamine and endorphins) increases your motivation to engage in the activity
- Increased engagement leads to more practice
- More practice leads to skill improvement
- Skill improvement allows you to take on greater challenges
- Greater challenges that match your new skill level trigger more flow

This self-reinforcing cycle explains why flow activities often become passions that people pursue with remarkable dedication. The state itself is so rewarding that it motivates continued engagement, leading to mastery over time.

Flow in the Body: Beyond the Brain

While we've focused primarily on the brain, flow isn't just a neural phenomenon—it involves your entire nervous system and physiology:

Heart Rate Variability and Flow

Heart Rate Variability (HRV)—the variation in time between heartbeats— is a key indicator of autonomic nervous system function2. Research shows that during flow:

- HRV often moves into a coherent pattern

- The sympathetic (activation) and parasympathetic (relaxation) branches of your nervous system find optimal balance
- Your cardiovascular system operates more efficiently

This physiological coherence contributes to the sense of energized calm characteristic of flow states.[12]

Respiration and Flow

Breathing patterns typically shift during flow, moving toward what researchers call "resonant breathing"—a rate of about 5-7 breaths per minute that maximizes HRV coherence and gas exchange efficiency.

This optimal breathing happens naturally in flow states, but can also be deliberately cultivated to help induce flow (as we'll explore in later chapters).

Muscle Tension Optimization

In flow, muscle tension reaches an optimal state—enough tension to support necessary movement and posture, but without excess tension that would waste energy or restrict movement[14].

Athletes call this "being loose but not loose"—a state of readiness without rigidity. Musicians describe it as "relaxed technique." This optimized muscle tone contributes to the sense of effortlessness in flow.

The Neuroscience of Flow Triggers

Understanding the neural mechanics of flow raises an important question: How do we activate these mechanisms intentionally? Research has identified several reliable "triggers" that help initiate the neurological shifts associated with flow:

1. Challenge-Skill Balance

When you engage in an activity that stretches your abilities without overwhelming them (typically about 4% beyond your current skill level), your brain responds with increased focus and engagement. This optimal challenge:

- Raises dopamine and norepinephrine to attention-enhancing levels

- ▸ Creates the right conditions for transient hypofrontality
- ▸ Activates both problem-solving and skill execution networks

2. Clear Goals and Immediate Feedback

When your brain knows precisely what it's aiming for and can tell how it's doing, uncertainty is reduced. This:

- ▸ Decreases activity in the analytical prefrontal cortex
- ▸ Allows attention to focus completely on the task
- ▸ Creates the conditions for implicit learning systems to activate

3. Novelty, Complexity, and Unpredictability

Novel situations, complex challenges, or unpredictable environments trigger the brain's orienting response—a state of heightened awareness and information processing. This:

- ▸ Increases dopamine release
- ▸ Enhances pattern recognition
- ▸ Creates the focused attention that precedes flow

4. Deep Embodiment

Activities involving multiple sensory streams and coordinated physical movement engage larger portions of your nervous system, creating the conditions for neural synchronization. This is why flow often emerges more readily in embodied activities like sports, dance, or hands-on creation.

5. Risk (Real or Perceived)

When you perceive an element of risk—whether physical risk in adventure sports or social risk in creative expression—your brain responds with:

- ▸ Heightened focus
- ▸ Increased adrenaline and dopamine
- ▸ Suppression of non-essential processes (including self- consciousness)

These triggers don't guarantee flow, but they significantly increase the probability of these neural mechanisms activating. In later chapters, we'll explore how to deliberately incorporate these triggers into your activities to enhance flow access.

The Individual Flow Profile: Why Your Experience is Unique

While the fundamental mechanisms of flow are universal, how these states manifest for you personally depends on your unique neurological makeup, which is influenced by:

Neurochemical Baseline and Sensitivity

Each person has different baseline levels of neurotransmitters like dopamine and serotonin, as well as varying sensitivity to changes in these chemicals. This affects:

- How easily you enter flow
- Which types of activities most reliably trigger flow for you
- The subjective quality of your flow experiences

Personality and Cognitive Style

Research suggests that certain personality traits correlate with flow proneness:

- **Autotelic personality**: A natural enjoyment of challenge and engagement
- **Openness to experience**: Willingness to explore new activities and perspectives
- **Need for cognition**: Enjoyment of thinking and problem- solving
- **Absorption capacity**: Ability to become completely engaged in experiences

Nervous System Regulation Capacity

Your autonomic nervous system has its own unique patterns of activation and regulation, affecting:

▸ How quickly you can shift into flow-conducive states
▸ Your resilience in maintaining flow amid distractions
▸ The intensity of flow states you can comfortably experience

This individual variation explains why some people find flow most easily through physical activities, others through creative expression, others through analytical problem-solving, and still others through interpersonal connection.

Understanding your personal flow profile—which we'll explore more deeply in the next chapter—allows you to work with your unique neurological makeup rather than against it.

Beyond Peak Moments: The Flow Lifestyle

Flow isn't limited to occasional peak experiences. With the right conditions and practices, these states can become more accessible and integrated into your daily life.

Research at the Flow Research Collective and other institutions has found that people who experience flow regularly show:

▸ Higher levels of overall well-being
▸ Greater resilience to stress
▸ Accelerated skill development
▸ More consistent creative output
▸ Stronger sense of meaning and purpose

The neural mechanisms of flow aren't reserved for extraordinary circumstances or exceptional individuals. They represent natural capacities of your nervous system that can be systematically cultivated.

As you continue through this book, remember that the practices and principles we'll explore aren't creating something artificial—they're helping you access what your nervous system is already designed to do under the right conditions.

"Flow isn't a rare accident—it's a biological signature of presence."

Understanding the science of flow doesn't diminish its wonder—it gives you the knowledge to work with your nervous system rather than against it. In the next chapter, we'll build on this foundation by helping you discover your unique Flow Profile—the personal patterns, preferences, and pathways that shape your relationship with flow.

~ § ~

REFLECTION: YOUR BRAIN ON FLOW

Before moving on, take a moment to reflect on your own experiences in light of what you've learned:

• **Think about a recent flow experience.** Based on what you now know about the neuroscience, what mechanisms were likely at work? Did you notice time distortion, self- consciousness fading, or any other classic flow markers?

• **Which flow triggers seem most relevant** to your experiences? Are you more responsive to challenge, risk, novelty, or embodiment as entry points to flow?

• **Consider your personal neurological tendencies**. Are you naturally more prone to flow during physical activity, creative work, analytical problems, or social connection? How might this reflect your unique neural makeup?

• **How might you apply this understanding** to design more flow-conducive conditions in your life and work?

This practice provides you with a chance to reflect on how to work with your nervous system to find flow.

~ § ~

"The brain is an instrument of rhythm—train it gently, and it will play the song of focus."

Yoga Connection: *Patanjali described the ideal posture as sthira sukham asanam—a balance of steadiness (sthira) and ease (sukha). That same harmony defines the mind's optimal state for flow: stability of attention paired with relaxation and effort. When you bring equal parts focus and softness to your work or meditation, the nervous system finds coherence, and awareness becomes both alert and serene.*

Chapter Three.

The Flow Profile Assessment

Discover your Unique "Flow Fingerprint"

~ / ~

Your flow isn't one-size-fits-all.

We each have a unique "flow fingerprint" — the way we enter, sustain, and return to our best states of focus, creativity, and ease. Knowing yours can completely change how you apply the strategies in this book.

In addition to printing a static version here, I've created an interactive Flow Type Quiz you can take in just 5-10 minutes on your phone, tablet, or computer. You'll get instant results, plus a personalized action guide with the practices from this book that will give you the biggest results fastest.

Take your quiz online now:

TheTransformativeFlow.com/quiz

You'll discover:

- Your primary flow type and what it means
- The strengths you naturally bring to your work, sport, or creative life
- Common pitfalls for your type — and how to avoid them
- The most effective practices from this book for you

The quiz is free for readers and comes with a downloadable PDF guide so you can revisit your results anytime.

Start now and unlock the fastest path into your personal flow.

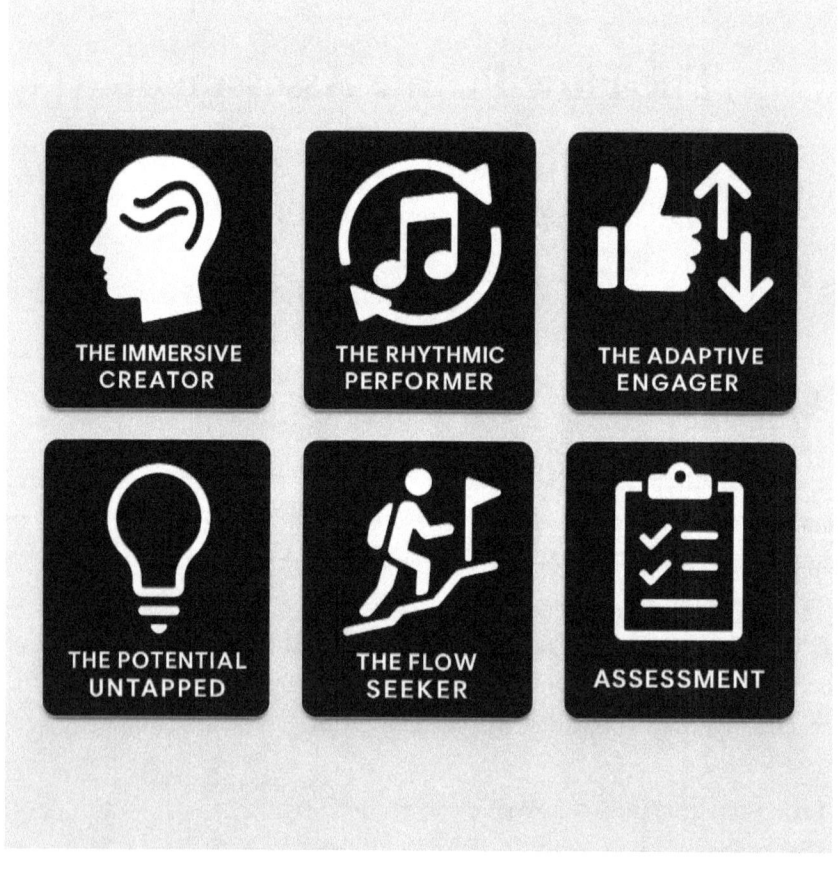

The Flow Profile Assessment

Discover Your Unique Flow Fingerprint

Before beginning your flow journey, take a moment to understand your personal relationship with flow. This assessment will reveal your Flow Type, identify your primary Flow Triggers, and highlight your key Flow Blockers. Use these insights to customize your practice and create a more aligned rhythm in your life and work.

PART I: FLOW FREQUENCY & AWARENESS

1. How often do you experience periods of complete immersion where time seems to disappear?[1]

A.   Daily or almost daily
B.   A few times a week
C.   A few times a month
D.   Rarely, maybe a few times a year
E.   I'm not sure I've ever experienced this

2. When was the last time you were so absorbed in an activity that you forgot to eat or didn't notice hours passing?[1]

A.   Within the past few days
B.   Within the past few weeks
C.   Within the past few months
D.   More than a year ago
E.   I can't recall a specific instance

3. After deep engagement in work or a creative activity, I typically

feel:[2]

A. Energized and fulfilled, even if physically tired
B. Satisfied but depleted
C. Mentally exhausted
D. Anxious about whether my output was good enough
E. Relieved it's over

4. When faced with a challenging task that requires my full attention, I:[1]

A. Look forward to it as an opportunity to get into the zone
B. Feel confident I can handle it with some focused effort
C. Vacillate between confidence and doubt
D. Feel nervous and often procrastinate
E. Try to delegate it or find a way around it

5. I would describe my relationship with deep focus as:[3]

A. Natural and accessible – I drop in easily
B. Available when I create the right conditions
C. Inconsistent – sometimes I can access it, sometimes not
D. Elusive – I know what it feels like but rarely achieve it
E. Foreign – I'm almost always at least somewhat distracted

PART II: YOUR FLOW ENVIRONMENT

6. My workspace or creative environment is:[6]

A. Intentionally designed to support my focus and creativity
B. Generally conducive to concentration with minor distractions
C. Varies widely in its suitability depending on the day
D. Often chaotic or distracting
E. Hostile to deep work (constant interruptions, noise, etc.)

7. When I need to concentrate deeply, I prefer:[3]

A. Complete silence
B. Ambient background noise (coffee shop, etc.)
C. Instrumental music
D. Music with lyrics
E. It doesn't make much difference to me

8. My relationship with digital devices during focused work is:[3]

A. I systematically eliminate digital distractions (notification off, phone away)
B. I try to minimize interruptions but keep devices accessible
C. I intend to stay focused but often get pulled into checking email/messages
D. I frequently multitask between focused work and device usage
E. My devices are a constant companion and source of interruption

9. The time of day when I tend to find the deepest focus is:[9]

A. Early morning
B. Late morning to midday
C. Afternoon
D. Evening
E. Late night

10. My physical environment affects my ability to concentrate:[6]

A. Profoundly – I'm very sensitive to my surroundings
B. Significantly – I need certain conditions to focus well
C. Moderately – I notice it but can usually adapt
D. Minimally – I can focus in most environments if necessary
E. Hardly at all – I can tune out almost anything

PART III: FLOW ACTIVITIES & DOMAINS

11. I most easily lose track of time when I am:[1]

A.   Engaged in creative expression (art, music, writing, etc.)
B.   Solving complex problems or puzzles
C.   In physical motion (sports, dance, yoga, etc.)
D.   In deep conversation or teaching
E.   Absorbed in reading or learning

12. When working on a challenging project, I find flow most often when:[1]

A.   I have complete autonomy and ownership
B.   I have clear guidelines but creative freedom within them
C.   I'm collaborating with others who share my passion
D.   I'm working against a deadline or with some pressure
E.   I have very explicit step-by-step direction

13. The types of challenges that engage me most deeply are:[1]

A.   Creative challenges that require invention or expression
B.   Intellectual puzzles that require analysis and problem-solving
C.   Physical challenges that require bodily skill and presence
D.   Social challenges that involve understanding or connecting with others
E.   Organizational challenges that require creating structure from chaos

14. When I'm in flow, I'm most likely to be:[1]

A.   Alone in a personally curated environment
B.   Alone but in a shared space (library, coffee shop, co-working)
C.   Working alongside others on individual tasks
D.   Actively collaborating with a partner or small team
E.   Part of a larger group with shared focus (performance, game, etc.)

15. My most consistent flow experiences have happened during:[1]

A. Professional work or study

B. Creative hobbies or personal projects

C. Physical activities or movement

D. Social connection or communication

E. Contemplative practices (meditation, journaling, etc.)

PART IV: FLOW BLOCKERS & CHALLENGES

16. The factor that most commonly disrupts my focus is:[3]

A. External interruptions and distractions

B. Internal thought spirals or worry

C. Physical discomfort or restlessness

D. Boredom or lack of challenge

E. Overwhelm or excessive challenge

17. When I struggle to find flow, it's often because:[3]

A. I haven't created the right environmental conditions

B. I'm emotionally preoccupied or stressed

C. I'm physically depleted or unwell

D. I don't find meaning or purpose in the task

E. I'm afraid of failure or judgment

18. After a period of intense productivity or creativity, I typically:[3]

A. Feel energized and eager to continue

B. Feel satisfied and naturally move to rest

C. Push through fatigue to accomplish more

D. Feel empty or flat and seek stimulation

E. Crash completely and require extended recovery

19. When facing an important deadline or performance, my focus

typically:[3]

A. Sharpens naturally – pressure helps me find flow
B. Remains steady – I can maintain my normal rhythm
C. Becomes erratic – alternating between hyper-focus and distraction
D. Fragments – stress makes it harder to concentrate
E. Collapses – pressure leads to avoidance or panic

20. The emotion that most often prevents me from entering flow is:[3]

A. Anxiety or fear
B. Anger or frustration
C. Sadness or disappointment
D. Boredom or apathy
E. Excitement or overstimulation

PART V: FLOW RECOVERY & SUSTAINABILITY

21. After a deep flow session, I typically:[4,9]

A. Take intentional time to rest and integrate
B. Naturally shift to less demanding activities
C. Keep working but at a reduced intensity
D. Try to maintain the high as long as possible
E. Collapse from exhaustion

22. My approach to breaks during focused work periods is:[4,9]

A. Scheduled, intentional breaks that involve movement or nature
B. Taking breaks when I naturally reach a stopping point
C. Working until completion then taking an extended break
D. Frequently interrupted by unplanned distractions that serve as de facto "breaks"
E. Pushing through without breaks, even when productivity declines

23. My sleep patterns and their effect on my ability to find flow are:[4,9]

A. Consistent and supportive – good sleep enables my flow states
B. Generally adequate with occasional disruptions
C. Irregular but I adapt reasonably well
D. Chronically insufficient, noticeably affecting my focus
E. Severely disrupted, making deep focus rarely possible

24. The role of physical movement in my flow practice is:[4,9]

A. Essential – regular movement directly enables my focus
B. Important – I notice better focus when I exercise regularly
C. Helpful but inconsistent in my routine
D. Minimal – I don't notice much connection between movement and focus
E. Non-existent – I rarely engage in intentional physical activity

25. When it comes to balancing different types of activities in my life:[4,9]

A. I have a clear rhythm that alternates focused work, physical activity, rest, and play
B. I maintain a reasonably balanced schedule with some variety
C. I tend to hyperfocus on work at the expense of other domains
D. I struggle to find consistent patterns and often feel scattered
E. My schedule is largely dictated by external demands rather than my own rhythm

Scoring Your Assessment[1,6]

Count the number of each letter you selected and note the totals here:

‣ A responses: _____
‣ B responses: _____
‣ C responses: _____
‣ D responses: _____
‣ E responses: _____

Your Flow Profile

PART I: Flow Awareness & Access

Questions 1-5

- Primarily A/B: **Flow Fluent** – You have natural access to flow states[1]
- Primarily C: **Flow Familiar** – You recognize and access flow sometimes[1]
- Primarily D/E: **Flow Potential** – You have yet to develop consistent flow access[1]

PART II: Flow Environment

Questions 6-10

- Primarily A/B: **Environment Master** – You create conditions that support flow[6]
- Primarily C: **Environment Adaptive** – You work with varying conditions
- Primarily D/E: **Environment Challenged** – Your surroundings often work against you

PART III: Flow Domains

Questions 11-15

- Your highest concentration of responses indicates your primary Flow Domain:[1]
- Primarily A: **Creative Flow** – Expression and creation are your flow channels
- Primarily B: **Cognitive Flow** – Analysis and problem-solving bring you into flow
- Primarily C: **Kinesthetic Flow** – Movement and physical engagement create your flow
- Primarily D: **Social Flow** – Connection and communication activate your flow

▸ Primarily E: **Contemplative Flow** – Learning and reflection are your flow pathways[2]

PART IV: Flow Blockers

Questions 16-20

▸ Your highest concentration of responses reveals your primary Flow Blocker:[3]
▸ Primarily A: **External Disruption** – Your environment interrupts your flow
▸ Primarily B: **Internal Disruption** – Your thoughts or emotions interrupt flow
▸ Primarily C: **Physical Disruption** – Your body's signals interrupt flow
▸ Primarily D: **Meaning Disruption** – Lack of purpose or engagement blocks flow
▸ Primarily E: **Challenge Disruption** – Imbalanced difficulty levels block flow

PART V: Flow Sustainability[4,9]

Questions 21-25

▸ Primarily A/B: **Rhythm Aware** – You honor the natural cycles of focus and rest
▸ Primarily C: **Rhythm Challenged** – You push through without fully honoring recovery
▸ Primarily D/E: **Rhythm Depleted** – Your patterns work against sustainable flow

Understanding Your Flow Type

Based on your overall pattern of responses, you'll fall into one of the five Flow Types. These typologies adapt and synthesize established models from foundational flow theory and contemporary positive psychology.[1,2] Each type has distinct strengths and growth opportunities:

The Immersive Creator

Highest number of A responses

Strengths: You naturally access flow states, especially in creative or self-directed activities. You intuitively understand the conditions that support your flow and actively create them. Your relationship with flow is conscious and cultivated.[1]

Growth Areas: You may sometimes prioritize flow experiences over practical needs or become frustrated in environments that don't support your ideal conditions. Learning to find micro-flow in less-than-ideal circumstances can expand your flexibility.

Flow Strategy: Protect your flow practices while developing the adaptability to find presence even in challenging conditions. Consider sharing your flow expertise with others who struggle.

The Rhythmic Performer

Highest number of B responses

Strengths: You have established reliable patterns that support focused work and recovery. You balance structure and flexibility, allowing flow to emerge within intentional frameworks. You understand your personal rhythms and honor them.[4,9]

Growth Areas: You might benefit from occasionally disrupting your patterns to discover new flow triggers. Your comfortable routines, while supportive, might limit exposure to novel flow catalysts.

Flow Strategy: Maintain your supportive routines while introducing purposeful novelty. Experiment with new environments, challenges, or collaborations to expand your flow repertoire.

The Adaptive Engager

Highest number of C responses

Strengths: You can find flow in varying conditions and have flexibility in your approach. You recognize flow when it arrives and have moderate awareness of what helps or hinders it. Your adaptability serves you well in changing circumstances.[2]

Growth Areas: Your inconsistent access to flow might benefit from more intentional design and awareness. Identifying specific patterns could help make your flow experiences more reliable.

Flow Strategy: Start tracking your flow experiences more systematically. Note the conditions, times, and activities when flow arrives naturally, then deliberately replicate these conditions.

The Potential Untapped

Highest number of D responses

Strengths: You recognize the experience of flow and have had meaningful experiences with it, though they may be infrequent. You have a sense that more is possible and are motivated to develop greater access to flow states.6

Growth Areas: Environmental factors, internal blocks, or lack of structure may be limiting your flow experiences. Learning specific techniques to address your primary blockers will expand your access.

Flow Strategy: Focus on removing obstacles rather than chasing peak experiences. Begin with small, regular periods of distraction-free focus on activities that naturally engage you.

The Flow Seeker

THE FLOW
SEEKER

Highest number of E responses

Strengths: You're at the beginning of your flow journey with the most room for transformation. You likely have experienced flow without recognizing it or naming it, and have untapped potential for developing this capacity.[3]

Growth Areas: Your relationship with focus, presence, and immersion may need foundational development. Starting with basic attention practices will build your capacity.

Flow Strategy: Begin with short periods (10-15 minutes) of completely undistracted focus on a single, engaging activity. Build gradually, noticing shifts in your experience of time and self-awareness.

Your Personalized Flow Prescription

Based on your primary Flow Type and dominant Flow Blockers, here's your customized approach:[4,6,9]

For Immersive Creators:[1]

THE IMMERSIVE CREATOR

- ▸ **Morning Practice**: Begin your day with your preferred creative ritual for 20-30 minutes before engaging with devices
- ▸ **Environmental Design**: Invest in creating multiple spaces that support different types of flow
- ▸ **Expansion Challenge**: Practice finding "micro-flow" in traditionally non-flow activities (meetings, errands, transitions)

For Rhythmic Performers:[9]

THE RHYTHMIC PERFORMER

- ▸ **Block Protection**: Guard your established flow periods vigilantly while experimenting with their timing and duration
- ▸ **Novel Input**: Introduce new influences, environments, or collaborators to your work rhythm monthly
- ▸ **Recovery Ritual**: Develop a specific post-flow integration practice to fully absorb insights before moving on

For Adaptive Engagers:

THE ADAPTIVE
ENGAGER

- ▸ **Flow Tracking**: Keep a daily flow journal noting when, where, and how you access flow states
- ▸ **Trigger Testing**: Experiment with different pre-work rituals to see which most reliably induces flow
- ▸ **Environmental Upgrade**: Improve your primary workspace based on your findings about your optimal conditions

For Potential Untapped:

THE POTENTIAL
UNTAPPED

- ▸ **Distraction Detox**: Implement a systematic plan to reduce your primary flow blockers
- ▸ **Focus Ladder**: Build focus gradually, starting with 10-minute deep work sessions and increasing by 5 minutes weekly
- ▸ **Sensory Anchors**: Create specific environmental cues (music, scent, location) that signal "flow time"

For Flow Seekers:

THE FLOW
SEEKER

- ▸ **Attention Foundation**: Practice basic meditation or single- pointed focus for 5 minutes daily
- ▸ **Flow Hunting**: Try activities from different domains (creative, cognitive, kinesthetic) to discover your natural flow channels
- ▸ **Success Spotting**: Note even brief moments of absorption or timelessness in your day

Remember, this assessment is a starting point for self-awareness, not a fixed categorization.[1,2] Your relationship with flow will evolve as you practice. Reassess every 3-6 months to track your progress and refine your approach.

"Flow isn't found—it's remembered. And what's remembered can be strengthened."

Start with your **personalized prescription** today, and watch as **your capacity for presence, immersion, and rhythm expands.**

~ § ~

REFLECTION PROMPT

• What small adjustments to your space could invite more creativity or calm?

• Where in your home or work environment do you feel most inspired or alive?

• How do light, sound, and movement shape your internal rhythm?

~ § ~

"Environment is the invisible teacher—its lessons whisper through color, space, and air."

Yoga Connection: *Saucha, the first niyama, means clarity and purity—not only of body, but of environment and thought. When you declutter your space, you declutter your perception. A clean environment amplifies energy flow, mirroring the inner spaciousness that supports creative focus. Your workspace, your home, even your mental landscape— each becomes a vessel for flow when intention meets simplicity. Clarity first, then creation.*

PART II.

APPLICATIONS

~ / ~

"Every moment offers a doorway into deeper presence."

Chapter Four.

Flow in Work & Productivity

"You don't need more time. You need more traction."

~ / ~

The conference room was thick with skepticism. Around the polished table sat men who had spent decades in heavy industry—army veterans, engineers approaching retirement, supervisors who had seen every safety initiative come and go. And there I was, barely out of college, the new Health and Safety Manager tasked with implementing what many saw as impossible: transforming a facility with a recent fatality, fresh amputations, and hearing loss cases into a model of Paul O'Neill's legendary safety vision.

Just a few years earlier, our independent aerospace extrusion and aluminum bat tubing facility had been acquired by ALCOA Corporation. We hadn't yet fully adopted the revolutionary standards that O'Neill had established during his transformative tenure as CEO—the same transformation now studied as Harvard Business School's most famous organizational change case. The resistance was palpable. These were proud professionals who had survived dangerous work for decades.

I had started as an industrial hygienist, learning the facility's operations and building relationships across all shifts. By the time I sat at that strategic table as department head, I had earned respect through competence, availability (showing up throughout our 24/7 operations), and a fundamentally different approach to safety leadership. Rather than embracing the traditional "safety head honcho oversight" atmosphere that tends to create adversarial relationships, I had developed something entirely different. I had learned something crucial about flow that most safety managers miss: **sustainable change doesn't come from compliance—it comes from honoring people's expertise while creating conditions where excellence feels natural.**

Within eighteen months, we achieved what seemed impossible: a 70% reduction in injury rates at a facility that was already considered to have "acceptable" safety numbers. More remarkably, we did it while improving quality metrics and maintaining production targets. The secret wasn't stricter rules or more inspections. It was understanding that peak performance—whether individual or collective—emerges when you align human nature with organizational goals.

Beyond Time Management: The Flow Paradigm

My experience at ALCOA revealed something profound about productivity that extends far beyond manufacturing floors. Most organizational approaches to performance are built on the same flawed assumption that dominates personal productivity: **if we can just control external variables–time, process, compliance–we can force better results.**

But human performance doesn't work that way. Whether you're managing a 24/7 aerospace facility or designing your own workday, the fundamental truth remains: **your state determines your output far more than the systems you impose upon it.**

For decades, we've approached productivity through the lens of time management. We slice our calendars into smaller segments, pack more tasks into each hour, and seek efficiency hacks to compress work into tighter timeframes. Yet despite an endless stream of time management systems, productivity apps, and efficiency techniques, most professionals report feeling more overwhelmed and less fulfilled than ever. The problem isn't that these approaches don't work—it's that they're built on a fundamental misconception about human performance.

Flow research reveals that people in flow states can:

- Accomplish in hours what might otherwise take days
- Make creative connections that would be missed in normal consciousness
- Produce higher quality work with greater innovation
- Complete complex tasks with lower perceived effort
- Emerge from deep work energized rather than depleted[2]

This isn't about working harder or longer—it's about working differently. Flow-based productivity doesn't ask you to sacrifice wellbeing for achievement. Instead, it aligns peak performance with optimal experience, creating a sustainable approach to accomplishment.

At ALCOA, we discovered that when people feel genuinely seen for their expertise, when their work environment supports rather than fights their natural rhythms, and when they have genuine agency in how they approach their tasks, extraordinary results become almost inevitable.

The Three Modes of Work

Not all work is created equal. To implement flow-based productivity effectively, we need to distinguish between three fundamentally different modes of working–a distinction that becomes crucial in our industrial transformation:

1. Shallow Work

Shallow work involves routine, low-cognitive-demand tasks that can be performed with divided attention. Examples include: basic email correspondence, administrative tasks, simple data entry, routine meetings, low-stakes decisions.

Characteristics of shallow work:

- Can be performed while partially distracted

- Doesn't significantly deplete mental energy
- Often involves executing established processes
- Limited creative or innovative potential
- Usually feels like "busy work"

While shallow work is necessary in most roles, it's rarely where meaningful contribution or fulfillment comes from. Yet studies show the average knowledge worker spends 60-70% of their time in this mode.[3] In our manufacturing environment, this was the paperwork, routine checks, and administrative compliance that could drain energy from the work that truly mattered.

2. Deep Work

Deep work, a term popularized by computer scientist Cal Newport, involves cognitively demanding tasks that require uninterrupted focus. Examples include: strategic planning, complex problem-solving, analytical thinking, creative conceptualization, and focused learning.

Characteristics of deep work:

- Requires full attention and concentration
- Draws on significant mental resources
- Generates substantial value
- Usually advances meaningful goals
- Often feels challenging but worthwhile

Deep work is where professional value creation happens. It's the thinking, creating, and solving that can't be easily automated or outsourced. Yet despite its importance, most knowledge workers manage less than 2-3 hours of genuine deep work per day.[4]

At ALCOA, this was the precision work, problem-solving, and innovative thinking that our veteran employees excelled at when given the right conditions.

3. Flow Work

Flow work represents the optimal zone where deep work becomes not just focused but immersive. It's **characterized by all the flow state markers we've discussed** in previous chapters:

- Complete absorption in the task
- Merging of action and awareness
- Loss of self-consciousness
- Distorted sense of time
- Intrinsic reward

Examples of flow work might include:

- A programmer losing track of time while solving a complex coding challenge
- A writer finding that words come effortlessly, almost as if the story is writing itself
- A designer experiencing a surge of creative solutions that seem to emerge organically
- An experienced machinist whose hands seem to know exactly how to adjust equipment for optimal performance
- A strategist seeing connections between seemingly unrelated factors

The critical distinction between deep work and flow work is not just the depth of focus, but the quality of experience. Deep work can feel effortful and demanding (though rewarding). Flow work, while still challenging, takes on a quality of effortlessness and intrinsic joy.

Honoring Expertise: What I learned from working with seasoned professionals is that flow work often emerges when someone's accumulated wisdom and skill meet the right challenge. The key is creating conditions where that expertise can flourish rather than prescribing how it should be applied.

Mapping Your Energy, Not Just Your Time

Traditional productivity focuses on managing time. Flow-based productivity focuses on managing energy and state–a principle that proved essential when managing round-the-clock operations with diverse teams.

This shift begins with understanding your personal energy patterns. Unlike time, which is constant and linear, your energy follows cycles that can be mapped and optimized.

Chronobiology: Your Internal Clock

My role at ALCOA wasn't enforcement—it was advocacy.

The facility I walked into had already experienced an employee fatality before I arrived, along with amputations and widespread hearing loss. This was serious industrial work: a foundry with 700-degree molten aluminum pits, tubing operations, aerospace extrusion. They already took safety seriously—you don't work around molten metal without respecting the obvious dangers. But the subtler issues—cumulative strain, fatigue patterns, the way bodies break down slowly rather than catastrophically—those weren't the focus.

As the health and safety manager across two 24/7 aerospace facilities, spanning all shifts, I had an unusual vantage point. I watched the same workers perform dramatically differently at different times. A night shift operator who struggled with complex troubleshooting at 3 AM would handle the identical problem effortlessly at the start of his shift. A morning-sharp supervisor made her worst decisions in early afternoon.

But what struck me most wasn't the pattern—it was how rarely anyone talked about it. Workers pushed through fatigue as if admitting it were weakness. Supervisors scheduled critical tasks without considering when their people would be doing them. The culture said: override your body, don't listen to it.

I took a different approach. Through the ergonomics program I developed and led across four production centers, I became a constant advocate for something radical in industrial settings: listen to your body. Not as soft advice, but as safety strategy. Know when you're sharp. Know when you're not. Speak up before a problem becomes an incident.

This wasn't top-down enforcement. It was more heart-centered than that—helping workers recognize that protecting themselves wasn't about following rules imposed from above, but about valuing their own bodies and long-term wellbeing. I stayed in supervisors' ears too, helping them see that early reporting of discomfort or fatigue wasn't a nuisance but a gift—small interventions that prevented large injuries.

The science backing this approach is called chronobiology.[5] Your body operates on layered rhythms. The **circadian rhythm**—a roughly 24-hour cycle—influences everything from alertness and body temperature to hormone production and cognitive function. Most people peak analytically 2-4 hours after waking, dip in early afternoon (the post-lunch slump is biological, not laziness), rise again in late afternoon, and decline after 9-10 hours awake.

Individual chronotypes vary: "larks" peak early, "owls" hit stride in afternoon or evening, "third birds" fall between. At ALCOA, we couldn't ignore this. A quality-critical inspection performed by an owl at 6 AM wasn't the same as one performed at 2 PM.

Layered on top are **ultradian rhythms**—roughly 90-minute cycles of higher and lower energy pulsing through your day.[6] Each cycle has a peak phase followed by a natural trough. The restlessness that arrives about 90 minutes into focused work isn't procrastination—it's your body signaling time for recovery. Fighting through it costs enormous effort and yields diminishing returns.[7]

At the facility, we noticed operators naturally clustered their breaks around 90-minute intervals—not because we told them to, but because their bodies demanded it. We stopped fighting this and started designing around it.

What we built at ALCOA wasn't just a safety program. It was permission—institutional permission—to honor these rhythms rather than override them. Workers who reported early fatigue weren't seen as complainers; they were seen as professionals managing their own capacity. Supervisors who adjusted task timing based on crew energy weren't coddling people; they were optimizing performance.

The result: morale improved. Quality improved. Injury rates dropped 70%. Not because we enforced more rules, but because we helped people listen to what their bodies already knew.

The principle applies whether you're on a factory floor or at a desk: **you can't override biology, but you can align with it**. The first step is giving yourself permission to listen.

Strategic Work Allocation: The Right Work at the Right Time

Once you understand your energy patterns, you can strategically align different types of work with your optimal states—a principle we applied both individually and organizationally at ALCOA.

Flow-Conducive Work belongs in your peak energy periods—those windows when flow is most accessible. This is your strategic problem-solving, creative work, complex analysis, anything requiring both cognitive depth and innovation. Protect these windows fiercely. Clear goals, distraction-free environment, challenge calibrated to skill level, rapid feedback mechanisms—stack the conditions in your favor. Don't waste your peak on email.

The most dangerous incidents at ALCOA happened when workers performed flow-requiring tasks during their troughs. The solution wasn't more training—it was better scheduling.

Focus-Based Work fits your secondary peaks—analytical tasks requiring sustained attention but not necessarily full flow. Data analysis, detailed planning, methodical research, structured learning. Time-blocking works well here: 25-50 minute focused intervals, minimized interruptions, single-tasking, clear completion criteria. You're working hard but not at the edge of your capabilities.

Administrative Work goes in your troughs. Email, scheduling, routine documentation, simple decisions. Batch similar activities together. Create templates. Set time boundaries so these tasks don't expand to fill your better hours. Your low-energy periods aren't wasted—they're strategically allocated to work that doesn't require your best.

The insight isn't complicated: match work type to energy state. But the discipline to actually do it—to protect your peak hours from the tyranny of the inbox, to trust that administrative tasks will get done in their designated slots—that's where most people fail.

At ALCOA, we built this into shift design. The most cognitively demanding safety-critical tasks were scheduled during each shift's peak periods. Routine documentation happened during natural troughs. The result: better quality work with less effort and fewer errors.

§ ~

ENERGY MAPPING EXERCISE

To discover your personal energy patterns, try this simple tracking exercise for one week:

• **Create an energy log** with hours of your workday listed vertically

• **Rate your energy, focus, and creative capacity** on a scale of 1-10 each hour

• **Note what you're doing** during high and low periods

• **Track flow states** when they occur, marking duration and activity

• **Identify patterns** after a week of data collection

This practice provides you with valuable data about your own energy patterns.

~ § ~

Most people discover surprising consistencies in their daily energy patterns, including:

▸ Specific hours when focus comes easily
▸ Times when creative thinking flourishes
▸ Periods when analytical work is most efficient
▸ Natural dips when recovery is most needed

This data becomes the foundation for strategic work planning based on energy states rather than just calendar slots.

From Theory to Practice:
The Flow-Based Workday

Let's translate these principles into a practical framework for designing your workday around flow rather than just time management:

1. Day Design: The 90-Minute Flow Block Method

Instead of approaching your day as eight continuous hours, restructure it around 90-minute "flow blocks" separated by intentional recovery periods:

Morning Flow Block (your first peak energy period)

▸ Begin with a 5-minute flow entry protocol (breathing, intention-setting)

- Focus on your most important creative or complex task
- Work without interruption for 90 minutes
- Complete with a 3-minute integration practice

Recovery Period (20-30 minutes)

- Physical movement (walking, stretching)
- Nature exposure if possible
- Non-work-related mental engagement
- Physiological reset (hydration, nourishment)

Mid-Morning Flow Block

- 3-minute re-entry practice
- Second most important complex work
- 90 minutes of focused engagement
- Brief integration

Lunch Recovery (45-60 minutes)

- Complete disengagement from work
- Social connection if energizing
- Mindful eating
- Possible brief rest (20-minute nap if appropriate)

Afternoon Focus Block

- Analytical or methodical work matching afternoon energy
- Structured approach with clear boundaries
- Possible use of time-blocking techniques

Administrative Period

- Batch processing of emails and communications

> ‣ Quick-decision items
> ‣ Planning and organization
> ‣ Low-energy tasks

This structure typically yields 3-4 hours of genuine flow or deep work daily— far exceeding the average knowledge worker's 1.5 hours of focused time, and with significantly higher quality output.

2. Environment Design:
Creating Flow Conditions

Environment shapes state. This might seem obvious, but most people design their workspaces for aesthetics or convention rather than cognitive performance.

At ALCOA, our ergonomics program revealed something important: a poorly positioned control panel didn't just risk injury—it prevented operators from entering the focused states where their expertise could truly shine. Physical discomfort is a constant low-level distraction. Your brain can't fully absorb in a task while also processing "my back hurts" signals. This principle applies whether you're operating industrial machinery or sitting at a computer.

Your physical environment communicates what kind of thinking should happen there. Dedicated spaces for different work modes (flow work, focus work, administrative work) create automatic state transitions. Visual cues prime your brain before you consciously choose to focus. Distraction removal—not just minimization but actual removal—eliminates the willpower tax of resisting temptation. Comfort optimization isn't luxury; it's cognitive performance infrastructure. And if you can incorporate natural elements, do—research consistently shows nature connection supports attention restoration.

Your digital environment matters equally. During flow blocks, notifications aren't just interruptions—each one costs 23 minutes of recovery time to return to full focus.[8] Disable everything non-essential. Consider separate browser profiles or even separate devices for deep versus shallow work. Use focus software that makes distraction actively difficult. Minimize on-screen visual clutter. And consider state-specific soundscapes—the right audio environment can accelerate the transition into flow.

The goal isn't a perfect environment—it's a deliberately designed one. Every element either supports your intended state or undermines it. There's no neutral.

Your physical and digital environments powerfully shape your capacity for flow. Strategic design can either remove barriers or reinforce them:

Physical Environment

- **Dedicated spaces:** Create distinct areas for different work modes (flow work, focus work, administrative work)
- **Visual cues:** Use environmental signals that prime your brain for the intended state
- **Distraction minimization:** Remove or hide items not relevant to current work
- **Comfort optimization:** Ensure ergonomics support extended focus periods
- **Nature connection:** Incorporate natural elements that support attention restoration

Digital Environment

- **Notification elimination:** Disable all non-essential alerts during flow blocks
- **App segregation:** Use different browser profiles or even devices for deep versus shallow work
- **Focus tools:** Implement software that limits distractions during flow periods
- **Visual simplification:** Minimize on-screen clutter and visual noise
- **State-specific soundscapes:** Create audio environments that support different work modes

Ergonomics as Flow Design: At ALCOA, our ergonomics program became a bridge between safety and performance. When we redesigned workstations to reduce physical strain, we also enhanced cognitive performance.

An awkwardly positioned control panel didn't just risk injury–it prevented operators from entering the focused states where their expertise could truly shine. This principle applies whether you're operating industrial machinery or sitting at a computer.

3. The Recovery Paradox:
Why Rest Creates Results

In conventional productivity, breaks are necessary evils—time away from 'real work.' In the flow paradigm, strategic recovery drives peak performance. This is counterintuitive but essential.

The Science of Productive Recovery

Research in performance psychology reveals several critical functions of properly designed recovery periods:[9]

Attention Restoration - Your capacity for focused attention is a finite resource that depletes with use. Studies show that specific recovery activities can rapidly restore this capacity:

- Exposure to nature (even brief or via images)
- Non-directed attention activities (walking, simple tasks)
- Sensory shift experiences (music, touch, taste)
- Brief meditation or breathwork

Creative Incubation - Many complex problems are solved during periods of apparent "non-work." When you step away from active problem-solving:

- Your default mode network activates, processing information differently
- Remote associations form between previously unconnected ideas
- Fixed perspectives and assumptions loosen
- Insight and intuition have space to emerge

Neurochemical Reset - Extended focus periods create specific neuro-chemical conditions that eventually degrade performance:

- Stress hormones accumulate
- Dopamine receptors downregulate
- Glucose and oxygen consumption in key brain regions creates fatigue

‣   Cognitive flexibility diminishes

Strategic recovery periods reset these conditions, preparing your brain for the next flow session.

Recovery by Design

Not all breaks are created equal. The most effective recovery activities share specific qualities:[8]

Complete Psychological Detachment

True recovery requires genuinely disconnecting from work thoughts:

‣   Physical removal from the work environment
‣   Engaging activities that require different mental resources
‣   Avoidance of work-adjacent topics or concerns
‣   Permission to fully release work responsibilities temporarily

Active Rather Than Passive

While rest is important, the most restorative breaks often involve:

‣   Gentle physical movement
‣   Nature engagement[8]
‣   Social connection (if energizing rather than depleting)
‣   Creative expression without performance pressure
‣   Learning for enjoyment rather than application

Physiological Support

Effective recovery addresses basic physical needs that support cognitive function:

‣   Hydration
‣   Appropriate nourishment
‣   Movement after sedentary focus
‣   Breath regulation
‣   Posture reset

By treating recovery as a strategic productivity tool rather than time "off," you create the conditions for sustained high performance without burnout.

The Flow Productivity Toolkit

Based on the principles we've explored, here are specific practices you can implement immediately to enhance your workday flow:

~ § ~

1. THE FLOW ENTRY PROTOCOL

Use this sequence before important work sessions to prime your nervous system for flow:

The 5-Minute Flow Entry Protocol:

• **Clear the space** (1 minute): Remove distractions, organize immediate workspace.

• **Center the body** (2 minutes): Three conscious inhales/exhales, brief posture adjustment, release physical tension (tense and relax if needed)

• **Focus the mind - intention setting** (1 minute): State a clear specific goal for the session, connect to a meaningful purpose or value, visualize successful completion.

• **Bonus options for environment optimization** (1 minute): Close unnecessary digital windows/apps, adjust physical comfort (lighting, sound, temperature), activate flow triggers (music, scent, objects), add gentle movement and/or mantra, and/or add a specific action that signals "flow time."

This simple practice can significantly reduce the time to enter flow.

~ § ~

2. THE TASK ALIGNMENT FRAMEWORK

When faced with multiple priorities, use this decision matrix to identify which tasks deserve your flow sessions:

Quadrant 1: Flow Priority

• High complexity/creativity required

- Significant value or impact
- Intrinsically engaging to you
- Benefits substantially from flow state

Quadrant 2: Focus Block

- Moderate complexity
- Important but not necessarily urgent
- Requires concentration but not full flow
- Systematic approach works well

Quadrant 3: Batch Processing

- Low complexity
- Administrative or routine
- Can be handled in blocks during energy dips
- Benefits from efficiency systems

Quadrant 4: Eliminate/Delegate

- Low value relative to time required
- Doesn't leverage your unique capabilities
- Could be automated, delegated, or simplified
- Drains energy without proportionate return

Applying this framework helps ensure your limited flow capacity is invested where it creates maximum value.

~ § ~

From Individual to Collective Flow

While we've focused primarily on individual productivity, the principles of flow-based work apply equally to teams and organizations. In fact, collective flow—sometimes called "group flow" or "team flow"—represents one of the most powerful applications of these concepts.

Creating Conditions for Team Flow

Research on high-performing teams reveals several conditions that foster collective flow states:[10]

Shared Mental Models

- Clear, compelling purpose understood by all members
- Aligned understanding of roles, processes, and goals
- Common language and frameworks
- Transparent decision-making criteria

Balanced Autonomy and Coordination

- Individual freedom within clear boundaries
- Defined coordination points without micromanagement
- Skills matched appropriately to challenges
- Distributed leadership based on expertise rather than hierarchy

Psychological Safety

- Environment where risk-taking feels acceptable
- Open exchange of ideas without fear of judgment
- Constructive conflict focused on concepts not personalities
- Learning orientation rather than performance orientation

Information Flow Optimization

- Right information available at right time
- Minimal bureaucratic barriers to communication
- Rapid, honest feedback
- Shared access to relevant data and insights

When these conditions align, teams can achieve collective flow states where the group's output far exceeds the sum of individual contributions.

The Systems Integration Approach: Beyond Compliance to Ownership

The breakthrough at ALCOA came when we stopped treating safety as a separate compliance issue and started integrating it with existing systems that already had enthusiastic buy-in. Rather than creating parallel processes, we wove health and safety standards into the quality improvement initiatives that were already being measured, rewarded, and celebrated.

This systems integration approach worked because it honored what was already working while elevating standards. We used kanban boards and other Toyota Production System methodologies that the teams were already excited about, simply adding safety metrics alongside quality indicators. When someone prevented an injury through better ergonomic practices, it was celebrated the same way as when they improved product quality—because we demonstrated they were fundamentally the same thing.

Building Psychological Safety for Early Reporting: The cornerstone of our transformation was creating an environment where employees felt genuinely heard and protected when reporting concerns—particularly near misses and small injuries that traditional safety programs often overlook. This was revolutionary in an industrial setting where workers typically fear repercussions for speaking up about safety issues.

The psychological impact was profound. When people no longer feared punishment for reporting, their nervous systems could operate for them rather than against them. Instead of operating from a defensive, survival-focused state that impairs cognitive function, employees could access the clear thinking and pattern recognition that comes with psychological safety. They felt seen, heard, and valued—core conditions for both individual and collective flow states.

By establishing clear protocols that protected people who identified potential hazards, we gained invaluable early warning data for pattern recognition. This focus on near misses and minor incidents—rather than waiting for major accidents—allowed us to prioritize improvements based on actual emerging risks rather than assumptions or past incidents. The data showed us exactly where our attention was most needed, creating a predictive rather than reactive safety culture.

The key was designing the reporting system to be constructive rather than overwhelming. We created efficient triage processes to distinguish between issues requiring immediate attention and those that could be addressed through systematic improvements. This prevented the early reporting culture from becoming burdensome while maintaining the psychological safety that made it effective. Employees could see that their reports led to meaningful action, which reinforced their engagement in the process.

Honoring Individual Expertise: What made this approach sustainable was recognizing that our veteran employees had decades of accumulated wisdom about how things actually worked versus how they were supposed to work on paper. Rather than dismissing their experience, we created frameworks for capturing and leveraging that expertise. When someone with thirty years of experience said "this could be dangerous," we had systems in place to investigate and act on that intuition, even if it couldn't be immediately documented or measured.

The Intrinsic Motivation Shift: We discovered that when people understand the deeper purpose behind safety standards—protecting themselves and their colleagues—compliance transforms into ownership. Instead of doing the minimum to meet regulations, people began identifying improvements and innovations that made their work both safer and more efficient. This shift from extrinsic to intrinsic motivation is one of the key conditions for flow states, both individually and collectively.

Redefining Productivity: From Output to Impact

As we conclude this chapter, it's worth questioning the very definition of productivity. Traditional metrics focus on output—tasks completed, hours worked, deadlines met. Flow-based productivity invites a shift toward impact, energy, and experience:

- Not just how much you produce, but the quality and significance of what you create
- Not just how efficiently you work, but how fully you engage with your work

‣   Not just what you accomplish, but who you become through the process

This redefinition aligns productivity with deeper human needs—not just achievement, but meaning; not just efficiency, but aliveness; not just doing more, but being more present in what you do.

At ALCOA, we learned that when you focus on creating conditions where people can bring their full expertise and energy to their work, productivity improvements follow naturally. The 70% reduction in injuries wasn't achieved through compliance-focused monitoring—it emerged from an environment where people felt valued, heard, and empowered to contribute their wisdom to collective safety and excellence.

The paradox of flow-based productivity is that by focusing less on traditional productivity metrics and more on the quality of your working experience, you often end up more productive by conventional measures. But the true value goes beyond measurable output—it transforms work itself from something you endure to something that energizes and fulfills you.

Honoring Individual Experience and Wisdom: Whether you're leading organizational change or optimizing your personal productivity, the principle remains the same: sustainable excellence emerges when we create conditions that honor individual expertise while aligning it with collective goals. This becomes even more important as we move into creative work— the subject of our next chapter—where the relationship between individual expression and collaborative innovation becomes even more nuanced and essential.

~ § ~

REFLECTION PROMPT

Think about your typical workday:

• When are you most likely to experience flow states naturally?

• What type of tasks seem to facilitate flow for you?

• How might your existing expertise and experience be better honored in your current work structure?

• What one change could you make to better align your work with your natural energy and wisdom?

This practice provides you with a chance to reflect on how to optimize flow states for productivity.

~ § ~

"Productivity isn't about doing more—it's about doing what matters from a state that honors your energy."

Work doesn't have to drain you. It can become the very space where you return to rhythm, where your accumulated wisdom meets meaningful challenge, where individual excellence serves collective flourishing. Let your schedule be an instrument—not a cage.

Yoga Connection: *The yogic concept of "dharana" (focused concentration) teaches that attention is directed, not forced. Practitioners develop the ability to place their awareness deliberately while maintaining relaxed alertness—the same quality of attention that characterizes flow states in work. Traditional yoga sequencing also honors energy rhythms, with more energizing practices (like sun salutations) in the morning and more restorative practices in the evening. More profoundly, yoga philosophy recognizes that individual practice (svadhyada) serves collective wellbeing (seva)–the same integration we see in flow-based organizations.*

Chapter Five.

Flow in Creativity & Innovation

"Creativity isn't something you chase. It's something you allow."

~ / ~

The wedding party had disappeared.

As the photographer responsible for capturing a crucial post-ceremony portrait session, this was the stuff of nightmares. The bride and groom, along with twenty family members, had vanished somewhere in the resort or one of its golf courses—a sprawling 85-acre location with multiple levels, paths, and hidden areas. The timeline was tight, the sun was setting, and the coordinator was growing increasingly anxious.

"We need to find them now," she insisted, reaching for her phone to start making calls.

"Wait," I said, placing a hand gently on her arm. "Let me try something first."

Instead of rushing into panic mode, I closed my eyes for a brief moment and took three deep breaths. I let go of the mental scrambling and opened myself to a different kind of intelligence—one I had learned to trust in critical moments.

When I opened my eyes, I had a sudden, clear intuition: "They're by the water, near the bridge." It wasn't logical for a group that size. We had planned for photos closer to the resort. But the impression was distinct.

"This way," I said with quiet certainty, and began walking toward an area we hadn't discussed using.

Sure enough, as we rounded the corner, there was the entire group, arranged perfectly with the waterway's bridge as their backdrop. The bride looked up, smiled, and called out, "We found the most amazing spot!"

The resulting images became the centerpiece of their album. Had I remained in analytical problem-solving mode—checking the original locations, making calls, following logical search patterns—I would have missed the magical combination of perfect light, composition, and authentic joy that made those photographs exceptional.

This wasn't luck. It was creative flow—a state where intuition, pattern recognition, and spontaneous innovation converge. And while it might seem mysterious, this state follows recognizable patterns that we can learn to access intentionally.

The Creative Paradox: Effort vs. Emergence

The more desperately we try to force creativity, the more elusive it becomes. Yet when we create the right conditions and then step back, ideas often emerge with surprising ease and clarity.

This paradox reflects the dual nature of the creative process—it requires both directed effort and receptive allowing. Understanding this dynamic is key to working with rather than against your creative nature.

The Limitations of Forced Creativity

Our conventional approach to creativity often resembles brute-force effort: demanding ideas appear on command, pushing through creative blocks with sheer willpower, judging half-formed ideas before they have a chance to develop, and expecting linear progress from initial concept to final completion.

This forcing approach activates the wrong neural networks. When we apply pressure to be creative, we trigger a cascade of counterproductive responses: increased activity in the analytical prefrontal cortex, stress responses that inhibit associative thinking, self-consciousness that restricts experimental thinking, and narrowed perception that limits novel connections. The result is often creative work that feels labored, derivative, or technically correct but lacking the spark of originality.

The Flow Alternative: Directed Allowing

Flow offers a different approach to creativity—what we might call "directed allowing."[6] This involves:

‣ Creating optimal conditions for ideas to emerge
‣ Directing attention without forcing outcomes
‣ Balancing structure with openness
‣ Trusting the natural rhythm of the creative process

When we enter flow states during creative work, we access a fundamentally different neurological configuration: reduced activity in self-critical brain regions, increased synchronization between neural networks, optimal neurochemistry for novel associations, and enhanced pattern recognition that enables intuitive leaps.

The result is work that often surprises us with its originality, coherence, and depth—work that feels less like something we produced and more like something we discovered or channeled.

The Creative Flow Cycle

Creativity isn't a single event but a cyclical process with distinct phases. Understanding this cycle helps us work with rather than against the natural rhythm of innovation.

Building on the work of Graham Wallas, Jacob Getzels, and contemporary creativity researchers, we can identify four key phases in the creative flow cycle.[1]

Preparation: Filling the Well

Before creative flow can occur, we need material to work with—the inputs that will later combine into new patterns and possibilities. This is the phase of active gathering: information, skills, questions, immersion in the domain.

Your brain is in analytical mode here—high prefrontal cortex activity, beta brainwaves dominant, focused attention on specifics. You're not creating yet; you're loading the system.

The counterintuitive key to preparation is breadth. When preparing for challenging portrait sessions, I would study not just other photographers' work but paintings, films, psychology. I practiced technical skills until they became automatic, explored locations in advance, and defined what story I wanted the images to tell. This groundwork wasn't the creative act itself, but it created the conditions for creative flow to emerge during the actual shoot.

The principle: prepare widely, not just deeply. The most innovative connections often come from cross-pollinating ideas between unrelated domains.

Incubation: The Power of Stepping Back

This phase defies everything our productivity-obsessed culture believes about creativity. Some of the most important creative work happens when we stop consciously working on the problem.

Here's what's actually occurring beneath awareness: your unconscious mind is processing information, forming new neural connections, weakening habitual associations, integrating diverse inputs. The default mode network—the brain's background processing system—becomes highly active. Alpha and theta brainwaves replace the busy beta rhythms of focused work. Your prefrontal cortex relaxes its grip, allowing more diffuse, associative thinking to emerge.

This is why you get your best ideas in the shower. Your conscious mind is occupied with a simple task, freeing your unconscious to work on harder problems.

Between wedding ceremonies and receptions, I developed a habit of taking 15 minutes to myself—not reviewing images or planning shots, but simply walking around the venue without my camera, observing light patterns, interactions, and spaces. This mental stepping-back consistently led to more innovative approaches during the reception coverage.

The practical applications:

- Build deliberate incubation periods into creative projects
- Engage in activities that occupy the conscious mind while leaving the subconscious free (walking, showering, routine tasks)
- Change environments to stimulate new perspectives
- Alternate between different creative problems
- Respect the incubation phase rather than forcing solutions

Incubation isn't procrastination. It's your brain doing exactly what it's designed to do—connecting dots while you're not watching.

Illumination: When Insight Arrives

Illumination is the "Aha!" moment—when scattered elements suddenly click into coherent form. It arrives without warning: in the shower, on a walk, in that liminal space before sleep. Your brain has been working on this in the background, and now it delivers the solution as a felt sense of rightness, often accompanied by a surge of energy that says yes, this.[4]

Neurologically, this moment shows gamma wave bursts, synchronization across brain networks, and a rush of dopamine and norepinephrine. It's brief but powerful.

You can't force illumination, but you can create conditions that invite it— and crucially, you can learn to notice when it arrives. Many breakthroughs are missed because we're too busy to register them.

While directing a complex multi-person photoshoot, I noticed that my best compositional ideas emerged right after I stepped back from adjusting details and simply observed the scene as a whole. I began deliberately building this "step back and see" moment into my process, often counting to ten while taking in the entire visual field. This micro-incubation consistently triggered creative insights about what was missing or what could be enhanced.

The key practice: create capture systems. Keep notebooks, voice recorders, or note apps always accessible. Insights are fragile—they fade within seconds if not recorded.

Verification: Bringing Ideas to Form

The final phase transforms insights into tangible creative work through deliberate crafting and refinement. This is where the analytical mind returns—but now it's serving the vision rather than blocking it.

Verification requires alternating between intuitive and logical thinking, testing ideas against reality, and accepting the iterative nature of creative work. It's less glamorous than illumination but equally essential. Ideas without execution are just pleasant daydreams.

When editing image collections, I developed a three-pass system: the first pass was purely intuitive, marking images that created an immediate emotional response; the second pass applied technical criteria and narrative considerations; the final pass integrated both perspectives. This approach consistently produced selections that were both emotionally resonant and technically strong.

The challenge of verification is balancing perfectionism with completion. The work must be good enough—not perfect, because perfect doesn't ship.

When Knowing Precedes Knowledge

Many creatives report accessing information during flow that they couldn't have known consciously—solutions to problems they hadn't studied, techniques they hadn't learned, connections between concepts they hadn't explored.

Is this:

- Enhanced subconscious processing surfacing under optimal conditions?
- Access to collective knowledge (Jung's "collective unconscious")?
- Perception of information from outside normal space-time bounds?
- Pattern recognition so refined it appears mystical?

Rupert Sheldrake calls this "morphic resonance"—accessing information through fields rather than individual memory. Yogananda called it "superconsciousness"—awareness beyond brain-based cognition.

The source remains mysterious. The phenomenon is well-documented. Creative flow seems to open channels to information beyond obvious sources.

I've experienced this myself—knowing where that wedding party would be before I had any logical reason to know it. The opening story of this chapter wasn't luck. Something in that moment of stillness accessed information my conscious mind couldn't have possessed.

Whether this represents enhanced pattern recognition, unconscious processing, or something more mysterious is a question I explore in the Afterword. For now, what matters is practical: creating the conditions where this knowing can emerge, and learning to trust it when it does.

Understanding Creative Blocks: Flow Interruptions

Creative blocks aren't simply the absence of ideas—they're active interruptions to the natural flow of creativity. By identifying specific blockers, we can address them precisely rather than struggling against a vague sense of "being blocked."

The Inner Critic Block: Self-Consciousness in Action

The Inner Critic arrives as self-consciousness in action, whispering that your ideas aren't good enough while you're still in the process of discovering them. When your inner critic activates prematurely, it interrupts the generative process, triggers performance anxiety, narrows creative exploration, diminishes risk-taking, and creates self-fulfilling creative failure.

Neuroscience Behind It: Heightened activity in the dorsolateral prefrontal cortex—the brain's self-monitoring center—directly interferes with the neural patterns of flow. This creates the paradoxical situation where trying harder to be creative makes you less creative.

FLOW-BASED SOLUTION:

- Create a "judgment-free zone" for early-stage creation
- Develop rituals that symbolically set aside the critic
- Use timed creation sessions with deferred evaluation
- Practice separating generation from refinement
- Cultivate self-compassion for creative struggles

The Overwhelm Block: Too Many Possibilities

Sometimes creativity stalls not from a lack of ideas but from too many competing possibilities and no clear direction.

Neuroscience Behind It: When faced with excessive options, the brain's executive function systems become overloaded, leading to decision paralysis and increased activity in the anterior cingulate cortex—the brain region associated with conflict monitoring.[10]

FLOW-BASED SOLUTION:

- Create productive constraints that narrow possibilities
- Establish clear creative principles or guidelines
- Use randomization techniques to force decisions
- Break large creative projects into defined segments
- Focus on process rather than all potential outcomes

The Depletion Block: Emptied Creative Resources

Creativity requires psychological and neurological resources that can be temporarily depleted through overwork, stress, or lack of diverse inputs.

Neuroscience Behind It: Sustained creative effort without replenishment leads to reduced dopamine (motivation), increased cortisol (stress), and diminished activity in the default mode network (imagination and association).

FLOW-BASED SOLUTION:

- Design deliberate cycles of creation and replenishment
- Curate diverse inputs that cross disciplinary boundaries
- Create "creative compost"—collection systems for inspiring material
- Engage in completely different creative activities as cross- training
- Prioritize sleep, movement, and nature exposure

The Perfectionism Block: Fear Disguised as Standards

Perhaps the most insidious block, perfectionism wears the mask of high standards while actually functioning as fear—of failure, judgment, vulnerability, being seen before you're ready.

Your brain treats imperfection as threat. The threat-detection system activates, triggering subtle fight-flight-freeze responses that inhibit exactly the open, exploratory state creative flow requires. You're trying to create while your nervous system is preparing for attack.

The antidote isn't lowering your standards—it's separating creation from evaluation. Create in low-stakes conditions: timed sessions where "nothing counts," projects no one will see, deliberate experiments in productive failure. Track and celebrate imperfect action. Use time constraints to override the perfectionist's endless revision loops.

Most importantly: distinguish between excellence and perfection. Excellence is achievable and serves the work. Perfection is impossible and serves fear. Ship excellent work. Let perfection go.

The CREATES Method:
A Flow-Based Creativity System

The CREATES method draws from both scientific research and practices of master creators across disciplines. It applies to any creative domain, from arts to business innovation.

C **Conditions & Container**
Deliberately design the physical, temporal, and psychological continer for creativity

R **Release Control**
Temporarily let go of outcomes to access creative flow

E **Engage the Body**
Incorporate physical movement an(sensory experience in the creative process

A **Access Altered States**
Intentionally shift consciousness through specific methods

T **Trust the Process**
Develop faith in your own creative rhythm over time

E **External Feedback**
Strategically seek input at appropriate stages of creation

S **Sustainable Rhythms**
Build resilient creative cycles of work and renewal
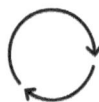

C: Conditions & Container

Creativity flourishes within the right conditions and boundaries. Rather than waiting for inspiration, deliberately design:

PHYSICAL ENVIRONMENT:

‣   Dedicated creative space with minimal distractions
‣   Environmental cues that trigger creative states
‣   Tools readily accessible to reduce friction
‣   Sensory elements that support creative thinking (light, sound, etc.)

TEMPORAL CONTAINER:

‣   Defined time boundaries for creative sessions
‣   Rhythmic alternation between focused creation and rest
‣   Alignment with personal energy patterns
‣   Protection from interruptions during key creative periods

PSYCHOLOGICAL CONTAINER:

‣   Clear parameters for the current creative challenge
‣   Permission structures for experimentation
‣   Emotional safety for risk-taking
‣   Designated "play space" separate from evaluation

Example Practice - The Creative Sanctuary: Set up a physical space used only for creative work. Include objects that symbolize creativity to you, ensure comfort without promoting sleep, remove digital distractions, and establish a brief entry ritual that signals to your brain that you're entering a different mode of thinking.

R: Release Control

Creativity requires a balance between intention and surrender. To access flow, we need to temporarily release our grip on outcomes and process.

TECHNIQUES FOR RELEASING CONTROL:

‣   Freewriting/free creation: Continuous creation without stopping to judge or correct

‣ Time-based creation: Setting a timer and creating without evaluation until it sounds

‣ Process focus: Attention on the experience rather than the result

‣ Constraint-based play: Using arbitrary limitations to bypass overthinking

Example Practice - The 100 Bad Ideas Exercise: When facing a creative challenge, set a goal of generating 100 deliberately bad solutions. This releases the pressure for quality, bypasses the inner critic, and often leads to surprisingly innovative approaches hiding among the intentionally flawed ideas.

E: Engage the Body

Creativity isn't just mental—it's deeply physical. Our most innovative thinking often emerges when we engage our bodies and senses.

BODY-BASED CREATIVE PRACTICES:

‣ Movement breaks: Short physical activity between creative sessions

‣ Walking generation: Problem-solving or ideation while walking

‣ Embodied exploration: Physically acting out concepts or challenges

‣ Cross-sensory exposure: Engaging non-dominant senses in your creative field

Example Practice - The Creation Walk: Take your creative challenge on a 20-minute walk.[5] Begin by clearly stating the problem or opportunity. Walk for 10 minutes without trying to solve it, simply observing your surroundings. Then allow your mind to make connections between what you're seeing and your creative challenge. Speak ideas into a voice recorder as they emerge.

A: Access Altered States

Creative breakthroughs often emerge from non-ordinary consciousness. Intentionally accessing these states creates conditions where new connections can form.

METHODS FOR ALTERED STATE ACCESS:

‣ Meditation and mindfulness: Practices that shift brainwave patterns

- Hypnagogic capture: Recording ideas from the edge of sleep
- Breathwork: Using breathing patterns to change consciousness
- Flow triggers: Applying specific conditions that induce flow states

Example Practice - The Theta Bridge: Sit comfortably with your creative challenge in mind. Hold a small object (like a stone) in your hand, extending your arm slightly. Close your eyes and breathe deeply while maintaining awareness of the object. As you drift toward sleep, your hand will relax and drop the object, waking you. Immediately record any insights that emerged in this theta-wave state between waking and sleeping.

T: Trust the Process

Creative flow requires faith in the process even when outcomes aren't immediately visible. Developing trust in your creative rhythm allows for deeper engagement.

TRUST-BUILDING PRACTICES:

- Creative tracking: Documenting your process to recognize patterns
- Success anchoring: Recalling previous creative breakthroughs
- Process orientation: Defining success by engagement rather than output
- Creative continuity: Maintaining consistent creative practice regardless of results

Example Practice - The Creative Journal: Maintain a dedicated journal that tracks not just ideas but your entire creative process—including blocks, breakthroughs, questions, and observations about your working patterns. Review regularly to identify your personal creative rhythm and build trust in your unique process.

E: External Feedback

While premature evaluation kills creativity, appropriately timed external input can spark new directions and refinement.

STRATEGIC FEEDBACK APPROACHES:

- Staged feedback: Different types of input at different creative stages

- Diverse perspectives: Gathering viewpoints from varied backgrounds and expertise
- Specific queries: Asking for particular types of feedback rather than general opinions
- Implementation filtering: Systems for processing feedback without losing vision

Example Practice - The Feedback Frame: When seeking input on creative work, provide a specific frame for the feedback you need: "I'm looking for input on X aspect specifically" or "This is at the Y stage of development, so I'm most interested in feedback on Z." This focuses input where it's most useful and protects work from inappropriate criticism.

S: Sustainable Rhythms

Sustainable creativity depends on rhythmic alternation between generation and renewal. Designing these rhythms intentionally prevents depletion and supports consistent creative flow.

RHYTHMIC DESIGN ELEMENTS:

- Creation-integration cycles: Alternating between making and absorbing
- Cross-pollination: Scheduling deliberate exposure to diverse influences
- Creative fallow periods: Planned intervals for regeneration
- Momentum maintenance: Practices that maintain connection during breaks

Example Practice - The Season System: Map your creative work to natural seasonal rhythms:

- Spring: Exploration and divergent thinking
- Summer: Active development and maximum output
- Fall: Refinement and completion
- Winter: Rest, reflection, and gathering new inputs This creates sustainable engagement without burnout.

Flow Triggers for Creative Breakthrough

While creativity benefits from all the flow triggers we explored in Chapter 3, certain triggers are particularly powerful for creative applications:

Optimal Challenge:
The Creativity Sweet Spot

Creative flow emerges when we're working at the edge of our capabilities— where the task is difficult enough to demand full engagement but not so difficult that it overwhelms us.

APPLICATION

Begin by assessing your current skill level with brutal honesty, then choose projects that stretch without breaking you. Gradually increase complexity as your capabilities develop, and create sub-challenges within larger projects to maintain optimal difficulty.

Example from Visual Storytelling: When I found myself growing comfortable with standard wedding coverage, I began setting specific creative challenges for each event: "Tell this story using only silhouettes," or "Create a complete narrative using reflections." These self-imposed constraints pushed me beyond my usual approaches without being overwhelming, consistently triggering creative flow states.

Deep Embodiment:
Beyond Mental Creativity

Some of the most powerful creative flow states occur when we fully engage our bodies in the creative process.

APPLICATION:

- Incorporate movement into ideation processes
- Pay attention to physical sensations during creation
- Use your body as a creative instrument
- Explore ideas through gesture, posture, and action
- Create with your whole sensory system, not just your mind

Example from Photographic Direction: I discovered that physically demonstrating poses or expressions to subjects created far more authentic results than verbal instructions. By embodying the emotion or quality I wanted to capture, I entered a flow state that subjects intuitively responded to, creating a feedback loop of creative energy.

Rich Environment:
Sensory Stimulation for Creativity

Our surroundings dramatically influence creative capacity.[9] Environments rich in meaningful stimuli can trigger associations and insights that wouldn't emerge in sterile settings.

APPLICATION:

- Curate environments with diverse sensory inputs
- Rotate creative spaces to prevent habituation
- Use environmental elements as random stimuli
- Match environments to creative stages
- Create contrast between preparation and insight environments

Example from Editing Process: I created different environmental presets for different stages of image editing: a clean, minimal setup for initial selection; a more stimulating environment with music and visual references for creative processing; and a comfortable, relaxed setting for final refinement. These environmental shifts reliably triggered different creative states.

Immediate Feedback:
The Creative Dialogue

Creativity flourishes when we can see the results of our actions quickly, creating a dynamic conversation between creator and creation.

APPLICATION:

- Structure work to provide fast feedback
- Create rough prototypes early in the process
- Establish personal feedback metrics
- Use technology to accelerate feedback loops
- Develop your critical eye while maintaining creative momentum

Example from On-Location Photography: Reviewing key images briefly during shoots provided immediate feedback that guided creative decisions. Rather than shooting blindly or constantly checking every image (which breaks flow), I developed a rhythm of working intensely, then briefly reviewing at natural transition points, creating a flow-friendly feedback system.

Collective Creativity: Flow in Creative Collaboration

While we often think of creativity as solitary, some of the most innovative work emerges from collective flow states[7]—when groups enter synchronized creative consciousness.

The Science of Group Flow

Research on creative teams reveals that collective flow follows similar patterns to individual flow but with additional dimensions:

- **Shared attention:** Group members focus on a common challenge or vision
- **Complementary skills:** Diverse capabilities that balance and enhance each other
- **Clear communication:** Information flows freely without excessive processing
- **Blended egos:** Individual identities temporarily merge into collective purpose
- **Emergent structure:** Order arises organically rather than through rigid planning

When these conditions align, groups can achieve creative results far beyond what individuals could accomplish alone.

Designing for Collective Creative Flow

Based on research and experience facilitating creative teams, these practices foster group flow:

Establish Psychological Safety

- Create environments where risk-taking feels acceptable
- Separate idea generation from evaluation
- Acknowledge and normalize creative struggles
- Celebrate productive failure
- Focus critique on work, not people

Design Effective Creative Sessions

- Begin with connective activities that build trust
- Establish clear creative parameters
- Use structured divergence before convergence
- Incorporate movement and environment changes
- Balance individual ideation with collective building

Maintain Creative Momentum

- Document ideas visibly during sessions
- Designate specific roles (facilitator, recorder, timekeeper)
- Create action bridges between sessions
- Establish clear next steps after creative meetings
- Celebrate progress and small wins

Example from Collaborative Photography: When photographing large events with a team, I discovered that our most innovative coverage came when we established clear roles and areas of responsibility but with deliberate overlap zones. We created a simple system of nonverbal cues to communicate opportunities without breaking flow, and began each event with a brief ritual that aligned our creative vision. This approach consistently produced more cohesive and creative results than either strict division of labor or unstructured collaboration.

The Mindset Shift: From Creator to Channel

Perhaps the most profound shift in accessing creative flow comes from reframing our relationship to the creative process itself. Rather than seeing ourselves as the source of creativity, we can experience ourselves as channels, or couriers, through which creativity flows.

This perspective aligns with both the subjective experience of flow states ("the book seemed to write itself") and the neuroscience of creativity (reduced activity in brain regions associated with self-reference during peak creative states).

From Control to Service

This mindset shift involves moving:

▸ From forcing creative output to creating conditions for emergence
▸ From ownership of ideas to stewardship of the creative process
▸ From self-conscious creation to being in service to the work itself
▸ From creator identity to creative vessel identity

Practice - The Morning Vessel: Begin creative sessions with this brief contemplation: "I am a channel for creativity that wants to emerge through me. My job is not to force or direct it, but to create the conditions for its natural expression, and to bring my skills to its service."

From Separation to Connection

The flow state dissolves the perceived boundary between creator and creation.[8] This shift involves:

▸ Recognizing creativity as a relationship rather than a possession
▸ Experiencing ideas as discovered rather than manufactured
▸ Seeing creative blocks as disconnection rather than failure
▸ Approaching creation as dialogue rather than monologue

Practice - The Creative Conversation: When starting a creative project, explicitly frame it as a conversation: "I am entering a dialogue with this work. I will bring my full presence and skills, but I will also listen to what the work itself needs to become."

From Product to Process

Flow thrives when we shift attention from outcomes to the creative journey itself:

- Valuing the experience of creating as inherently worthwhile
- Finding joy in the act rather than just the accomplishment
- Measuring success by engagement rather than just results
- Treating creation as a practice rather than a performance

Practice - Process Celebration: At the end of each creative session, regardless of outcomes, note three aspects of the creative process that you valued or enjoyed. This builds association between creativity and intrinsic reward rather than external validation.

~ § ~

REFLECTION PROMPT

Consider a recent creative experience:

• **What conditions** helped you drop into creative flow?

• **Which phase of the creative cycle** (preparation, incubation, illumination, verification) do you tend to rush or skip?

• **What personal blocks** most commonly interrupt your creative flow?

• **How might you apply** one principle from this chapter to enhance your creative process this week?

"Flow isn't a switch to flip—it's a door we walk through with the right key."

~ § ~

Creativity isn't random—it's responsive. Learn the rhythm, and it will meet you there.

Yoga Connection: *In yogic philosophy, the concept of "ishvara pranidhana" (surrender to the divine) parallels the creative flow experience of becoming a channel rather than forcing outcomes. Traditional practices like trataka (steady gazing) develop the capacity for sustained, relaxed attention that supports creative flow, while pranayama techniques alter consciousness in ways that enhance creative insight. These practices recognize that our most original thinking often emerges when the "small self" steps aside.*

Chapter Six.

Flow in Sports & Movement

"Your body is not a barrier to flow. It's the bridge."

~ / ~

The soccer ball rose to perfect arc against the Norwegian sky.

Time seemed to stretch as I tracked its descent, feeling the positions of opponents and teammates without needing to look. My body was already moving—not from conscious command but from a deeper intelligence. As the ball dropped, I knew exactly where my foot needed to be, the precise angle required, the perfect amount of force to redirect it to my teammate making a run toward goal.

For an instant, time stretched like elastic. I felt every player's movement without needing to look — the geometry of possibility unfolding in real time. My body was already there before thought could catch up. When foot met ball, I wasn't deciding; I was *listening* — to rhythm, to instinct, to the intelligence of movement itself.

That moment of *total coherence* was my first taste of embodied flow. Years later, I would recognize the same quiet power in a yoga sequence, in the effortless snap of a camera shutter, and even at a workstation redesigned for harmony of posture, lighting, and breath.

The form changes — soccer field, studio, office — but the principle is constant: when body, mind, and environment synchronize, awareness becomes seamless. Flow moves through you as easily as air through open lungs.

The Somatic Gateway to Flow

Flow is not purely a mental event; it's the emergent property of a finely tuned human system.[1] The nervous system, muscles, senses, and environment collaborate in real time to regulate arousal, focus, and perception.

The Body–Brain Feedback Loop

Every movement sends information upward; every thought sends information downward.[2]

Posture influences mood, and breath modulates neurochemistry.[3] Even subtle shifts — unclenching the jaw, widening the chest — can transform internal dialogue.

Embodied Cognition

Neuroscience confirms what ancient yogic philosophy always taught: we *think* through our bodies.[4] Gestures, orientation, and rhythm shape conceptual understanding. Physical practice literally sculpts neural pathways that support adaptability and creativity.

Interoception: The Inner Compass

Interoception — the awareness of internal states — is the nervous system's compass for presence.[5] Training it through slow breathing or mindful movement enhances both emotional stability and intuitive timing. The more refined your interoception, the earlier you sense when you're drifting from alignment — and the faster you can return to flow.

Three Somatic Pathways to Flow

1. Rhythmic Movement

Repetitive motion — running, cycling, swimming, chanting, drumming — stabilizes neural oscillations and induces transient hypofrontality, the quieting of the analytical mind.[6]

Practice: maintain a steady tempo, attune to breath–movement synchrony, and extend duration gradually.

2. Challenge-Based Movement

Sports and skill-intensive play activate the balance of skill × challenge = flow.[7] Immediate feedback, risk, and clear goals compress perception of time and silence self-talk.

Practice: calibrate difficulty just above current capacity. Focus on process, not outcome; use mistakes as data for refinement.

3. Awareness-Based Movement

Slow, mindful modalities — tai chi, qigong, gentle yoga — heighten subtle sensation and interoception.[8]

Practice: replace ambition with curiosity. Feel the breath trace the movement. Let precision arise from awareness rather than effort.

Most people access flow through a hybrid of all three. The key is flexibility: knowing when your system needs rhythm, challenge, or awareness to re-enter coherence.

The Athlete's Mindset: Preparation for Flow

Elite performance is not random magic — it's trained receptivity. Athletes cultivate conditions where flow is *most likely* to occur.[9]

1. Deliberate Practice and Edge Work

Great performers spend more time at the threshold between mastery and failure than anywhere else. Each repetition edges the nervous system toward greater precision. Recovery is built into the design, not added afterward.

2. Visualization and Mental Rehearsal

The brain doesn't distinguish vividly imagined movement from physical rehearsal.[10] When an athlete mentally runs the play or swimmer feels each stroke in advance, the motor cortex primes neural circuits for efficiency.

Practical cue: visualize in first-person perspective with full sensory immersion — texture, temperature, sound — for 3–5 minutes pre-performance.

3. Pre-Performance Rituals

Rituals stabilize attention and anchor physiology. The consistent sequence — lacing shoes, breathing pattern, mantra — signals safety and readiness.

This is the athlete's version of *entering sacred space*: routine as gateway to transcendence.

4. Recovery and Integration

Flow without recovery becomes depletion.[11] Sleep, nourishment, and play recalibrate neurotransmitter balance, allowing future flow to arise naturally.

The Athletic Body in Flow

When skill and challenge align, attention becomes both laser-focused and panoramic.[12]

Perception sharpens: colors brighten, time slows, noise fades to rhythm. Movements unfold automatically, guided by body intelligence rather than analysis. It feels effortless precisely because every neural circuit is optimized for action.

In those moments, identity dissolves. You are not *doing*; you are *being done*.

From Sidelines to Workspaces

Years after that Norwegian sky, I found myself in steel-toed boots rather than cleats — walking factory floors as an **industrial hygienist and certified ergonomist** for ALCOA.

There, I learned a different form of performance science: how lighting, noise, and workstation design influence attention, fatigue, and flow.

We adjusted desk heights to match anthropometric ranges, tuned LED color temperature to daylight rhythm, installed acoustic baffles to quiet the brain's constant vigilance.

Accident rates dropped. Focus increased. People moved with less strain, more ease.

Ergonomics, I realized, is simply applied compassion: creating environments where bodies can breathe.

And when the body breathes, the mind follows.

Designing for Flow: Ergonomic Micro-Practices

- **Posture Resets:** stand, reach, and open the chest every 30 minutes.
- **Visual Horizons:** alternate near and far focus to refresh ocular muscles.
- **Lighting Rhythm:** bright → midday; warm → evening — cue the circadian clock.
- **Noise Awareness:** steady low-frequency hum supports concentration; erratic noise erodes it.
- **Two-Minute Movement Protocol:** shoulder rolls → hip circles → full-body shake → deep exhale.

Environment is never neutral. It either constrains or catalyzes flow.

The Nervous System & Breath Rhythms

Flow emerges in the state of *calm alertness* — balanced sympathetic drive with parasympathetic grounding.[13]

- **Extended Exhale (4-in / 8-out):** before high-stakes performance.
- **Balanced Breath (5-in / 5-out):** between tasks.

- **Energizing Breath (6-in / 4-out):** when fatigue dulls focus.
- **5-5-5 Reset:** inhale 5 – hold 5 – exhale 5 × 3 cycles.

Release & Grounding

Tension is the silent saboteur of flow.

Try this **two-minute release**: drop jaw → shoulder rolls → neck arcs → hip circles → whole-body shake.

Then engage the **5-4-3-2-1 sensory scan**: five things seen, four touched, three heard, two smelled, one tasted.

In less than a minute, awareness returns to present-time reality.

Movement as Lifestyle

Flow is sustained by rhythm, not intensity.

Morning Activation: stretch, sunlight, slow breath.

Workday Micro-Flows: brief walks or mobility drills between deep-focus blocks.

Evening Integration: gentle yoga, gratitude movement, or slow walk under stars.

Sleep & Recovery: same bedtime, dark room, digital sunset.

These cycles keep the physiology of flow replenished rather than exhausted.

Integrating Movement Wisdom Everywhere

At Work: Respect ultradian rhythms; schedule effort and recovery like training intervals.

In Relationships: Regulate your body first; coherence is contagious.

In Creativity: Follow rhythm, not rigidity. Let movement unlock the idea that words cannot.

Every arena is a practice field.

Whether you're running a mile, running a meeting, or running toward a dream, the principles are the same: presence, rhythm, recovery, and trust in the body's intelligence.

The body is not the vehicle for consciousness; it is consciousness embodied.

Meet yourself there — and flow will meet you.

~ § ~

REFLECTION PROMPT

Consider your relationship with movement and flow:

• **When have you experienced** flow states through physical activity?

• **Which of the three somatic pathways** to flow (rhythmic, challenge-based, or awareness-based) most resonates with you?

• **How might you incorporate** brief movement practices to enhance flow in your daily activities?

• **What patterns have you noticed** in how your physical state affects your mental and emotional experience?

"You're not trying to control your body—you're remembering how to listen to it."for productivity.

~ § ~

Flow isn't found in the mind alone. It begins with the body. The more fluent you become in your somatic signals, the more easily you'll recognize the rhythm of your own return.

Yoga Connection: *Yoga means "to yoke" — to unite what we habitually divide. Through "asana" (posture), "pranayama" (breath), and "dharana" (focus), it trains the nervous system for sustained, embodied awareness.*[14] *The yogic concept of "asana" originally referred not just to physical postures but to finding a position that is both steady (sthira) and comfortable (sukha). This balance between effort and ease creates the physical foundation for meditation and expanded awareness. Similar principles appear in movement practices across cultures, suggesting a universal recognition that certain qualities of physical engagement create the conditions for flow states. Its purpose is not escape from the body but entry into its deepest intelligence — where the sacred and the physical are one seamless motion.*

Chapter Seven.

Flow in Relationships
& Communication

"Connection is the current. Flow is the bridge."

~ / ~

I can't get this couple to relax," whispered my second shooter as we prepared for an engagement session with a particularly stiff pair of clients.

Despite picture-perfect location and lighting, the couple looked uncomfortable and posed in every frame. Their smiles were fixed, their interaction mechanical.

"Let's try something different," I said to the couple. "For the next few minutes, forget about the portrait session and our cameras completely. I'd like you to simply take turns telling each other the story of how you met—but with a twist. Each of you should tell it from the other person's perspective, as if you were them."

They looked skeptical but played along. As they began speaking, something remarkable happened. Their bodies softened. Genuine laughter erupted. They started correcting each other's versions with playful touches and knowing glances. Memories sparked spontaneous gestures and expressions.

I nodded subtly to my second shooter, who began photographing from a distance with a long lens. Meanwhile, I continued guiding their conversation, keeping them engaged with each other rather than aware of the camera.

The resulting images captured something authentic that posed instructions never could have—the genuine connection between two people sharing a moment of mutual presence.

This wasn't just a photography technique. It was an example of relational flow—that remarkable state when connection becomes effortless, authentic, and generative. The same state that transforms ordinary conversations into meaningful exchanges, workplaces into collaborative communities, and casual encounters into moments of genuine human recognition.

In this chapter, we'll explore how flow principles apply beyond individual experience to the space between people—how connection itself can become a flow state, and how we can create the conditions for more meaningful, energizing relationships across all domains of life.

The Science of Shared Flow

While we typically think of flow as an individual experience, research increasingly reveals that some of the most powerful flow states happen between people rather than within them. This phenomenon—variously called interpersonal flow, group flow, or relational flow—has distinctive characteristics and benefits.

The Neuroscience of Connection

Recent advances in social neuroscience have dramatically expanded our understanding of the brain's social nature and the neurological basis of human connection. Our brains are equipped with specialized neural mechanisms that allow us to "tune in" to others. Mirror neuron networks activate when we observe others' actions, creating internal simulation of their experience. Motor resonance systems subtly mimic the movements and expressions of those around us, while limbic resonance circuits allow emotional states to synchronize between individuals.

These mechanisms create what neuroscientist Stephen Porges calls "neuroception"—the unconscious assessment of whether situations and people are safe, dangerous, or life-sustaining—a crucial foundation for relational flow.

During meaningful connection, our brains literally sync up. EEG studies show neural oscillations (brainwaves) aligning between people in conversation. This "neural coupling" increases with the quality of understanding and connection, becoming strongest during mutual engagement and shared purpose. Phrases like "being on the same wavelength" reflect this literal neural reality.

Effective connection also triggers specific neurochemical cascades. Oxytocin increases during positive social connection, supporting trust and bonding. Dopamine rewards positive social interaction, making connection intrinsically satisfying. Endorphins are released during shared laughter and synchronized movement, while serotonin rises in contexts of positive social recognition. This biochemistry explains why quality connection feels not just emotionally satisfying but physically rewarding—creating a natural high similar to other flow states.

Characteristics of Relational Flow

When people enter flow together, several distinctive phenomena emerge that differ from individual flow experiences. Collective creativity becomes accessible, where groups generate insights and solutions that none of the individuals could have reached alone. Synchronized action develops as movements, timing, and responses become naturally coordinated without explicit planning. Shared time perception occurs, where groups lose track of time together and experience similar temporal distortion. Most remarkably, there's often a dissolution of individual ego boundaries, where the sense of separate self softens and participants experience themselves as part of a larger, flowing whole.

The Anatomy of Flow Conversations

Not all conversations are created equal. Flow conversations have specific characteristics that distinguish them from routine social exchange or even productive discussions. Understanding these elements allows you to cultivate more meaningful, energizing interactions across all areas of life.

Presence Over Performance

The foundation of any flow conversation is mutual presence—each person being genuinely available to the moment and to each other rather than performing predetermined roles or pushing personal agendas. This presence creates psychological safety where people feel free to express authentic thoughts and responses. It also enables real-time responsiveness, allowing the conversation to evolve organically based on what's emerging rather than following a fixed script.

When people show up with genuine curiosity about each other's perspectives and experiences, something magical happens. The conversation becomes less about convincing or impressing and more about shared discovery. Each person becomes interested in understanding not just the content of what others are saying, but the person behind the words.

Generative Building

Flow conversations don't just involve taking turns speaking. Instead, participants build on what's emerging through what improvisational theater calls "yes, and" responses that extend and develop ideas rather than blocking or redirecting them. They identify patterns across seemingly separate contributions and draw connections to previously shared content. Most importantly, they name the emergent insights that arise from the exchange itself.

This building creates conversational coherence that turns individual contributions into something larger. When people experience their ideas being incorporated rather than just acknowledged, psychological ownership of the conversation becomes distributed. This creates the conditions for collective creativity to emerge—where the group discovers ideas that no individual brought to the table.

The Power of Collaborative Inquiry

Instead of debates where people advocate for fixed positions, flow conversations often involve collaborative inquiry where participants explore questions together. Rather than trying to win or convince, everyone becomes genuinely curious about discovering new understanding. Questions shift from evaluative ("Is that right?") to exploratory ("What would happen if…?" or "How might we understand this differently?").

This collaborative approach activates the neural reward systems associated with insight and learning. It moves people out of defensive postures and into creative exploration, making new discoveries possible.

Flow in Different Relationship Contexts

While the fundamental principles of relational flow remain consistent across contexts, their application varies based on the relationship type and purpose.

Intimate Relationships: Beyond Transactional Connection

Intimate relationships offer perhaps the richest potential for relational flow, yet often become constrained by routines, expectations, and unaddressed patterns. Common flow blockers include accumulated resentments that restrict emotional availability, comfort patterns that reduce novelty and challenge, assumptions of understanding that limit curiosity, and merged identity that diminishes generative difference.

Flow-enhancing practices for intimate relationships involve creating regular opportunities for fresh discovery. This might include curiosity rituals where partners ask genuine questions about each other's evolving thoughts and feelings, or new territory experiences—shared activities that place both people in learning mode together. Appreciation specificity helps, where partners notice and name particular qualities rather than offering generic positivity. Calibrated vulnerability, or appropriately timed sharing of deeper thoughts and feelings, also supports relational flow.

The Daily Temperature Check: In my own relationship, we developed a simple daily practice that significantly enhanced our connection. Each evening, we would share a moment when we felt close to each other during the day, a moment when we felt distant or disconnected, and something we appreciate about each other right now. This brief ritual created regular opportunities for attunement, prevented small issues from accumulating, and maintained our awareness of the relationship as an evolving, living system rather than a fixed entity.

Professional Relationships: Creating Collective Intelligence

Teams and work relationships can access forms of flow that dramatically enhance both creativity and effectiveness. Professional flow emerges when clear purpose and shared goals align with complementary skills and mutual respect. The most effective teams develop what researchers call "collective intelligence"—the ability to think and solve problems together in ways that transcend individual capabilities.

Creating conditions for professional flow requires establishing psychological safety where team members feel free to take risks and make mistakes. It involves developing shared language for important concepts and creating rituals that support both individual contribution and group cohesion. Regular appreciation practices help team members feel valued for their unique contributions, while constructive feedback systems allow continuous learning and adaptation.

Team Flow in Action: During a remote collaboration for one of many graduate program's writing projects while attending the University of Southern California, I worked with a team of executives and recent college graduates that had never collaborated before. We established what were essentially brief 3-minute connection rituals between each session where we shared what we were noticing in our shared document, what we needed, and what was emerging for the next segment. These micro-connections allowed real-time coordination, emerging pattern recognition, and energy recalibration. They created a shared awareness that allowed the team to function as an integrated system rather than just individuals with assigned roles, resulting in more comprehensive and cohesive coverage.

Community and Social Flow

Beyond intimate and professional relationships, flow principles can transform how we engage in our communities and casual social interactions. Community flow emerges when groups gather around shared purpose with mutual respect for individual differences. It requires creating inclusive spaces where diverse perspectives can contribute to collective intelligence.

Effective community flow often involves ritual and ceremony that help individuals transition from separate concerns to shared awareness. It benefits from rotating leadership so different voices and perspectives can guide the group's attention. Story sharing helps create continuity between past, present, and future while honoring both individual experience and collective wisdom.

Extended Mind: Shared Consciousness?

Couples in deep rapport finish each other's sentences. Parents "know" when children are in danger miles away. Team flow creates shared awareness transcending verbal communication.

Materialist neuroscience explains this through subtle behavioral cues— micro-expressions, tone shifts, unconscious mimicry. But research suggests something additional might be happening:

Rupert Sheldrake's studies on telephone telepathy and the sense of being stared at show effects beyond chance. HeartMath Institute documents electromagnetic fields extending beyond bodies, affected by emotional states. Mirror neurons suggest we're wired for consciousness sharing.

Does consciousness extend beyond individual brains, creating fields we can tune into? Or do we just get very good at reading subtle signals in close relationships?

Whether you interpret interpersonal flow as enhanced perception or genuine field effects, cultivating coherence seems to enhance connection. The mechanism invites investigation. The experience is undeniable.

Building a Flow-Based Relationship System

Moving beyond individual interactions, we can design entire relationship systems to support sustained connection and collective flow across all our relationships.

Regular Rhythm: The Backbone of Relational Flow

Just as individual flow benefits from rhythm, relationships thrive when they include regular patterns that support connection. Daily touchpoints provide brief but focused connection moments and check-ins that maintain relational awareness. Small rituals reinforce belonging, while transition moments between separate activities create opportunities for reconnection.

Weekly deepening involves more extended, uninterrupted connection time where partners or team members can reflect on patterns and experiences, address emerging issues before they become problems, and celebrate progress and positive developments. Periodic renewal through retreats or dedicated time for relationship focus allows for review of larger patterns and direction, recommitment to shared values and vision, and innovation and experimentation with new possibilities.

Feedback Systems: The Learning Engine

Flow-based relationships incorporate regular feedback that allows continuous learning and adaptation. Appreciation practices involve specific, timely positive feedback that recognizes contribution and impact, acknowledges growth and development, and celebrates shared achievements. Constructive engagement means directly and respectfully addressing concerns, focusing on patterns rather than isolated incidents, and connecting feedback to shared values and goals.

Process reflection includes regular assessment of how (not just what) people are doing together, attention to energy patterns and dynamics, identification of emerging strengths and challenges, and collaborative design of experiments and adjustments.

The Monthly Relationship Review: For important ongoing relationships, scheduling a regular review using specific prompts can transform relationship quality. Questions like "What's been working well in our relationship?" "What patterns have created challenge or friction?" "What do we each need more or less of?" and "What experiment should we try in the coming month?" create a container for continuous improvement without waiting for problems to force change.

From Theory to Practice: Building Flow-Based Teams

Creating sustained collective flow requires deliberate culture-building. Several key practices help transform any group into a flow-generating system.

Psychological safety building involves normalizing and learning from mistakes, encouraging appropriate vulnerability, welcoming questions and concerns, and demonstrating curiosity toward differing perspectives. Shared language development means creating team-specific terms for important concepts, establishing clear distinctions for commonly confused ideas, and building vocabulary for nuanced feedback.

Ritual integration includes designing transition moments between activities, creating celebration practices for achievements, establishing reflection points in work processes, and developing renewal rituals for maintaining energy. Story cultivation involves collecting and sharing examples of success and learning, developing narrative about team identity and purpose, creating continuity between past, present, and future, and using storytelling to integrate new members.

These practices transform a collection of individuals into a cohesive system capable of achieving flow states that transcend what any member could experience alone.

Flow isn't just a solo journey. It's a field we co-create. When we show up with full presence, the space between us becomes sacred. True connection doesn't require perfect words—it asks for presence, permission, and rhythm.

~ § ~

REFLECTION PROMPT

Consider your approach to connection and communication:

• In which relationships do you most easily experience flow-based connection?

• What conditions or practices help you move from transactional to transformative interaction?

• Which relational flow blocker most commonly interrupts your connections?

• What one practice from this chapter could most enhance the quality of your key relationships?

"True connection doesn't require the perfect words—it asks for presence, permission, and rhythm."

~ § ~

Flow isn't just a solo journey. It's a field we co-create. And when we show up with full presence, the space between us becomes sacred.

Yoga Connection: *The yogic principle of "sangha" (community) recognizes that certain developments only emerge through intentional connection with others. Traditional yoga wasn't just an individual practice but included relation-based elements meant to dissolve the illusion of separation. Modern practices like partner yoga and AcroYoga explicitly use physical connection to create states where individual boundaries soften and shared flow emerges— demonstrating how embodied connection can facilitate transpersonal awareness.*

PART III.

MECHANISMS

~ / ~

"Your breath is the bridge."

Chapter Eight.

Unlocking the Flow Gateway

"Flow isn't a switch to flip–it's a door we walk through with the right key."

~ / ~

The timeline was collapsing at the high-profile Indian wedding at Central Park's Boathouse.

I'd been hired through Sonal Shah, an ambitious wedding planner on her way to becoming globally recognized and one of New York City's premier luxury event coordinators serving celebrities and billionaires. The stakes were high—not just for the couple's once-in-a-lifetime celebration, but for my career as well. Success here could lead to an ongoing partnership with Sonal's team, potentially opening doors to international destination weddings and a significantly expanded client base.

As I navigated the complex multi-day event, challenges mounted. The weather shifted unpredictably, forcing last-minute location changes except for the all-important capture of heading out through the rain to where the couple first met in New York's Central Park. And, throughout it all, cultural traditions I was still learning needed to be captured with both respect and artistry.

What saved the day wasn't just my technical preparation—though the backup equipment, location scouting, and shot lists certainly helped. What truly made the difference was my ability to shift into a flow state precisely when the pressure was highest.

Instead of fighting against the evolving circumstances, I took a deliberate breath and released my attachment to how things "should" be. I turned my full attention to what was actually unfolding. I noticed the quality of light as it filtered through trees at an unplanned location. I observed subtle interactions between family members that told deeper stories than the posed portraits I'd originally envisioned.

Within moments, my entire experience transformed. Time seemed to expand. Creative solutions appeared effortlessly. I found myself moving intuitively through the space, anticipating moments before they happened, seeing compositions that I might have missed had everything gone according to plan.

The resulting images not only delighted the couple and impressed the planner—some would be selected for publication in an international wedding magazine. But more importantly, I had discovered something crucial about flow states: they weren't random accidents that happened to me when circumstances aligned perfectly. They were experiences I could access intentionally, even under challenging conditions, by understanding and activating specific triggers.

That wedding represented a professional crossroads. Sonal was impressed enough to discuss bringing me onto her team for international events, including week-long celebrations in India. It was an enticing opportunity, but with young children at home, I ultimately chose a different path—one that prioritized family over career expansion.

Yet the lesson about flow stayed with me far beyond that decision. I had learned that optimal experience wasn't about controlling external circumstances. It was about creating internal and external conditions that allowed natural performance to emerge—a skill applicable across every domain of life.

On that NYC Central Park wedding shoot day with Sonal, just like many others in all types of circumstances where panic might have a chance to take over, where the mind fragments between competing demands and everything becomes reactive scrambling. I had noticed the familiar tightness in my chest that signals stress building, I employed what I now call the "Flow Gateway Protocol"—a series of mental moves that consistently shifted me from scattered overwhelm into centered presence. Within thirty seconds, my perception sharpened. Time seemed to slow down. The chaos transformed from threatening overwhelm into a dynamic puzzle I could navigate with clarity and even enjoyment.

The shift wasn't magical. It was the result of understanding how to deliberately activate the psychological conditions that make flow accessible—even in challenging circumstances.

While Chapter 6 explored how the body serves as a gateway to flow through movement and somatic awareness, this chapter focuses on the mind's role in unlocking optimal states. We'll explore how specific mental practices, attention training, and cognitive strategies can create reliable pathways to flow regardless of external conditions.

The Psychology of Flow Access

Flow isn't just a state that happens to you—it's a state you can learn to enter deliberately through specific mental practices. Understanding the psychological infrastructure of flow gives you tremendous leverage in accessing these states when you need them most.

The Attention Revolution

At its core, flow is an attention phenomenon. Every flow experience involves a particular quality of attention: focused yet flexible, intense yet effortless, concentrated yet expansive. Learning to cultivate this quality of attention is perhaps the most direct pathway to flow mastery.

The Paradox of Flow Attention: Flow attention has a paradoxical quality that distinguishes it from both scattered distraction and forced concentration. It's focused without being tight, engaged without being effortful, concentrated without being narrow. This quality emerges naturally when specific psychological conditions are met.

The key is understanding that attention isn't something you force but something you guide. Like learning to ride a bicycle, there's a subtle balance point where effort and ease meet. Too much force and you lose the fluidity; too little engagement and you lose the focus.

Mental Preparation: Setting the Stage

Just as athletes have pre-performance routines that prepare their bodies for optimal performance, you can develop mental preparation routines that prepare your psychology for flow. These routines serve multiple functions: they signal to your nervous system that it's time to shift into a different mode, they clear mental clutter that might interfere with focus, and they activate the specific psychological triggers that support flow emergence.

The Clear-Set-Prime Protocol:

CLEAR THE MENTAL SPACE: Before entering any flow-requiring activity, spend two to three minutes clearing your mental environment. This involves acknowledging any preoccupations or concerns and either addressing them briefly or consciously setting them aside. Like closing browser tabs on a computer, this frees up mental processing power for the task at hand.

SET CLEAR INTENTIONS: Flow thrives on clarity of purpose. Set specific but flexible intentions for your session. Rather than vague goals like "be creative," establish clear direction like "explore three different approaches to this design challenge." This gives your attention something concrete to organize around while maintaining openness to emergent discoveries.

PRIME YOUR STATE: Engage in a brief practice that activates the particular quality of attention your activity requires. This might involve visualization, brief breathing techniques, or mental rehearsal. The key is consistency—using the same priming routine signals to your brain that it's time to enter flow mode.

The Role of Challenge and Curiosity

Flow emerges most readily when your mind encounters the optimal balance of challenge and capability—what researchers call the "challenge-skill sweet spot." But this balance isn't just about external difficulty; it's about how you frame and approach whatever you're doing.

Curiosity as a Flow Catalyst: One of the most reliable ways to access flow is through genuine curiosity. When you approach any activity with authentic interest in what you might discover, your attention naturally becomes engaged and focused. Curiosity transforms even routine tasks into opportunities for exploration and learning.

This works because curiosity activates the brain's reward systems in ways similar to flow itself. When you're genuinely interested in something, dopamine release increases, supporting sustained attention and engagement. The mind naturally enters a state of open, focused awareness—precisely the condition that supports flow emergence.

The Art of Reframing: You can cultivate the challenge-skill balance through how you frame your activities. If a task feels too easy, you can introduce constraints or explore new approaches. If it feels overwhelming, you can break it into smaller components or focus on process rather than outcome. The key is learning to adjust your mental approach to find that sweet spot where you feel stretched but not stressed.

Advanced Flow Triggers: The Mental Pathways

Beyond the basic conditions for flow, there are specific psychological triggers that can reliably activate optimal states. These triggers work by shifting your brain into the particular neural patterns associated with flow experiences.

The Constraint Paradox

One of the most counterintuitive flow triggers is the strategic use of constraints. While we might assume that unlimited freedom supports creativity and performance, research consistently shows that appropriate limitations actually enhance flow by providing clear boundaries that focus attention and stimulate creative problem-solving.

Creative Constraints: Set specific limits on your process, materials, or time. A writer might commit to using only words that begin with certain letters, or a designer might limit themselves to three colors. These constraints force your brain to find novel solutions within defined parameters, often leading to more innovative outcomes than unlimited freedom would produce.

Time Constraints: Working within specific time boundaries can powerfully trigger flow by creating urgency without anxiety. The pressure of limited time forces your attention into the present moment while preventing the perfectionism that often blocks flow. Start with periods that feel challenging but achievable, then gradually extend as your flow capacity develops.

The Power of Process Focus

Flow states are characterized by absorption in the process itself rather than preoccupation with outcomes. Learning to shift your attention from results to process is one of the most reliable ways to access flow, especially in high-pressure situations.

Process Questions: Train yourself to ask process-oriented questions during your activities: "What am I noticing right now?" "How might I approach this differently?" "What wants to emerge here?" These questions keep your attention grounded in the immediate experience rather than jumping ahead to worry about results.

The Next Right Step: When you feel overwhelmed by the scope of a project or unclear about direction, focus exclusively on identifying and taking the next right step. This practice grounds you in concrete action while maintaining forward momentum. Each step completed successfully builds confidence and clarity for the subsequent step.

Identity and State Shifting

One of the most sophisticated flow triggers involves temporarily shifting your identity to align with the state you want to access. This works because our sense of self profoundly influences what we believe is possible and how we approach challenges.

Flow Personas: Develop specific "flow personas"—versions of yourself that embody the qualities you want to express during different activities. For creative work, you might cultivate your "Explorer" identity that's curious and experimental. For analytical tasks, you might access your "Detective" identity that loves solving puzzles. These aren't fake identities but different facets of your authentic self.

Embodying Excellence: Before important sessions, spend a few minutes embodying the energy and presence of someone performing at their peak in your field. This isn't about comparison or imitation but about accessing states of excellence that already exist within you. What would it feel like to approach this work with complete confidence and skill?

The Flow Gateway Protocol: A Comprehensive System

Building on the principles we've explored, here's a comprehensive protocol for accessing flow states consistently across different activities and contexts.

Phase 1: Preparation (5-10 minutes)

Environmental Setup: Optimize your physical environment for the specific type of flow you're seeking. This includes removing distractions, adjusting lighting and sound, and ensuring you have all necessary resources easily accessible.

Mental Clearing: Use the technique that works best for you to clear mental clutter. This might involve brief journaling, meditation, or simply taking a few conscious breaths while mentally acknowledging and releasing any preoccupations.

Intention Setting: Establish clear but flexible goals for your session. Include both process intentions (how you want to approach the work) and outcome intentions (what you hope to accomplish), while remaining open to emergent discoveries.

Phase 2: Activation (3-5 minutes)

State Priming: Engage in whatever practice most reliably shifts you toward your desired state. This might involve movement, breathing, visualization, or listening to specific music. The key is consistency—using practices that your nervous system recognizes as signals to enter flow mode.

Attention Focusing: Begin focusing your attention on your chosen activity through gentle, progressive engagement. Start with broad awareness and gradually narrow your focus as you become more absorbed in the process.

Challenge Calibration: Assess the difficulty level of your intended work and adjust either the challenge or your approach to find the optimal balance. This might involve adding constraints if the work feels too easy or breaking things into smaller steps if it feels overwhelming.

Phase 3: Entry (Variable duration)

Process Immersion: Begin your activity with complete attention to the process itself. Release concern about outcomes and focus entirely on the quality of your engagement. Trust that good outcomes emerge naturally from process excellence.

Flow Maintenance: As you work, gently redirect your attention back to the immediate experience whenever you notice it wandering to outcomes, comparison, or self-evaluation. Use breath awareness as an anchor when you need to return to presence.

Responsive Adjustment: Stay alert to your changing state and make micro-adjustments as needed. This might involve changing your pace, taking brief breaks, or adjusting your approach based on what's emerging.

Troubleshooting Common Mental Flow Blocks

Even with solid preparation and technique, you'll encounter mental states that resist flow. Understanding how to work with these blocks skillfully can transform obstacles into gateways.

The Perfectionism Trap

Perfectionism is one of the most common flow blockers because it shifts attention from process to outcome while creating the kind of self-consciousness that fragments the effortless quality of flow. When you notice perfectionist thoughts arising, redirect your attention to curiosity and experimentation.

The "Good Enough" Principle: Give yourself permission to produce work that's good enough rather than perfect. This doesn't mean accepting poor quality but rather recognizing that flow emerges from willingness to engage imperfectly with full presence rather than waiting for perfect conditions or guaranteed success.

Mental Resistance and Starting Inertia

Sometimes the biggest barrier to flow is simply getting started. Mental resistance can make even enjoyable activities feel overwhelming, creating a cycle where avoidance increases anxiety, which increases resistance.

The Two-Minute Rule: Commit to engaging with your activity for just two minutes with absolutely no pressure to continue beyond that. This removes the psychological pressure that often triggers resistance while taking advantage of momentum—once you start, continuing often feels natural.

Resistance as Information: Instead of fighting mental resistance, get curious about what it might be telling you. Are you approaching the task in a way that doesn't serve you? Do you need to adjust your energy level, environment, or expectations? Sometimes resistance dissolves when you address its underlying message.

Analysis Paralysis

Overthinking can prevent the spontaneous emergence that characterizes flow states. When you find yourself caught in analytical loops, shift from thinking about your work to engaging directly with it.

Action as Antidote: The most effective way to move beyond analysis paralysis is through small, concrete actions. Make a mark, write a sentence, test an idea. Physical engagement with your work often dissolves mental loops that pure thinking cannot resolve.

Designing Your Personal Flow System

Every person has unique psychological patterns, challenges, and strengths that influence their flow access. The final step in mastering mental gateways to flow is designing a personalized system that works with your specific tendencies.

Flow Pattern Recognition

Spend two weeks tracking your flow experiences with particular attention to the mental conditions that support or hinder your access. Notice what thoughts, mental states, and preparation practices most reliably lead to flow. Also observe what mental patterns most consistently block flow for you.

Daily Flow Notes: Keep brief daily notes about your flow experiences, including what mental preparation you used, what challenged or supported your access, and what you learned about your unique patterns. This creates a personalized database of what works for you.

Customized Gateway Design

Based on your pattern recognition, design a personal flow gateway that incorporates your most effective mental practices. This should include your optimal preparation routine, your most reliable attention-focusing techniques, and your preferred methods for working with resistance and blocks.

Minimum Viable Practice: Also develop a shortened version of your gateway for situations when time is limited. This might be a three-minute routine that includes the most essential elements of your longer preparation sequence.

Integration and Evolution

Your flow gateway should evolve as your skills and circumstances change. Plan regular reviews of your system, experimenting with new techniques and retiring practices that no longer serve you. The goal isn't to find the perfect system but to develop an evolving relationship with your own optimal functioning.

The mind is not just the site where flow happens—it's the doorway through which flow enters your experience. By understanding how to prepare your psychology, trigger optimal states, and work skillfully with mental blocks, you transform flow from an occasional accident into a reliable capacity.

Your gateway to flow isn't just about technique—it's about developing a relationship with your own potential for excellence. Each time you practice accessing flow deliberately, you're not just improving your performance in that moment; you're training your nervous system to recognize and create the conditions for optimal functioning across all areas of your life.

The key is patient practice combined with genuine curiosity about your own patterns and possibilities. Flow mastery isn't about forcing yourself into optimal states but about creating conditions where these states naturally emerge. When you understand your personal pathway to flow, you hold the key to transforming not just what you accomplish but how you experience the process of living itself.

~ § ~

• What practices or environments help you hold steady focus without tension?

• How does your attention shift when you become fully immersed in the present moment?

• What does "discipline" mean to you when it comes to concentration and ease?

"Focus is not force—it is remembering to stay where the life energy already flows."

~ § ~

Yoga Connection: *Before concentration (dharana) comes pratyahara—the yogic practice of sense withdrawal. Not numbing or escaping, but consciously choosing what receives your attention. In a world of infinite stimulation, pratyahara is revolutionary: the deliberate turning inward that creates space for flow to emerge. You cannot enter the gateway while still grasping at every distraction. Pratyahara teaches us to release our grip on the outer world so the inner current can carry us.*

Chapter Nine.

The Mind-Body Connection

"Your body is not a barrier to flow. It's the bridge."

~ / ~

The camera felt heavy in my hands as I stood at the edge of the reception hall. It had been a grueling day—eight hours of continuous shooting at a particularly emotional wedding, with family dynamics that required careful navigation. My mind was sharp, but my body was sending unmistakable signals of fatigue.

In my early career, I would have ignored these physical warnings, pushing through with sheer determination. The result would have been increasingly mechanical images as my creative edge dulled with exhaustion.

But I had learned a different approach. Finding a quiet corner, I took sixty seconds to check in with my body—noticing the tension in my shoulders, the shallow quality of my breathing, the subtle fog creeping into my awareness.

Instead of fighting these sensations, I responded to them directly: rolling my shoulders, taking five deep breaths, stretching my spine, and drinking water.

This brief somatic intervention created an immediate shift. The mental fog lifted. My perception sharpened. My movements became more fluid and intuitive. When I returned to shooting, I found myself noticing subtle emotional exchanges and anticipating moments with renewed clarity. The final hour of coverage produced some of the day's most powerful images.

This wasn't just a physical recharge. It was a recalibration of my entire system—a direct demonstration of how our mental and physical states exist not as separate domains but as a single integrated reality.

When we talk about flow, we often focus on mental aspects—attention, focus, and cognitive states. But flow isn't just something that happens in the brain. It emerges from the dynamic relationship between mind, body, and environment. Understanding this integration opens new pathways to accessing flow and maintaining it through challenging circumstances.

In this chapter, we'll explore the intimate connection between physical and mental states, how somatic awareness becomes a gateway to flow, and how simple body-based practices can transform your capacity for presence, creativity, and optimal performance.

The Nervous System and Flow

At the core of the mind-body connection is your nervous system—the biological infrastructure that determines your capacity for presence, engagement, and optimal performance. Once you understand how this system works, you gain powerful leverage for shifting your state when flow feels inaccessible.

Your autonomic nervous system operates largely beneath conscious awareness, governing everything from heart rate to digestion to immune response. It runs on two complementary branches: the sympathetic system, which mobilizes you for action (accelerating heart rate, sharpening alertness, preparing muscles for movement), and the parasympathetic system, which restores and recovers (slowing the heart, deepening breath, facilitating repair).

Here's what matters for flow: optimal states require a dynamic balance between these systems. Enough sympathetic activation for energy and engagement. Enough parasympathetic influence for relaxation and presence.

Too much activation creates anxiety; too much relaxation creates lethargy. The sweet spot—where you feel simultaneously energized and calm—is where flow lives.

This explains something you've probably noticed: flow feels both activating and peaceful at once. That's not a contradiction. It's your nervous system finding its optimal operating point.[1]

Beyond Fight-or-Flight: The Polyvagal Revolution

The simple sympathetic/parasympathetic model is useful but incomplete. Dr. Stephen Porges' Polyvagal Theory reveals a third neural circuit that changes everything we understand about flow access.[3]

Think of your nervous system as having three modes, each with its own logic:

The **ventral vagal system**—what Porges calls the social engagement system—comes online when you feel genuinely safe. This is where flow lives. In this state, your face and voice become expressive, you can read others' emotions accurately, and you have access to your full creative and cognitive capacity. Your physiology supports connection, nuance, and optimal performance.

The **sympathetic system** activates when you perceive challenge or threat. It generates the energy for action—useful for deadlines and high-stakes moments—but at higher intensities, it narrows your focus and makes flow harder to access. Some sympathetic activation supports flow; too much blocks it.

The **dorsal vagal system** is the emergency brake. When threat feels overwhelming, this ancient circuit shuts you down—creating numbness, dissociation, the foggy feeling of "checking out." Flow is impossible from this state.

The hierarchy matters: you can only access flow when your nervous system perceives sufficient safety. This isn't about positive thinking or pushing through—it's biology. When your system detects threat, it prioritizes survival over optimal performance, redirecting resources away from the neural networks that support flow.

The good news? You can deliberately signal safety to your nervous system through specific practices. That's what the rest of this chapter is about.

Nervous System Regulation for Flow Access

Based on this understanding, we can approach flow not just as a mental state but as a whole-system condition that requires appropriate nervous system regulation.[5] These practices help create the physiological foundation for flow:

Breath: Your Direct Line to State Change

Your breath is the one autonomic function you can consciously control—which makes it your most immediate lever for shifting nervous system state. Different patterns send different signals to your brain about safety and energy needs.

When I need to calm an activated system before a high-stakes shoot, I extend my exhales: four counts in, six to eight counts out. This directly activates the parasympathetic system, quieting mental chatter and releasing excess tension. It's my go-to for any situation requiring calm, focused presence.

When I need to raise energy without creating anxiety—say, after a long editing session when I need to engage with clients—I flip the ratio: five to six counts in, four counts out. This gently activates the sympathetic system, increasing alertness without the jittery edge.

For transitions between different types of work, balanced breathing (equal counts in and out) creates nervous system coherence—a reset that prepares you for whatever comes next.

~§~

THE 60-SECOND RESET

When you need to shift state quickly, try this:

- Inhale for 5 counts
- Hold for 5 counts

- Exhale for 5 counts

- Repeat 3-5 times

This simple practice can fundamentally change your nervous system state in under a minute. I use it before important conversations, challenging creative sessions, and any moment when I notice I've drifted from presence.

The key insight: breath isn't just about relaxation. It's a precision tool for dialing in the exact state your current activity requires.[6]

Physical Release: Tension as Flow Blocker

Physical tension—especially in the neck, shoulders, jaw, and hips—sends continuous signals of threat to your nervous system, making flow states neuro-logically inaccessible.[8] Regular tension release practices counteract this effect.

These physical releases are particularly important during extended focus periods, as tension accumulates unconsciously during concentration and gradually blocks flow if not addressed.

Sensory Grounding: Anchoring in the Present

Your sensory systems provide direct channels to your nervous system state.

Deliberate sensory engagement can shift you from stress or dissociation into the present moment—a prerequisite for flow:[9]

THE 5-4-3-2-1 TECHNIQUE

When feeling scattered or disconnected:

Notice 5 things you can see
Acknowledge 4 things you can touch
Identify 3 things you can hear

Recognize 2 things you can smell

Note 1 thing you can taste

SENSORY CONTRAST PRACTICE

Create deliberate sensory contrast to sharpen presence:

+ Temperature contrast (warm hands on cool surface)

+ Texture exploration (rough and smooth surfaces)

+ Sound dynamics (loud sound followed by silence)

+ Visual narrowing and widening (focus on detail, then expand to full field)

When I needed to quickly reset during a demanding photoshoot, I developed a 30-second sensory routine: feeling the texture of my camera, noticing three distinct sounds in the environment, focusing on a distant object and then a close one, and taking three conscious breaths. This brief practice consistently shifted me from scattered to centered, creating the conditions for flow to reemerge.

Interoception: Learning to Listen

There's a sensory system you probably never learned about in school—one that might matter more for flow than all five traditional senses combined.

Interoception is your ability to sense your body's internal state: the subtle signals of hunger, fatigue, emotional activation, and physical need that most of us have learned to override or ignore.[10]

The science is fascinating: specialized receptors throughout your body continuously monitor everything from organ states to blood composition to temperature variations, sending this information to brain regions that create your felt sense of how you're doing from the inside.[10] But the practical application is what matters here.

Research increasingly shows that people with more developed interoceptive awareness make better decisions, regulate emotions more effectively, and—crucially—have more consistent access to flow states.[11] They catch problems before they become crises.

They know when to push and when to rest. They maintain conditions for optimal performance because they can actually feel when those conditions are shifting.

In my photography work, I discovered this the hard way. Early in my career, I'd ignore body signals—hunger, thirst, fatigue—until they screamed so loudly I couldn't function. My images from those sessions showed it: technically competent but somehow lifeless, missing the subtle emotional moments that require presence to catch.

Learning to listen changed everything.

Developing Interoceptive Intelligence

The good news is that interoceptive awareness can be systematically developed through specific practices:

BODY SCANNING PRACTICE

~Sit or lie comfortably with eyes closed
~Gradually direct attention through the body from feet to head
~Notice sensations without trying to change them
~Observe with curiosity rather than judgment
~Start with 5-minute scans, gradually extending to 10-15 minutes

BREATH SENSING

~Place one hand on your chest and one on your abdomen
~Notice the sensations of breath without changing your breathing
~Observe subtle differences between inhalation and exhalation
~Track the brief pauses between breaths
~Practice for 3-5 minutes daily

HUNGER-FULLNESS TRACKING

~Before eating, rate your hunger on a 1-10 scale
~Notice specifically where and how you feel hunger
~Halfway through eating, pause and reassess

~After eating, note fullness sensations
~Practice connecting specific sensations to the number scale

EMOTION LOCATION EXERCISE

When experiencing a distinct emotion:

~Close your eyes and scan your body
~Identify where you physically feel the emotion
~Note the quality of the sensation (temperature, weight, movement)
~Track how the sensation changes over 1-2 minutes

I discovered this in my own work. Before important sessions, I developed what I call "the pre-shoot check-in"—a 30-second interoceptive scan before beginning important sessions. This quick assessment helped me identify if I needed water, movement, food, or a brief rest before engaging fully with clients. By addressing these needs proactively, I prevented the subtle degradation of attention and presence that would otherwise occur, maintaining access to flow throughout longer 8- to 12-hour (or more) shoots.

The Interoception-Flow Connection

The link between interoceptive awareness and flow access appears through several pathways:

Early Adjustment Opportunity - Better interoception allows you to notice when your internal state is shifting away from optimal conditions. This early detection means you can make minor adjustments before flow is disrupted, rather than trying to recover after you're significantly off-balance.

Reduced Cognitive Load - When basic physical needs are addressed, your brain allocates fewer resources to monitoring discomfort, freeing up attention for the task at hand. This reduced cognitive load is essential for the absorption characteristic of flow.

State-Activity Matching - Enhanced interoceptive awareness helps you match activities to your current energetic state, or adjust your state to match necessary activities. This optimal pairing creates better conditions for flow than forcing mismatched states and tasks.

Feedback Refinement - Flow thrives on immediate feedback. Interoception provides an internal feedback channel that complements external information, creating richer data for your system to respond to and learn from.

By developing this internal sensing capacity, you essentially create an ongoing flow-readiness assessment system that operates largely beneath conscious awareness, helping maintain optimal conditions for presence and performance.

Embodied Cognition:
Thinking Through Your Body

Beyond nervous system regulation and interoceptive awareness, another crucial aspect of the mind-body connection is embodied cognition—the understanding that thinking itself is a whole-body process, not just a brain activity.[13]

Recent research in embodied cognition has identified several mechanisms through which physical states influence cognitive processes[13]:

- Posture effects on thinking[13]
- Gestural enhancement[13]
- Facial feedback[13]

Embodied experience forms the foundation of abstract thought.[13] This integration helps explain why movement, posture, and physical state shifts can transform mental blocks and enhance flow.[13]

PRACTICE: THE GESTURE LABORATORY

- Identify a challenging thinking task
- Experiment with different gesture patterns while working on it
- Notice which movements facilitate different aspects of thinking
- Develop a personal "gesture vocabulary" for different cognitive needs

Many great thinkers intuitively developed specific gestural patterns that supported their cognitive processes—from Einstein's thought experiments involving physically imagining riding on light beams to Richard Feynman's dynamic hand movements while solving physics problems.

Movement Integration for Cognitive Enhancement

Beyond posture and gesture, integrating specific movements into your thinking processes can significantly enhance flow:

WALKING THINKING

Use for: Problem-solving, idea generation, mental blocks

Method: Walk at moderate pace while focusing on a specific question

Duration: 10-30 minutes

Enhancement: Different walking environments (nature, urban, indoor) stimulate different thinking patterns

MOVEMENT BREAKS

Use for: Extended cognitive work, attention restoration

Method: 3-5 minutes of full-body movement every 30-45 minutes

Types: Stretching, brief exercise, dance, or free movement

Enhancement: Match movement quality to desired cognitive state afterward

CROSS-LATERAL MOVEMENT

Use for: Integrating different cognitive processes, whole-brain thinking

Method: Movements that cross the body's midline (right hand to left knee, etc.)

Duration: 1-2 minutes

Enhancement: Particularly effective before tasks requiring creative and analytical integration

When facing creative blocks during image editing, I developed a simple movement practice—standing up, doing 30 seconds of cross-lateral movements, then walking a specific pattern through my studio or grabbing a random book off my bookcase and turning to a random page while considering different approaches to the image. This brief embodied intervention consistently shifted my perspective and unlocked new creative possibilities that weren't accessible in my seated, focused state.

Somatic Awareness as a Flow Practice

Bringing together nervous system regulation, interoception, and embodied cognition, we can develop an integrated approach to somatic awareness that directly enhances flow capacity. These practices build the foundation for more reliable and sustainable flow experiences.

THE DAILY EMBODIMENT PRACTICE

This 10-minute daily practice builds your foundation for embodied flow:

ARRIVAL (I MINUTE)

- Stand in a comfortable, balanced posture

- Feel your feet connecting to the ground

- Take five slow, full breaths

- Notice your current physical and energetic state

RHYTHMIC MOVEMENT (3 MINUTES)

- Begin gentle movement synchronized with breath

- Allow the movement to gradually increase in range

- Explore different levels (low, middle, high)

- Follow what feels most needed in your body

TARGETED RELEASE (2 MINUTES)

- Identify areas of tension or holding

- Apply gentle pressure or stretching to these areas

- Breathe into any resistance

- Allow natural unwinding rather than forcing

STILLNESS INTEGRATION (2 MINUTES)

- Return to a comfortable seated or standing position

- Close your eyes and scan your body

- Notice the effects of the movement and release

- Feel the quality of presence in your body

INTENTION SETTING (2 MINUTES)

- Identify your desired state for upcoming activities

- Feel this state as a physical experience

- Set an intention for embodied awareness throughout your day

- Create a somatic anchor (a specific sensation or gesture) to recall this state

This practice builds the mind-body connection that serves as the foundation for flow, making it more accessible across different contexts and activities.

Somatic Check-ins: Micro-Practices

While the daily practice builds your foundation, brief somatic check-ins throughout the day help maintain embodied awareness and flow access:

THE 30-SECOND RESET (USE EVERY 60-90 MINUTES)

+ Pause your activity completely

+ Take three conscious breaths

+ Scan your body for tension, particularly in neck, shoulders, and jaw

+ Make any needed adjustments to posture and tension

+ Reconnect with your current purpose before continuing

THE STATE SHIFT PROTOCOL
(USE WHEN TRANSITIONING BETWEEN ACTIVITIES)

+ Complete the previous activity with a clear ending

+ Stand and shake out your body for 10-15 seconds

+ Roll your shoulders and stretch your spine

+ Take three breaths matched to your desired next state

+ Adjust your posture to support the upcoming activity

THE FLOW BLOCK SCAN
(USE WHEN FEELING STUCK OR DISCONNECTED)

~ Stop and acknowledge the block

~ Close your eyes and scan your body

~ Identify any physical constriction or tension

~ Apply gentle movement or pressure to these areas

~ Re-approach your activity from this more open state

These micro-practices take minimal time but maintain the somatic conditions that support flow, preventing the gradual accumulation of tension and disconnection that often disrupts optimal states.

The Mind-Body Integration Framework

With greater somatic awareness, you systematically integrate physical and mental aspects of experience—progressing from recognition of physical cues, to prompt response, to resonance with your context, and finally to full integration and embodied knowledge.[15]

Awareness Level 1: Recognition

- Notice physical sensations as they arise
- Identify emotional states through physical cues
- Recognize patterns of tension or activation
- Development practice: Daily body scanning and emotional location

Awareness Level 2: Response

- Address physical needs promptly (hydration, movement, etc.)

‣ Adjust posture and breathing to support current activities
‣ Apply appropriate regulation techniques when needed
‣ Development practice: Needs tracking and response journaling

Awareness Level 3: Resonance

‣ Feel subtle interactions between body and environment
‣ Sense energetic dynamics in social situations
‣ Experience physical dimension of creative and intellectual processes
‣ Development practice: Attention to subtle sensations during varied activities

Awareness Level 4: Integration

‣ Experience unified mind-body states rather than separate domains
‣ Access embodied knowledge directly
‣ Move fluidly between different somatic-cognitive states
‣ Development practice: Flow state tracking with somatic awareness

This progressive framework helps you develop the mind-body integration that characterizes mature flow experiences—where thinking, feeling, and action merge into a seamless whole.

A Ritual for Flow Reset

To bring together the concepts and practices from this chapter, here is a comprehensive flow reset ritual that addresses the full mind-body system. Use this 5-minute practice whenever you need to shift from fragmentation to integration, or before any activity where flow is desired:

THE 5-5-5 FLOW RESET RITUAL

PHASE I: RELEASE (I MINUTE)

- Stand in a comfortable position

- Shake out your entire body for 20 seconds

- Roll your shoulders, neck, and ankles

- Gently twist your spine in both directions

- Take three deep exhales with audible sighs

PHASE 2: REGULATE (1 MINUTE)

~ Place one hand on your chest and one on your belly

~Breathe in for 4 counts, hold for 2, out for 6

~ Repeat this pattern for 5-6 breath cycles

~ Feel your nervous system settling into balance

~ Notice the quality of alertness with ease

PHASE 3: RECONNECT (1 MINUTE)

+ Close your eyes and scan your internal state

+ Notice any hunger, thirst, or physical needs

+ Acknowledge any emotions present without judgment

+ Feel your feet connecting to the ground

+ Sense the space around your body

PHASE 4: REORIENT (1 MINUTE)

+ Open your eyes and take in your surroundings

+ Notice three things you haven't observed before

+ Feel the temperature and texture of the air

+ Listen for distant sounds beyond immediate space

+ Sense your position in the broader environment

PHASE 5: REFOCUS (1 MINUTE)

+ Set a clear intention for your next period of activity

+ Connect this intention to something meaningful

+ Adjust your posture to support this intention

+ Take three breaths with this purpose in mind

+ Begin your activity from this centered state

This reset ritual creates a clean transition between states, addressing each level of the mind-body system: physical tension, nervous system regulation, interoceptive awareness, environmental connection, and purposeful focus. The result is an integrated state where flow can emerge more naturally.

~ § ~

REFLECTION PROMPT

Consider your relationship with embodied awareness:

• When have you noticed a clear connection between your physical state and your capacity for presence or flow?

• Which aspects of somatic awareness (nervous system regulation, interoception, or embodied cognition) seem most relevant to your personal flow challenges?

• What patterns of physical tension or disconnection most commonly precede your flow blocks?

• What one practice from this chapter could you implement this week to enhance your mind-body integration?

> *"You're not trying to control your body—you're remembering how to listen to it."*

~ § ~

Flow isn't found in the mind alone. It begins with the body. The more fluent you become in your somatic signals, the more easily you'll recognize the rhythm of your own return.

> **Yoga Connection:** *The yogic concept of "embodied awareness" finds scientific validation in contemporary neuroscience. Traditional practices like pranayama (breath control) directly influence the autonomic nervous system, while asana (posture) affects not just physical flexibility but cognitive and emotional states. These ancient approaches intuitively recognized what science now confirms: that consciousness is a whole-body phenomenon, and that certain somatic practices create conditions where presence and flow emerge naturally.*[16]

Chapter Ten.

Breaking Through Flow Blocks

"Flow isn't a reward for perfection. It's a natural rhythm waiting to be remembered beneath noise."

~ / ~

The post-wedding editing session had stretched into its fifth hour. Despite having captured hundreds of beautiful images at the event, I found myself staring at the screen, unable to make even basic creative decisions.

Which images told the story best? How should they be processed? Every choice felt both crucial and impossible.

This wasn't simple fatigue—it was a full creative block. My usual flow state, where editing decisions came intuitively and time disappeared, seemed utterly inaccessible. Instead, I felt a tightening in my chest, a scattered attention pattern, and a growing sense of inadequacy. The more I tried to force the process, the more stuck I became.

In my earlier career, this experience would have triggered a spiral of self-criticism and increasingly desperate efforts to "push through," usually resulting in mediocre work and mounting frustration. But I had learned to recognize what was happening: I wasn't facing a skill deficit or a motivation problem. I was experiencing a specific type of flow block—one with identifiable causes and practical solutions.

Instead of continuing to struggle, I stepped away completely. I closed my laptop, went outside, and took a 20-minute walk with no goal beyond physical movement. I deliberately shifted my attention to sensory experiences—the feel of air on my skin, the sounds around me, the rhythm of my steps. When a thought about the project arose, I simply noticed it and returned to sensory awareness.

Upon returning, I didn't immediately resume editing. Instead, I spent five minutes freewriting about what I hoped the final collection would convey about the couple and their celebration. This reconnection to purpose, combined with the physical and mental reset, created a remarkable shift. When I opened the images again, the block had dissolved. Selections that had felt overwhelming now seemed obvious. Creative decisions flowed naturally. The next three hours passed in a state of absorbed engagement, resulting in one of my strongest wedding collections.

This wasn't magic or random luck. It was the result of understanding flow blocks—not as failures of character or ability, but as specific patterns of interference with natural flow states. By learning to identify my particular blocks and applying targeted strategies to address them, I had transformed a potentially disastrous creative session into a productive one.

In this chapter, we'll explore the nature of flow blocks, how to identify your personal blockers, and practical approaches to moving through resistance rather than being stopped by it. Instead of treating blocks as evidence of inadequacy, you'll learn to view them as valuable signals pointing toward deeper alignment with your natural rhythm.

Understanding Creative Blocks: Flow Interruptions

Creative blocks aren't simply the absence of ideas—they're active interruptions to the natural flow of creativity. By identifying specific blockers, we can address them precisely rather than struggling against a vague sense of "being blocked."

The Inner Critic Block: Self-Consciousness in Action

The most common creativity killer is excessive self-evaluation during creation. When your inner critic activates prematurely, it:

▸ Interrupts the generative process
▸ Triggers performance anxiety
▸ Narrows creative exploration
▸ Diminishes risk-taking
▸ Creates self-fulfilling creative failure[1]

Neuroscience Behind It: Heightened activity in the dorsolateral prefrontal cortex—the brain's self-monitoring center—directly interferes with the neural patterns of flow.[2] This creates the paradoxical situation where trying harder to be creative makes you less creative.

Flow-Based Solution:

▸ Create a "judgment-free zone" for early-stage creation
▸ Develop rituals that symbolically set aside the critic
▸ Use timed creation sessions with deferred evaluation
▸ Practice separating generation from refinement
▸ Cultivate self-compassion for creative struggles

The Overwhelm Block: Too Many Possibilities

Sometimes creativity stalls not from a lack of ideas but from too many competing possibilities and no clear direction.

Neuroscience Behind It: When faced with excessive options, the brain's executive function systems become overloaded, leading to decision paralysis and increased activity in the anterior cingulate cortex—the brain region associated with conflict monitoring.[3]

Flow-Based Solution:

- Create productive constraints that narrow possibilities
- Establish clear creative principles or guidelines
- Use randomization techniques to force decisions
- Break large creative projects into defined segments
- Focus on process rather than all potential outcomes

The Depletion Block: Emptied Creative Resources

Creativity requires psychological and neurological resources that can be temporarily depleted through overwork, stress, or lack of diverse inputs.

Neuroscience Behind It: Sustained creative effort without replenishment leads to reduced dopamine (motivation), increased cortisol (stress), and diminished activity in the default mode network (imagination and association).[4]

Flow-Based Solution:

- Design deliberate cycles of creation and replenishment
- Curate diverse inputs that cross disciplinary boundaries
- Create "creative compost"—collection systems for inspiring material
- Engage in completely different creative activities as cross- training
- Prioritize sleep, movement, and nature exposure

The Perfectionism Block:
Fear Disguised as Standards

Perhaps the most insidious block, perfectionism appears as high standards but functions as fear of failure, judgment, or vulnerability.

Neuroscience Behind It: Perfectionism activates the brain's threat- detection system, triggering a subtle fight-flight-freeze response that inhibits the open, exploratory state required for creative flow.[5]

Flow-Based Solution:

- Create "low-stakes" creative practices
- Track and celebrate imperfect action
- Use time constraints to override perfectionist tendencies
- Share work earlier in the process with trusted feedback sources
- Distinguish between excellence (healthy) and perfection (impossible)

The CLEAR Method:
Moving Through Flow Blocks

Understanding your blocks is only the first step. The next is developing a systematic approach to moving through them. This is where the CLEAR Method comes in—a simple five-step process starting with C:

C: CONNECT WITH THE BLOCK

Instead of fighting resistance, start by acknowledging it. Name what you're experiencing without judgment.

Practice: Block Mapping

- When you feel blocked, place your hand on your heart and take three slow breaths
- Ask: "What am I experiencing right now?" (Perfectionism? Overwhelm? Depletion?)
- Locate the sensation in your body – where do you physically feel it?
- Say aloud: "I notice [this block] is present right now."

This simple practice interrupts the spiral of frustration that often accompanies blocks. By naming your experience, you activate your prefrontal cortex in a constructive rather than destructive way.

Photography Example: When struggling with culling and editing decisions after large events, I developed a habit of "block mapping" whenever I felt stuck. Simply identifying "I'm in overwhelm block right now" and noticing the scattered attention and chest tightness that accompanied it created immediate relief. This naming separated me from the block—I wasn't my resistance anymore but simply experiencing a temporary state.

L: LOWER THE STAKES

Flow thrives when the challenge matters but failure feels survivable. When blocks appear, temporarily reduce the perceived stakes.

Practice: The Playground Shift

- Ask: "How would I approach this if it were just practice?"
- Set a defined time period (10-30 minutes) where "nothing counts"
- Give yourself permission to create something imperfect, messy, or experimental
- Focus on process rather than outcome

This practice bypasses the protective mechanisms that trigger blocks by creating psychological safety.

Client Example: A wedding photographer I mentored struggled with paralysis during couple portrait sessions, feeling the pressure of creating "portfolio-worthy" images with limited time. I suggested she start each session with what we called "warmup shots"—5 minutes where she explicitly told herself these images "didn't count" and she was just getting comfortable. The freedom this created consistently led to creative flow that continued throughout the real session, and ironically, many of her "throwaway warmups" became her most innovative portraits.

E: ENGAGE THE BODY

Flow isn't just mental – it's deeply physical. Shifting your somatic state can bypass cognitive blocks.

Practice: The 3-Minute Reset

- Stand up and shake your body vigorously for 30 seconds

- Perform 5 large, exaggerated movements (stretching, bending, reaching)
- Take 3 deep breaths, extending the exhale
- Return to your task with refreshed attention

This practice utilizes the body-brain connection to reset your nervous system and interrupt thought patterns that maintain blocks.

Research Validation: A 2018 Stanford study found that even brief movement breaks increased creative problem-solving ability by 41% compared to continued sitting.6 The effect was most pronounced when the movement involved full-body engagement rather than just standing.

Personal Example: During complex editing sessions, I developed what I called "the editor's reset"—standing up, shaking out my hands and arms, doing five full-body stretches, and taking three audible exhales before sitting back down. This three-minute investment consistently dissolved decision fatigue and restored creative flow, saving hours of frustrated effort.

A: ALIGN WITH PURPOSE

Reconnect with why your work matters – to you, to others, to something larger than yourself.

Practice: Purpose Touchstone

- Write 1-3 sentences completing: "This work matters because..."
- Keep this visible in your workspace
- Place your hand on this statement and read it aloud before beginning work
- Connect the task at hand, however small, to this larger purpose

This practice activates your brain's intrinsic motivation centers, producing dopamine and making focus more accessible.

Client Transformation: A commercial photographer experiencing burnout and creative blocks transformed her relationship with challenging corporate assignments by developing a purpose statement focused not on the technical aspects but on "bringing humanity and dignity to how people see themselves in professional contexts." Reconnecting with this purpose before difficult shoots shifted her experience from depleting to energizing, allowing flow states to emerge even in highly constrained commercial environments.

R: REDUCE THE FRICTION

Identify and eliminate the specific environmental or procedural friction points that trigger your blocks.

Practice: Friction Audit

‣ Track your work sessions for one week, noting exactly when flow breaks
‣ Identify patterns: What consistently interrupts your focus?
‣ Create specific interventions for your top three friction points
‣ Implement one solution at a time, testing its effectiveness

This practice makes block patterns visible and addressable rather than mysterious and overwhelming.

Personal Example: I discovered through tracking that my flow consistently broke approximately 45 minutes into editing sessions when I would compulsively check email—not from notifications, but from habitual anxiety about client messages. Rather than relying on willpower, I implemented a simple system: scheduled 10-minute email checks at specific times, with a timer and clear boundaries. This created the psychological safety to fully immerse in editing without the background worry, extending my flow sessions from 45 minutes to 2+ hours.

The Flow Block Recovery System

Sometimes, despite your best efforts, flow remains elusive. In these moments, you need a reliable system to reset and realign rather than forcing what isn't coming.

This three-part system helps you navigate persistent blocks without spiraling into frustration or self-judgment:

1. The 15-Minute Rule

If you've been struggling to find flow for more than 15 minutes, it's time to shift approach rather than continue pushing.

Implementation:

▸ Set a timer when you begin focused work
▸ If flow hasn't begun to emerge after 15 minutes, initiate the Pivot Protocol
▸ This prevents the negative reinforcement that comes from prolonged struggle

Scientific Basis: Research on ultradian rhythms (natural attention cycles) indicates that forcing focus beyond approximately 15 minutes of resistance creates diminishing returns and can actually strengthen block patterns.[7] The 15-minute threshold represents an optimal intervention point before negative reinforcement occurs.

2. The Pivot Protocol

When the 15-Minute Rule activates, don't abandon work entirely – pivot to a different type of value creation.

Four Types of Pivots:

▸ **Task Pivot:** Switch to a different aspect of the same project
▸ **Energy Pivot:** Match your current energy level with appropriate work
▸ **Environment Pivot:** Change your physical location or setup
▸ **Mode Pivot:** Shift from creation to organization, learning, or reflection

Case Study: When wedding album design sessions stalled, I developed a systematic pivot approach. Rather than forcing the creative selection process, I would switch to organizing images by timeline (task pivot), move from my desk to a comfortable chair with a tablet (environment pivot), or shift from design work to writing accompanying text (mode pivot). These pivots maintained productivity while creating space for the original block to dissolve naturally.

3. The Integration Window

After any work session – flowing or blocked – take 5 minutes to integrate the experience before moving on.

Implementation:

▸ Ask: "What worked today? What didn't?"
▸ Note any patterns or triggers you observed
▸ Identify one small adjustment for next time
▸ Express gratitude for showing up, regardless of outcome

The Research: Studies show that this reflective practice accelerates learning and adaptation. A 2020 study from the European Journal of Work and Organizational Psychology found that teams who implemented brief reflection periods improved performance 25% faster than those who didn't.[8]

Personal Practice: I developed a post-editing integration ritual that took just 3-5 minutes but transformed my relationship with creative resistance. In a dedicated notebook, I would briefly note what worked in the session, what triggered blocks, and one specific adjustment for next time. This simple practice turned every session—even difficult ones—into valuable learning that improved my process over time.

When Flow Blocks Persist: The Deeper Work

Sometimes flow blocks signal a need for deeper recalibration. If you consistently experience blocks despite applying the tools above, consider these underlying factors:

Identity Transitions

Major life or career transitions often temporarily disrupt flow access as your identity reconfigures.

Signs This Might Be Happening:

▸ Your blocks emerged during or after a significant life change

- Work that once felt natural now feels foreign
- You feel uncertain about who you are in your current role

The Path Through: During identity transitions, flow often requires conscious redefinition rather than automatic access. Create exploratory spaces where you can experiment with new approaches without pressure for immediate results.

Personal Transition Example: When I tried to shift from mainly wedding photography to niche commercial and portrait work, I experienced persistent creative blocks despite having all the necessary skills. The blocks reflected not technical limitations but an identity transition—I was no longer the "documentary wedding photographer" I had defined myself as for years. Rather than forcing myself back into familiar patterns, I created exploratory projects that allowed me to discover who I was becoming as a photographer. These low-pressure experiments gradually revealed new modes of creative flow aligned with my evolving identity.

Value Misalignment

Sometimes persistent blocks signal that your work has drifted away from your core values.

Signs This Might Be Happening:

- You can access flow in personal projects but not professional ones
- You feel ethically uncomfortable with aspects of your work
- You find yourself questioning the impact of what you create

The Path Through: This calls for honest reassessment of alignment between your work and values. Sometimes small adjustments can bring things back into harmony; other times, larger realignments may be necessary.

Client Transformation: A photographer I coached experienced constant blocks when shooting certain types of commercial projects that had once energized her. Through deeper exploration, she realized she had developed ethical concerns about promoting overconsumption through her images.

Rather than abandoning her career, she gradually shifted her client base toward sustainable brands and purpose-driven companies. This realignment resolved her creative blocks without requiring a complete professional reinvention.

Nervous System Regulation

Chronic stress, trauma, or prolonged pressure can dysregulate your nervous system, making flow physiologically inaccessible.

Signs This Might Be Happening:

▸ You feel constantly on edge or shut down
▸ Your block is accompanied by physical symptoms
▸ Rest doesn't seem to restore your capacity
▸ Flow blocks emerged after a period of intense stress

The Path Through: This requires direct attention to nervous system regulation through practices that create safety and stability.

Recommended Practices:

▸ Regular nervous system regulation practices (breathwork, embodiment)
▸ Professional support if trauma is a factor
▸ Temporary reduction in performance pressure
▸ Nature immersion and movement practices

Personal Recovery: After an intensely stressful year with back-to-back major projects and personal challenges, I experienced unprecedented creative blocks that standard approaches couldn't touch. The blocks weren't about creativity but about a dysregulated nervous system. Recovery came through a three-month focus on regulation: daily breathwork, weekly nature immersion, reducing client load temporarily, and working with a somatic coach. This physiological reset restored flow access more effectively than any creativity technique could have.

Building a Personal Block-Busting System

Now that we've explored various approaches to breaking through flow blocks, it's time to design your personal system—one that addresses your specific blockers and leverages your natural strengths.

Step 1: Identify Your Primary Block Pattern

Begin by reflecting on your most common flow blockers:

Reflection Questions:

- When do you most frequently experience blocks in your work or creative practice?
- What thoughts, feelings, or sensations accompany these blocks?
- What patterns do you notice in terms of timing, environment, or context?
- Which type of block (Inner Critic, Overwhelm, Depletion, Perfectionism) most resonates with your experience?

Documentation Practice: Create a "Block Profile" by writing down:

- Your 1-2 most common block types
- The physical sensations associated with each
- The thoughts or messages that accompany them
- The contexts where they most frequently appear

Example Block Profile: "My primary flow blocker is the Inner Critic, which appears most strongly during initial creation phases. It manifests as tension in my shoulders and jaw, racing thoughts evaluating my work against imagined standards, and appears most reliably when I'm working on projects with high visibility or unfamiliar elements. My secondary blocker is Depletion, which typically follows periods of intensive output without adequate recovery."

Step 2: Design Your Personal CLEAR Protocol

Based on your Block Profile, create a personalized version of the CLEAR Method tailored to your specific patterns:

Personalization Guidelines:

- For each step (Connect, Lower, Engage, Align, Reduce), choose a specific practice that addresses your unique blocks

- Consider your natural strengths and preferences when selecting approaches
- Create simple, accessible practices that can be implemented in your actual work context
- Write out your protocol in clear, actionable language

Example Personal Protocol: For a photographer struggling with perfectionism during client sessions:

CONNECT: "I place my hand on my chest, take three breaths, and say: 'I notice perfectionism arising.'"

LOWER: "I consciously adopt a 'practice mentality' by telling myself the first 10 minutes are just warm-up shots that don't count."

ENGAGE: "I physically shift position, trying three completely different angles or perspectives without judging the results."

ALIGN: "I remind myself: 'This work matters because it helps people see their own beauty and worth.'"

REDUCE: "I limit my visible options by working with one lens for at least 15 minutes before considering changes."

Step 3: Create Environmental Supports

Design your physical and digital environments to support flow and minimize common blockers:

Environment Design Elements:

- **Visual reminders** of your CLEAR protocol in your workspace
- **Block-specific interventions** (e.g., a dedicated notebook for overwhelm, a timer for perfectionism)
- **Friction reduction tools** tailored to your patterns
- **Recovery stations** for addressing depletion when it appears

Implementation Example: A portrait photographer created what she called "Flow Stations" in her studio—dedicated spaces designed to address specific blockers:

- A "Reconnection Corner" with client vision boards and purpose statements (for alignment)
- A "Movement Zone" with space for physical reset practices (for embodiment)
- A "Decision-Free Zone" with pre-set lighting and backgrounds (for overwhelm)
- A "Playful Experimentation Area" with unusual props and perspectives (for perfectionism)

These environmental supports made her block-busting practices concrete rather than conceptual, significantly increasing their consistent application.

Step 4: Develop a Consistent Integration Practice

Create a simple but consistent reflection practice to accelerate your learning about personal blocks and effective solutions:

Integration Elements:

- Regular review of block patterns and successful interventions
- Documentation of new discoveries about your creative process
- Celebration of progress and successful block navigation
- Refinement of your personal protocol based on experience

Example Practice: A weekly "Flow Review" using a dedicated journal with four simple prompts:

- What blocks appeared this week, and in what contexts?
- Which interventions were most effective in moving through them?
- What new insights emerged about my creative process?
- How will I refine my approach based on these learnings?

This consistent integration transforms blocks from frustrating obstacles into valuable data that continuously improves your creative process.

From Blocks to Bridges:
The Opportunity in Resistance

As we conclude this exploration of flow blocks, it's worth considering a fundamental reframe: What if blocks aren't primarily obstacles but invitations? What if resistance isn't a problem but a signal pointing toward deeper alignment?

The Wisdom in Blocks

When viewed with curiosity rather than judgment, blocks often contain valuable information:

- **Inner Critic blocks** may signal areas where skill development or clearer standards would serve your work
- **Overwhelm blocks** often indicate a need for better structures or clearer priorities
- **Depletion blocks** reliably signal that recovery and input have been neglected
- **Perfectionism blocks** frequently point toward unaddressed fears or values conflicts

By approaching blocks as messengers rather than enemies, you gain access to the guidance they contain—using resistance as a compass rather than experiencing it as a barrier.

From Management to Partnership

This perspective invites a shift from managing blocks to partnering with them:

Management Approach:

- Views blocks as problems to be eliminated
- Relies on willpower and discipline

- Creates ongoing struggle with resistance
- Treats blocks as separate from the creative process

Partnership Approach:

- Views blocks as integrated parts of the creative cycle
- Works with the underlying energy and information
- Creates collaborative relationship with resistance
- Treats blocks as valuable elements of the creative process

This partnership doesn't romanticize struggle or suggest that blocks are pleasant. Rather, it acknowledges that resistance is a natural and informative part of any creative journey—not evidence of inadequacy but an expected aspect of meaningful work.

Artist's Insight: A fine art photographer shared a perspective that transformed my understanding of blocks: "I used to think my resistance was the enemy of my art. Now I see it's actually the guardian—it shows up most strongly when I'm approaching something significant, something that matters deeply. When I feel that resistance now, I thank it for highlighting what's important, then gently move through it toward what matters."

Sustainable Creativity Through Block Integration

Ultimately, the goal isn't to eliminate blocks but to develop the capacity to move through them with grace and wisdom—transforming resistance from a stopping point to a stepping stone.

This integration creates several powerful shifts:

From Frustration to Fascination

- Blocks become interesting data rather than personal failures
- Curiosity replaces condemnation as the primary response
- Each block becomes an opportunity for deeper self- understanding

From Fragmentation to Wholeness

- All aspects of the creative process are welcomed rather than rejected
- The full cycle of creativity is honored, including fallow periods
- Personal worth is separated from momentary states of flow or block

From Force to Fluidity

- Moving with resistance rather than against it conserves energy
- Natural rhythms of engagement and recovery create sustainability
- The creative process becomes more resilient and adaptive

By developing this integrated relationship with blocks, you create the conditions for sustainable creativity and more consistent access to flow—not because blocks disappear, but because they no longer have the power to derail your process or diminish your sense of capability.

~ § ~

REFLECTION PROMPT

Consider your relationship with creative blocks:

• Which of the block types described in this chapter most frequently appears in your work?

• What messages or assumptions typically accompany your blocks?

• Which element of the CLEAR method seems most relevant to your personal patterns?

• How might viewing your blocks as information rather than obstacles shift your creative process?

"Blocks don't mean you're broken. They're simply the gatekeepers asking if you're present enough to proceed."

~ § ~

Remember: Flow isn't a reward for perfection. It's a natural rhythm waiting to be remembered beneath the noise.

The goal is not to chase peak states. It is to become someone who knows how to return.

Yoga Connection: *In yoga philosophy, the concept of "duhkha" (suffering or discomfort) isn't seen as something to eliminate but as a teacher pointing toward greater awareness. Similarly, the principle of "pratipaksha bhavana" (cultivating the opposite) offers a way to work with challenging mental states by intentionally invoking their complement—similar to how the CLEAR method addresses specific block types with targeted practices. These ancient approaches recognized that obstacles aren't separate from the path but integral to it.*

Chapter Eleven.

The Transformative Power of Breath and Meditation

"Breath is the rhythm beneath the rhythm. When you return to it, you return to yourself."

~ / ~

It was the most important shoot of my career—a high-profile wedding at an exclusive venue with a client list that included celebrities and business leaders. Everything was on the line. As I prepared my equipment, I noticed my hands trembling slightly. My mind raced with concerns: What if the lighting is challenging? What if I miss crucial moments? What if my equipment fails?

The spiral of worry was familiar. In my early career, this anxiety would have followed me throughout the day, subtly compromising my creativity, presence, and technical execution. The resulting images would have been

competent but mechanical—lacking the intuitive timing and emotional connection that elevates photography from documentation to art.

But I had developed a different approach. Stepping away from my gear, I
found a quiet corner and closed my eyes. I began a deliberate breathing pattern: inhaling slowly for four counts, holding briefly, then exhaling for six
counts.

With each breath, I guided my attention fully to the physical sensations—
the expansion of my chest, the pause between breaths, the gradual release.

After just two minutes, the transformation was profound. My heart rate
slowed. The mental chatter quieted. My perception widened beyond my concerns to include the beauty of the venue, the energy of the gathering guests,
the quality of light filtering through windows. When I picked up my camera
again, I moved with fluid confidence rather than anxious tension.

That day produced some of my finest work—images infused with the
emotional richness and perfect timing that only emerge from complete presence. The difference wasn't better equipment or technical knowledge. It was
the quality of consciousness I brought to each moment, made possible by the
simplest yet most powerful tool available to us: conscious breathing.

Breath is our most accessible gateway to flow states. It's the doorway between the conscious and unconscious mind, the bridge between voluntary
and involuntary functions, the rhythm beneath all other rhythms in your life.
When approached with understanding and intention, breath and meditation
practices become powerful catalysts for accessing and sustaining flow.

In this chapter, we'll explore how these ancient practices align with
modern neuroscience, providing practical approaches to shifting your state,
sharpening your attention, and creating the conditions where flow emerges
naturally.

Breath as a Flow Regulator

Your breath is perhaps the most immediate and powerful tool for influencing your state. Understanding the mechanics and effects of different breathing patterns gives you direct access to your nervous system, energy levels, and
mental clarity.

The Science of Breath

Breath operates at a unique intersection in human physiology—it functions both automatically (you don't have to remember to breathe) and voluntarily (you can consciously control your breathing pattern). This dual nature creates a special opportunity:

The Autonomic Bridge

- Breath is the only autonomic function you can directly control
- Breathing patterns send immediate signals to your brain about safety or threat
- These signals trigger cascading effects throughout your nervous system
- By changing your breath, you change your neurophysiological state[1]

This mechanism explains why conscious breathing is such a powerful intervention—it provides direct access to systems that are otherwise beyond conscious control.

Key Physiological Effects

Specific breathing patterns create measurable changes in:

- Heart rate and heart rate variability
- Blood pressure and circulation
- Stress hormone levels (cortisol, adrenaline)
- Brain wave patterns and neural synchronization
- Muscle tension and physical activation
- Digestive and immune function

These effects aren't subtle or marginal—they represent significant state shifts that directly influence your capacity for attention, creativity, performance, and presence.

Breath Patterns for State Regulation

Different breathing patterns create different physiological and psychological effects. By understanding these patterns, you can deliberately shift your state to support various activities and needs.

The principle is simple: **exhale-emphasis calms, inhale-emphasis energizes, equal ratio balances**. From there, it's about learning which tool fits which moment.

The Calming Breath: Extended Exhale

This is the pattern I reached for in that quiet corner before the high-profile wedding shoot—and it's the one I recommend mastering first.

The practice: Inhale through the nose for 4 counts. Exhale through the nose or mouth for 6-8 counts. Maintain this ratio for 2-5 minutes.

What happens physiologically is immediate and measurable: your parasympathetic nervous system activates, heart rate and blood pressure decrease, cortisol and adrenaline drop, and heart rate variability increases (a marker of nervous system resilience).[2] This isn't subtle relaxation—it's a direct intervention in your stress response.

I developed a habit of using this pattern before crucial moments at events—just 30-60 seconds created a noticeable shift from anxious anticipation to grounded presence. The camera felt different in my hands. My perception widened. Moments I would have missed in an anxious state became visible.

Use it: Before activities requiring calm focus. When anxiety blocks creative flow. During breaks to reset from high-intensity periods. As preparation for any precision task.

The Energizing Breath: Emphasized Inhale

The opposite pattern for the opposite need.

The practice: Inhale through the nose for 5-6 counts. Exhale for 4 counts. Maintain a slightly faster overall pace. Continue for 1-3 minutes.

This gently activates your sympathetic nervous system—increasing heart rate, alertness, oxygen delivery, and cognitive processing speed. The key word is gently. You're not hyperventilating; you're dialing up energy without tipping into anxiety.

When editing sessions stretched into evening hours and my energy naturally dipped, two minutes of emphasized-inhale breathing restored alertness without the jittery effects of caffeine. This became essential for maintaining quality through long projects.

Use it: When energy is low but focus is needed. Before activities requiring vigor. To counteract afternoon dips.

The Balancing Breath: Equal Ratio

Sometimes you don't need to calm down or amp up—you need to center.

The practice: Inhale for 4-5 counts. Exhale for the same count. Focus on smooth transitions. Practice for 3-5 minutes.

This creates autonomic nervous system balance, synchronizes cardiovascular rhythms, and promotes coherent brainwave patterns. It's the reset button.

Before client consultations or team meetings, three minutes of equal-ratio breathing created a state of balanced alertness—neither too activated nor too relaxed—that supported clear communication and responsive listening.

Use it: To establish baseline regulation before complex tasks. During transitions between different activities. When seeking mental clarity for decisions.

The Flow-Inducing Coherence Breath

This is the precision tool—the pattern specifically designed to create the physiological conditions for flow.

The practice: Inhale through the nose for 5.5 seconds. Exhale through the nose for 5.5 seconds. Maintain precise timing with no pauses between breaths. Continue for 5-10 minutes.

Studies by the HeartMath Institute demonstrate that this specific rhythm—approximately 5.5-6 seconds per inhale and exhale, creating a full breath cycle of about 11-12 seconds—generates maximum heart rate variability coherence.[3] This physiological state is strongly associated with optimal cognitive function and flow access. Your heart rhythm, breathing, and blood pressure oscillations synchronize, and your brain follows.

I discovered that 5 minutes of coherence breathing before important photoshoots created a state of alert calm that significantly enhanced my ability to notice subtle moments, anticipate action, and make intuitive creative decisions. This became an essential pre-work ritual for any high-stakes creative project.

Use it: As preparation for activities requiring peak performance. Before creative sessions. As a daily practice to develop baseline coherence.

The Two-Minute Breath Reset

While comprehensive breathing practices bring cumulative benefits, sometimes you need a rapid state change in the middle of a demanding day. This protocol creates a remarkable shift with minimal time investment:

First 30 seconds—Awareness: Stop everything. Turn attention to your current breathing pattern. Notice rate, depth, any areas of restriction. Don't change anything yet. Just observe your current mental and emotional state. This pause alone begins the shift.

Next 30 seconds—Release: Take three deep breaths with audible exhales. Let your shoulders drop. Soften your jaw. Intentionally release any obvious tension you discovered in the awareness phase.

Final 60 seconds—Regulation: Choose the breath pattern that matches your need—extended exhale to calm, emphasized inhale to energize, equal ratio to balance. Complete 6-10 cycles with full attention on the physical sensations.

This brief practice can be implemented throughout your day—between activities, before important conversations, when facing challenges, or whenever you notice fragmentation. It creates a "state reset" that re-establishes conditions for flow without requiring significant time investment.

I used versions of this reset dozens of times during long wedding days. Between the ceremony and reception. Before the toasts. When I felt my attention scattering. Each two-minute investment paid back in hours of sustained presence.

Building a Breath Practice

Start simple: 5-10 minutes daily, same time each day, one pattern at a time. Begin with extended exhale breathing for weeks 1-2, then explore the others. Consistency matters more than duration. A 5-minute daily practice builds more capacity than occasional 30-minute sessions.

Research Validation: Studies show that consistent breath practice creates lasting changes in nervous system regulation. Research published in the Journal of Alternative and Complementary Medicine demonstrated that daily breath practice for 8 weeks significantly improved heart rate variability, stress resilience, and cognitive function—with effects persisting beyond practice sessions.[2]

A note for those reading this from crisis: when your nervous system is overwhelmed, even simple breath practices can feel impossible. Start smaller than you think necessary. Three conscious breaths. That's it. Don't aim for state change—aim for one moment of conscious contact with your body. Build from there.

From Breath to Meditation: Deepening the Practice

Conscious breathing is meditation's doorway. Every breath practice you've learned in this chapter is, in a sense, a meditation—you're directing attention, noticing when it wanders, returning it to your chosen focus.

Formal meditation simply extends this process. Instead of 2-5 minutes of breath focus, you sit for 10, 20, or 30 minutes. Instead of using breath purely for state change, you use it to train attention itself.

The payoff for flow is substantial. Regular meditators show increased activity in attention networks, enhanced ability to sustain focus, and faster recovery from distraction. They access flow states more readily and sustain them longer. The meditation cushion is, in effect, a gym for the attention muscles that flow requires.

My own meditation practice evolved slowly. Early attempts felt like failures—constant distraction, physical restlessness, impatient clock-watching. What changed everything was releasing the idea that meditation should feel a certain way. The practice isn't about achieving a state; it's about noticing what's happening and returning attention, again and again. That returning *is* the practice. And that skill—noticing distraction and redirecting without judgment—is exactly what flow requires.

In yoga, asana developed as a way to prepare the body and mind for meditation. Practiced with breath and awareness, it becomes meditation in motion, cultivating the same attentional stability trained in seated position.

Meditation: Training the Flow Muscle

While breathwork provides immediate state changes, meditation develops the fundamental capacity for sustained attention that underlies all flow experiences. Think of meditation not as a mystical practice but as direct training for your attention—the primary skill required for flow states.

The Neuroscience of Meditation

Research on meditation has exploded in recent decades, with thousands of studies documenting its effects on brain structure and function. Key findings with direct relevance to flow include:

Structural Brain Changes

▸ Increased gray matter in the prefrontal cortex (attention control)[5]
▸ Greater density in the hippocampus (memory and learning)[6]
▸ Reduced size of the amygdala (fear and stress response)
▸ Enhanced connectivity between brain regions[4]

Functional Improvements

▸ Strengthened attention networks[8]
▸ Improved emotional regulation
▸ Enhanced sensory processing
▸ More efficient switching between focused and open awareness
▸ Greater activation of default mode network (DMN) during rest[7]

Physiological Benefits

▸ Reduced inflammation markers
▸ Lower stress hormone levels
▸ Improved immune function
▸ Enhanced sleep quality
▸ Better autonomic nervous system balance

These changes don't require years of intensive practice. Research at Massachusetts General Hospital found measurable structural brain changes after just eight weeks of regular meditation practice—as little as 15-20 minutes daily.

Flow-Enhancing Meditation Styles

Different meditation approaches develop different aspects of attention and awareness. Understanding their unique benefits helps you choose practices that specifically support flow states:

FOCUSED ATTENTION MEDITATION

The Practice:

Direct attention to a single object of focus (breath, sound, image, etc.)

When attention wanders, gently return it to the chosen anchor

Continue this process of focusing and returning

Begin with 5-10 minutes, gradually extending duration

Neural Development:

- Strengthens selective attention networks[8]
- Develops the ability to maintain focus despite distractions
- Builds the "attention muscle" through the return process
- Enhances frontal lobe executive function

Flow Application:

- Develops the sustained attention component of flow
- Builds capacity to stay with challenging tasks
- Reduces susceptibility to distraction and interruption
- Strengthens the ability to direct attention intentionally[8]

Photography Application: I found that regular focused attention practice significantly improved my ability to maintain concentration during long event coverage, allowing me to stay alert and creative even after many hours behind the camera. The practice of continually returning attention directly translated to returning to presence during mentally demanding work.

OPEN MONITORING MEDITATION

The Practice:

Begin with brief focused attention to stabilize awareness

Then expand attention to include all arising experiences

Notice sensations, thoughts, sounds, emotions as they come and go

Maintain a stance of curious, non-judgmental awareness

Start with 5-10 minutes, gradually increasing

Neural Development:

- Enhances receptive attention and awareness
- Develops metacognitive monitoring capacity
- Reduces automatic reactivity to stimuli
- Increases cognitive flexibility and creativity

Flow Application:

- Supports the expansive awareness aspect of flow
- Develops the capacity to notice subtle cues and opportunities
- Enhances receptivity to emergent ideas and insights
- Builds the ability to hold multiple elements in awareness

Creative Application: Open monitoring practice proved invaluable for developing my creative perception—the ability to notice subtle emotional exchanges, fleeting expressions, and unexpected compositional opportunities that others might miss. This expanded awareness directly enhanced my capability to capture decisive moments rather than merely documenting events.

LOVING-KINDNESS MEDITATION

The Practice:

Generate feelings of goodwill toward yourself and others

Use mental phrases like "May I/you be happy, healthy, safe, at ease"

Gradually extend these wishes from self to loved ones, neutral people, difficult people, and all beings

Focus on the emotional quality rather than the words

Begin with 10-15 minutes

Neural Development:

- Activates positive emotion networks[9]
- Reduces activity in threat-detection systems
- Enhances vagal tone and parasympathetic activation
- Increases connectivity in empathy-related brain regions

Flow Application:

- Creates emotional security that supports creative risk-taking
- Reduces self-criticism that blocks flow states
- Enhances social connection that facilitates collaborative flow
- Develops intrinsic motivation through positive emotional states[9]

Client Interaction Example: I incorporated brief loving-kindness practice before meeting with clients, especially those who seemed nervous or uncomfortable being photographed. The resulting shift in my own emotional state created a more relaxed atmosphere where authentic connection could emerge, leading to more natural images and a better overall experience.

BODY SCAN MEDITATION

The Practice:

Systematically direct attention through the body

Notice sensations in each area without trying to change them

Maintain curious, accepting awareness of whatever is present

Move from feet to head or head to feet in a methodical progression

Start with 10-15 minutes

Neural Development:

- Enhances interoceptive awareness (internal body sensing)
- Strengthens insula activation (related to self-awareness)
- Improves connection between brain and body
- Develops somatic regulation capacity

Flow Application:

- Builds the embodied awareness essential for flow
- Enhances ability to notice and address physical tension

‣ Develops capacity to use body signals as information

‣ Strengthens the mind-body connection necessary for immersive states

Movement Application: Regular body scan practice dramatically improved my physical endurance during long events by helping me notice and address subtle tension patterns before they became problematic. It also enhanced my ability to use physical sensations as early indicators of optimal shooting positions, timing, and creative opportunities.

The Meditation-Flow Connection: Three Key Mechanisms

The connection between meditation and flow isn't coincidental—these practices develop foundational capacities that directly enable flow states:

1. Attention Training

Flow requires sustained, flexible attention—exactly what meditation develops. The process of continually bringing attention back to an anchor during meditation is essentially training the neural networks that support flow states.

The Mechanism:

‣ Meditation strengthens the anterior cingulate cortex and prefrontal regions

‣ These areas govern attention allocation and maintenance

‣ Stronger attention networks create greater capacity for immersion

‣ This directly enhances the absorption quality of flow

Research Finding: A 2018 study published in the Journal of Cognitive Enhancement found that three months of regular meditation practice increased participants' ability to maintain focus during complex tasks by 14% compared to control groups, with corresponding increases in flow experiences during challenging activities.

2. Default Mode Regulation

One of the main obstacles to flow is an overactive default mode network (DMN)—the brain regions responsible for self-referential thinking, mind-wandering, and rumination. Meditation helps regulate this network.

The Mechanism:

‣   Meditation decreases inappropriate DMN activation during tasks
‣   It strengthens the ability to disengage from self-referential thinking
‣   This reduces the self-consciousness that blocks flow
‣   It enables the fluid shifting between focused and receptive attention

Science Connection: Neuroimaging research published in Proceedings of the National Academy of Sciences showed that experienced meditators exhibited significantly different DMN activity patterns, with enhanced ability to disengage this network during tasks requiring focus—a neural signature also observed during flow states.[8]

3. Autonomic Nervous System Regulation

Flow emerges most readily when your nervous system is in a state of balanced arousal—neither too activated nor too relaxed. Meditation creates this balanced state.

The Mechanism:

‣   Regular practice increases parasympathetic tone
‣   This enhances recovery capacity and stress resilience
‣   Meditation improves autonomic flexibility and responsiveness
‣   This creates the psychophysiological conditions that support flow

Applied Finding: Research on concert pianists found that those who practiced meditation exhibited more consistent flow states during performances compared to equally skilled pianists without meditation practice. The distinguishing factor was their superior autonomic regulation under pressure—they maintained optimal arousal states rather than becoming either too anxious or too withdrawn.

Building a Meditation Practice for Flow

To use meditation as a flow-enhancing tool, consistency matters more than duration. These guidelines help establish a sustainable practice that directly supports flow capacity:

Start Small and Consistent

- Begin with just 5 minutes daily
- Prioritize consistency over duration
- Gradually increase by 2-3 minutes every two weeks
- Aim eventually for 15-20 minutes as your baseline

Use Appropriate Structure

- Set a clear beginning and end (timer or bell)
- Maintain a specific posture that's alert but comfortable
- Create a designated meditation space if possible
- Use the same time of day to leverage habit formation

Track Effects on Flow

- Note how different meditation styles affect your flow access
- Observe changes in your attention quality during activities
- Document improvements in recovery and state regulation
- Connect specific meditative skills to flow experiences

Address Common Challenges

- For restlessness: Use shorter sessions with greater frequency
- For sleepiness: Practice with eyes open or at different times of day
- For discouragement: Focus on process rather than results
- For inconsistency: Connect practice to existing habits

Personal Development: I began with just three minutes of daily breath-focused meditation. Even this minimal practice created noticeable improvements in my ability to maintain presence during challenging shoots. As I gradually extended to 15-20 minutes daily, the effects became more pronounced—not just in specific flow moments, but in my baseline capacity for sustained attention and emotional regulation. This made accessing flow states more reliable across all domains of work and life.

Integrating Breath and Meditation Into Daily Life

While formal practices bring significant benefits, the real power emerges when you integrate these approaches into your daily activities and work. This integration creates a continuous foundation for flow rather than isolated experiences.

Micro-Practices for Busy Lives

These brief interventions take minimal time but create meaningful shifts in state:

THE THREE-BREATH RESET (30 SECONDS)

Pause whatever you're doing

Take three full, conscious breaths

On the first breath, focus on physical sensations

On the second breath, release any obvious tension

On the third breath, set an intention for what follows

Return to activity with renewed presence

THE SENSORY MINUTE (60 SECONDS)

Stop and notice five things you can see

Acknowledge four things you can feel/touch

Identify three things you can hear

Recognize two things you can smell

Note one thing you can taste

This grounds attention in present-moment sensory experience

THE STATE SHIFT PROTOCOL (90 SECONDS)

When transitioning between activities, implement:

30 seconds of conscious breathing

30 seconds of physical movement or stretching

30 seconds of setting intention for the next activity

This creates clean transitions rather than carrying mental residue

Work Integration Example: During wedding days with multiple locations and changing conditions, I implemented the State Shift Protocol between major segments (preparation, ceremony, portraits, reception). This 90-second investment created psychological transitions that matched the physical ones, allowing me to approach each new segment with fresh attention rather than accumulated mental fatigue.

Activity-Specific Integrations

Different activities benefit from specific breath and awareness approaches:

For Creative Work:

▸ Begin with two minutes of coherence breathing
▸ Set a timer to prompt breath awareness every 30 minutes
▸ When feeling stuck, implement a three-minute body scan
▸ End sessions with conscious breathing to integrate the experience

For Analytical Tasks:

▸ Start with one minute of focused attention on breath
▸ Use equal-ratio breathing during complex problem-solving
▸ When encountering obstacles, pause for three conscious breaths
▸ Take brief standing breaks with movement and breathing every 45 minutes

For Social Engagement:

- Before important interactions, practice two minutes of loving-kindness
- Use brief breath awareness during listening to maintain presence
- When feeling reactive, take one conscious breath before responding
- After significant exchanges, take a moment for integration breathing

For Physical Activities:

- Begin with body scan to establish awareness
- Synchronize breath with movement when possible
- During rest periods, use conscious breathing for recovery
- Complete with integration breathing to absorb benefits

Client Preparation Example: Before meeting new clients, especially those nervous about being photographed, I developed a specific preparation sequence: two minutes of coherence breathing, one minute of loving-kindness practice focused on the client, and a clear intention-setting moment. This brief ritual transformed my presence in ways that clients consistently responded to, creating more authentic connection and natural images.

Environmental Integration

Your physical environment can support breath and meditation awareness:

Visual Reminders

- Place small symbols or objects that prompt awareness
- Use post-it notes with single words like "Breathe" or "Present"
- Set phone or computer backgrounds as awareness cues
- Position reminders at transition points (doors, stairs, etc.)

Technology Support

- Use apps that provide periodic mindfulness bells
- Set calendar reminders for brief awareness practices

‣ Create custom alerts with specific breathing instructions

‣ Use wearable devices that monitor breath or heart rate variability

Designated Spaces

‣ Create a specific meditation corner or area

‣ Establish different spaces for different types of attention

‣ Design environmental shifts to support state transitions

‣ Use consistent elements that signal practice time

Studio Implementation: In my photography studio, I created what I called "presence points"—specific locations marked with subtle visual cues that prompted breath awareness. One by the entrance (transition), one by my editing station (focus), one by the client meeting area (connection), and one by the equipment wall (preparation). These environmental triggers maintained awareness throughout my workflow, supporting consistent access to flow during diverse activities.

A Ritual for Flow Integration

To bring together the concepts and practices from this chapter, here is a comprehensive daily ritual that takes just 15 minutes but creates powerful conditions for flow:

THE 15-MINUTE FLOW FOUNDATION RITUAL

Phase 1: Arrival (2 minutes)

Sit in a comfortable, upright position

Close your eyes or soften your gaze

Take three deep clearing breaths

Scan your body for areas of tension

Notice your current mental and emotional state

Phase 2: Regulation (5 minutes)

Practice coherence breathing (5.5 seconds in, 5.5 seconds out)

Maintain gentle attention on the breath sensations

Allow thoughts to come and go without engagement

Return attention to breath whenever it wanders

Phase 3: Presence Expansion (5 minutes)

Shift to open monitoring awareness

Notice sensations, thoughts, emotions as they arise

Maintain a receptive, spacious quality of attention

Practice being with experience without pursuing or resisting

Phase 4: Integration (3 minutes)

Return attention to breath in a more relaxed manner

Visualize yourself moving through your upcoming activities with presence

Set a clear intention for how you wish to show up today

Take three final breaths to complete the practice

This ritual combines elements of breathwork and different meditation styles to create comprehensive preparation for flow states. Practiced consistently, it develops the foundational capacities that make flow more accessible across all domains of life.

~ § ~

REFLECTION PROMPT

Consider your relationship with breath and meditation:

• When have you noticed your breathing pattern affecting your mental or emotional state?

• Which aspect of attention—focus, awareness, or regulation— feels most relevant to your flow challenges?

• What patterns of breath or attention do you notice during your most absorbing flow experiences?

• What one practice from this chapter could you realistically implement this week?

"Breath is the rhythm beneath the rhythm. When you return to it, you return to yourself."

~ § ~

When you understand the profound connection between breath, attention, and flow, the simplest practices become powerful gateways. You don't need to master complex techniques or spend hours in meditation. You simply need to remember—again and again—to return to the breath that has been with you all along.

> **Yoga Connection:** *Pranayama (yogic breathing) and dharana (concentration) practices have been refining the science of breath and attention for thousands of years. Modern research increasingly validates what these traditions discovered through direct experience: that conscious breathing creates specific psychophysiological states, and that attention is a skill that can be systematically developed. The Sanskrit word "prana" refers not just to breath but to life force itself—recognizing that breath is the gateway to our most vital energy.*

PART IV.

INTEGRATION

~ / ~

"Mastery blooms in the garden of consistent practice."

Chapter Twelve.

Recovery and the Flow Cycle

"You're not lazy for needing rest. You're cyclical for being human."

~ / ~

The phone had finally stopped ringing. After ten back-to-back days of intense work—a grueling schedule of 12-hour days filled with constant decision-making, creative problem-solving, and emotional engagement—I had deliberately blocked off three days with no appointments, no deliverables, no emails.

Yet rather than feeling relief, I found myself pacing my apartment, restless and oddly guilty. Shouldn't I be answering inquiries? Shouldn't I be getting ahead on projects? The silence felt almost physically uncomfortable—like an itch I couldn't quite reach.

This tension was all too familiar—the voice that equated rest with laziness, recovery with weakness. In my early career, I had fully embraced the hustle culture narrative: that success required constant productivity, that breaks were for the uncommitted, that tiredness was something to push through rather than honor.

The results were predictable but painful: declining creative quality, recurring illnesses, strained relationships, and a growing disconnection from the work I once loved. My flow states—those Green Moments that had initially drawn me to creative work—became increasingly rare.

Through a mix of self-study, self-awareness through experience, and finding mentors in the creative process, I came to understand that the most valuable creative skill isn't necessarily technique nor vision, but It's understanding the natural rhythm between channeling or creating and recovering. Without honoring that rhythm, you'll either burn out or fade away.

This realized perspective really challenged everything I thought I knew about creative success. Could it be that my relentless push for productivity was actually undermining the very results I sought? What if rest wasn't the enemy of accomplishment but its essential partner?

What I discovered wasn't just a better scheduling approach but a fundamental truth about human performance and creativity: flow isn't a constant state but part of a natural cycle. When we honor all phases of this cycle—including the essential recovery phase—we don't just avoid burnout; we create the conditions for more reliable, sustainable, and profound flow experiences.

The Four Phases of the Flow Cycle: A Deeper Look

While the basic framework of the flow cycle is straightforward, understanding the neurobiological mechanisms behind each phase reveals why this cycle is fundamental to human performance rather than merely a productivity technique.

The Neurochemistry of Struggle

During the struggle phase, your brain creates a specific neurochemical profile designed to support sustained effort and learning:

▸ **Dopamine** increases in anticipation of potential reward, motivating continued effort

- **Norepinephrine** rises to sharpen attention and increase alertness
- **Cortisol** elevates moderately to mobilize energy resources
- **Glutamate** activity increases in learning-related neural pathways

This cocktail creates the "productive tension" necessary for skill acquisition and problem-solving. Neuroimaging studies show heightened activity in the prefrontal cortex and anterior cingulate cortex—regions associated with executive function, error detection, and conflict monitoring. This neurological state is essential for building the neural connections that will later support flow, yet it often feels uncomfortable, which is why many people avoid or abbreviate this critical phase.

I experience this phase every time I approach a new creative project. The initial struggle involves research, planning, and confronting the gap between vision and current skills. This period isn't comfortable; it involves confusion, false starts, and moments of self-doubt. But this productive struggle lays essential groundwork for what follows.

Why Struggle Matters:

Many people try to skip this phase, viewing it as merely unpleasant. But struggle serves crucial functions:

- It activates necessary neural networks
- It creates the conditions for subsequent insight
- It builds the skills that make flow possible
- It establishes the challenge level that triggers flow

The key isn't to eliminate struggle but to engage with it productively—working at the edge of your capabilities without tipping into overwhelm.

Release: The Pivot Toward Flow

The release phase involves a dramatic shift in brain activity:

- **Default Mode Network** (mind-wandering, self-reflection) temporarily activates
- **Task-Positive Network** (focused attention) momentarily decreases
- **Alpha brain waves** increase, creating a more relaxed but alert state
- **Prefrontal cortex** activity reduces, allowing more distributed neural processing

This neurological pivot is why stepping away from a problem often leads to sudden insights. When you deliberately disengage conscious effort, your brain doesn't stop working—it shifts to a different processing mode that excels at detecting distant connections and novel patterns. Neuroscientists call this "incubation"—the background processing that occurs when the conscious mind releases its grip on a problem.

I discovered the power of this phase after days of struggling with a challenging project. Frustrated and anxious about the deadline, I finally stepped away, taking a long walk in a nearby park. I deliberately focused on the sensory experience—the crunch of leaves underfoot, the patterns of sunlight through branches.

As I walked, my shoulders gradually relaxed. My breathing deepened. The mental loops of worry quieted. I wasn't trying to solve the problem anymore; I had fully released it.

Why Release Matters:

The release phase creates the neurological conditions for insights and flow:

- It allows the brain to form novel connections
- It reduces the cognitive fixation that blocks new perspectives
- It gives the nervous system time to recalibrate
- It creates psychological space for intuition to emerge

Many resist this phase, feeling that stepping away demonstrates lack of commitment. In reality, strategic disengagement is a sophisticated performance tool used by peak performers across domains.

Flow: The Neural Symphony

During flow itself, we see a distinctive neural configuration:

- **Transient hypofrontality:** The prefrontal cortex (particularly the dorsolateral prefrontal cortex) shows decreased activity, reducing self-monitoring and inner criticism[3]
- **Synchronous neural oscillations:** Different brain regions exhibit synchronized electrical activity, particularly in theta and gamma bands

- **Neurochemical cascade:** The brain releases dopamine (motivation and reward), norepinephrine (alertness), endorphins (pleasure, pain reduction), anandamide (lateral thinking), and serotonin (wellbeing)

This state creates what neuroscientist Arne Dietrich calls "optimal arousal"—your nervous system is neither too activated nor too relaxed but in a sweet spot that supports maximal performance with minimal perceived effort.3 Studies using EEG and fMRI during flow states show this unique neural signature across diverse activities from athletics to artistic creation, suggesting that flow represents a fundamental organization of human consciousness rather than a domain-specific phenomenon.

When I returned from my walk that day, the solution to my creative challenge appeared almost effortlessly. Without the forced concentration and anxiety that had blocked me earlier, I found myself in a state of fluid creativity. Hours passed unnoticed as I worked with a clarity and intuition that had been completely inaccessible during my previous struggle.

Why Flow Matters:

Flow represents optimal human experience and performance:

- It creates conditions for peak creative output
- It makes challenging work intrinsically rewarding
- It produces results that often exceed conscious capabilities
- It creates deep engagement and meaning

This state is where Green Moments frequently occur—those transcendent experiences of perfect alignment when time seems to expand and significance deepens. In flow, we experience not just heightened performance but heightened presence, making these moments especially rich and memorable.

Recovery: The Integrative Brain

The final phase—and perhaps the most neglected in our productivity-obsessed culture—is recovery: the period where we integrate experience and restore the resources expended during the previous phases.

The recovery phase involves yet another distinct neurobiological profile:

- **Parasympathetic nervous system dominance:** "Rest and digest" mode activates

- **Theta and delta brain waves** increase, supporting memory consolidation
- **Brain-derived neurotrophic factor (BDNF)** rises, promoting neural growth and repair
- **Default mode network** activates more fully, supporting meaning-making and integration

During this phase, the brain literally rebuilds itself based on recent experiences. Sleep research shows that the hippocampus (memory center) replays neural firing patterns from recent learning experiences, strengthening important connections while pruning others. This process, called "memory consolidation," transforms temporary memory traces into long-term skill and knowledge—but only when sufficient recovery time is allowed.

This was the phase I had been so reluctant to honor after my intensive work schedule. Yet when I finally surrendered to the recovery my system was demanding—truly unplugging, getting extra sleep, spending time in nature, allowing myself to simply be without producing—something remarkable happened. Not only did my energy return, but I found myself experiencing a deeper level of creative insight about my work.

Ideas and perspectives that had been just beyond my reach suddenly crystallized. Technical challenges that had been frustrating me resolved themselves in moments of quiet reflection. My relationship with my work itself transformed, shifting from pressure to possibility.

Why Recovery Matters:

Recovery isn't just about feeling better—it serves crucial functions:

- It consolidates learning and skills development
- It prevents the depletion that leads to diminishing returns
- It allows the integration of insights and experiences
- It builds the resources necessary for the next cycle

This neurobiological understanding explains why recovery isn't optional but essential. When we skip this phase, we interrupt the very processes that convert experience into lasting capacity.

Integration: Where Learning Becomes Knowing

The consolidation phase after flow—when insights integrate, skills solidify, and experiences crystallize into wisdom—may be when consciousness does its deepest work.

Sleep research shows memory consolidation requires specific neural processes. But contemplatives report something additional: integration isn't just storing information, but accessing deeper knowing.

Yogic tradition describes this as moving from intellectual understanding (jnana) to embodied wisdom (prajna). Not just learning about something, but knowing it directly through experience.

Whether this represents enhanced neural consolidation or consciousness accessing information beyond brain-based memory, the integration phase matters deeply for sustainable transformation. Honor it.

Why Recovery Matters

While each phase of the flow cycle plays an important role, recovery deserves special attention because it's the most frequently neglected yet crucial for sustainable performance.

The Biology of Restoration

Recovery isn't a passive process but an active biological necessity with specific mechanisms:

Neural Recovery

- The brain consumes approximately 20% of the body's energy
- Focused attention and creative work create high metabolic demands
- Recovery periods allow for waste clearance and nutrient delivery
- Sleep and rest enable essential memory consolidation

Hormonal Rebalancing

- Flow states involve the release of performance-enhancing hormones
- These same chemicals can become depleting when chronically elevated
- Recovery periods allow endocrine systems to rebalance
- This prevents the downregulation that leads to diminished response

Schedule a dedicated reflection day after major project completions — not a day off, but a day *on* in a different mode. Review what worked, what didn't, what you'd change. The insights that surface during deliberate pause are often more valuable than weeks of active problem-solving. Your brain doesn't stop working during downtime — it shifts to a different and equally crucial form of processing that can't happen under the pressure of execution.

The Myth of Continuous Productivity

Our cultural narratives often celebrate uninterrupted productivity and demonize rest. This perspective is not just unhealthy—it's fundamentally misaligned with how human performance actually works:

The High Cost of Continuous Output

- Attention is a finite resource that depletes with use[1]
- Creativity requires cycles of engagement and incubation
- Emotional capacity fluctuates rather than remaining constant
- Physical energy operates in ultradian rhythms (90-120 minute cycles)[2]

I learned this lesson on the soccer field before I had language for it. In the lead-up to the Norway Cup tournament, our training intensified — two-a-days, extra conditioning, indoor scrimmages. But our trainer, Mariano Albano, an Arizona Soccer Hall of Fame inductee, also built in mandatory rest days that felt agonizing at the time. We wanted to train more. He knew better. The tournament schedule — 21 games across three countries — would have broken a team running on fumes. The rest wasn't a concession. It was strategy. A professional athlete I met at a performance workshop shared how dramatically her approach to training had evolved. "Early in my career, I thought more training always meant better performance," she explained. "I'd push through fatigue, viewing it as weakness. Then I hit a wall—declining performance despite increased training hours, recurring injuries, loss of motivation."

Working with sports scientists, she discovered that her approach violated fundamental principles of human physiology. "Now my training schedule includes deliberate recovery phases—not just physical rest but active restoration practices." The result wasn't just better physical performance but enhanced mental clarity, emotional resilience, and creative tactical thinking—qualities that had deteriorated during her continuous-output phase.

Signs You're Skipping Recovery

Since our culture often fails to validate the importance of recovery, many high-performers miss crucial signals that their recovery needs aren't being met. Here are key indicators to watch for:

Physical Warning Signs

These bodily signals typically appear first:

Sleep Disruption

- Difficulty falling asleep despite fatigue
- Waking during the night with racing thoughts
- Unrefreshing sleep despite adequate duration
- Increased need for caffeine to maintain alertness

Energy Fluctuations

- Afternoon energy crashes that affect performance
- Paradoxical "tired but wired" sensations
- Morning fatigue despite sufficient sleep
- Reliance on stimulants to maintain basic function

"I used to brush off those signs," a successful composer told me during a collaborative project. "I'd have these bizarre energy patterns—completely wired at night despite exhaustion, then dragging myself through mornings. I figured that was just the price of a creative career."

He described recognizing the pattern: first came sleep disruption—lying awake with musical phrases and deadlines cycling through his mind. Then energy instability—alternating between hyperfocus and complete depletion within the same day. If he continued pushing, mild health issues would follow—tension headaches, digestive problems, lowered immunity.

"I finally realized these weren't random health fluctuations but direct communications from a system desperately seeking recovery. Now I treat those signals with the same seriousness I'd give to any critical feedback about my work."

Cognitive and Emotional Signals

As recovery debt accumulates, cognitive and emotional patterns emerge:

Attention Quality

- ‣ Difficulty sustaining focus on important tasks
- ‣ Increased distractibility during work periods
- ‣ Problems shifting attention between activities
- ‣ "Spinning wheels" on tasks that previously came easily

Creative Capacity

- ‣ Reliance on formulaic approaches rather than fresh thinking
- ‣ Difficulty generating multiple solutions to problems
- ‣ Decreased satisfaction with creative output
- ‣ Loss of the playful exploration that fuels innovation

"I knew something was wrong when I stopped experiencing creative breakthroughs," an accomplished designer shared during a conference. "My work was technically sound, but that sense of alignment and flow had disappeared. I'd lost the joy and discovery that originally drew me to design."

Her portfolio showed the pattern clearly—her earlier work displayed an innovative sensibility and distinctive voice that had gradually been replaced by technically competent but formulaic solutions. She had been delivering major projects back-to-back for three years without meaningful breaks.

"What I was experiencing wasn't a loss of skill but a depletion of the cognitive and emotional resources that fuel creative vision. My attention had narrowed, my emotional connection had dulled, and my intrinsic motivation had been replaced by obligation—all classic signs of recovery deficit."

Designing Your Recovery System

Understanding the importance of recovery is the first step. The next is designing a system that ensures you get the recovery you need—one that works with your specific life circumstances and professional demands.

Daily Recovery Rhythms

Effective recovery begins at the daily level, with practices that support the natural ultradian rhythms of energy and attention:

The 90-Minute Focus Block System

- Work in focused 90-minute intervals aligned with natural attention cycles
- Follow each block with a 15-30 minute recovery period
- Design different types of recovery based on preceding activity
- Track energy and focus quality to refine your personal optimal intervals

Morning Recovery Foundation

- Begin the day with practices that activate parasympathetic tone
- Examples include gentle movement, meditation, or nature exposure
- Start with 10-15 minutes before engaging work demands
- Create a clear transition ritual from recovery to engagement

A software engineer described how this approach transformed his productivity and wellbeing. "I used to code in marathon sessions, often 6-8 hours without meaningful breaks," he explained. "I thought interrupting my flow would hurt my productivity. What I didn't realize was that without recovery periods, I wasn't actually experiencing true flow—just increasing struggle with diminishing returns."

He restructured his approach: "Now I work in what I call 'Focused Pulses'—90-minute periods of complete concentration followed by 30-minute recovery intervals involving physical movement, nature exposure, or completely different mental activities. The quality of my code has improved dramatically, bugs have decreased, and creative solutions come more easily. Plus, I can maintain this pace day after day without the burnout that used to hit me regularly."

The key insight was that sustained productivity doesn't come from continuous work but from strategic oscillation between engagement and recovery. By honoring the natural rhythms of attention and energy, he maintained higher quality focus for far longer than through forced persistence.

Weekly Recovery Architecture

Beyond daily rhythms, weekly patterns create the foundation for sustainable performance:

The Strategic Recovery Day

- Designate one day weekly for active recovery
- Design this day around replenishment activities
- Include both physical and cognitive restoration
- Protect this time with the same commitment as work obligations

Input/Output Balancing

- Track the ratio of creative output to restorative input
- Aim for balance appropriate to your field and work demands
- Schedule specific input activities (reading, learning, experiencing)
- Recognize that input activities are productive investments, not indulgences

One powerful version of this: protect an entire day each week from client work, meetings, and deliverables. Devote it to creative restoration — learning, strategic thinking, movement, connections outside your industry. It sounds impossible when your task list is already overwhelming. But most people who try it discover they accomplish more in four focused days than they did in five fragmented ones — and their decision-making sharpens because they're responding rather than reacting.

Seasonal Recovery Integration

The largest timescale of recovery involves seasonal rhythms that support sustainable performance over years and decades:

Quarterly Renewal Periods

- Schedule 3-7 day recovery blocks every 90 days
- Design these periods around deeper restoration
- Include significant nature exposure when possible
- Create space for reflection and integration

Annual Restoration Planning

‣ Map intensive work periods and recovery needs across the year
‣ Plan proactive recovery before and after high-demand periods
‣ Schedule at least one extended restoration period annually
‣ Design these experiences based on personal renewal patterns

What some leaders have discovered is that seasonal rhythm isn't just about individual wellbeing but organizational sustainability and innovation. The predictable cycles of engagement and renewal create the psychological safety needed for risk-taking and creative thinking while preventing the cumulative depletion that leads to conservative, risk-averse decision-making.

Recovery Modalities:
The Science of Restoration

Different types of recovery activate different restoration mechanisms.

Understanding these modalities helps you design recovery practices matched to your specific needs:

Physical Recovery Modalities

The body's restoration systems provide the foundation for all other forms of recovery:

Movement-Based Recovery

‣ Light aerobic activity that promotes blood flow without stress
‣ Range of motion practices that relieve accumulated tension
‣ Nature-based movement that combines physical and attentional benefits
‣ Social movement that adds connection to physical restoration

Sleep Optimization

‣ Strategic napping protocols based on circadian timing
‣ Sleep environment design for maximum restoration
‣ Pre-sleep routines that enhance sleep architecture
‣ Chronotype-aligned sleep scheduling

After high-intensity work periods, a multi-system recovery protocol outperforms any single modality. Combine gentle movement with temperature regulation (alternating warm and cool exposure), specific breathing practices, and a complete technology fast until the following morning. The key is addressing multiple systems — physical, sensory, autonomic — rather than relying on rest alone.

Cognitive Recovery Modalities

The brain requires specific forms of restoration to maintain optimal function:

Attention Restoration

▸ Activities that involve "soft fascination" rather than directed attention
▸ Environments that support involuntary rather than voluntary focus
▸ Experiences that create cognitive interest without effort
▸ Practices that reset attentional capacity after extended focus

Cognitive Mode Switching

▸ Deliberate alternation between focused and diffuse thinking
▸ Activities that activate different cognitive networks
▸ Practices that engage right-brain processing after left-brain work
▸ Experiences that balance analytical and intuitive thinking

After intensive analytical or focused work, visit a museum, gallery, or natural space with no agenda. Don't take notes. Don't analyze. Let your attention rest in what environmental psychologists call "soft fascination" — interest without effort. This engages different cognitive networks while your primary work circuits recover. Many people find that insights from their focused work emerge spontaneously during these seemingly unrelated experiences. The goal isn't to shut down mental activity entirely but to let different modes complement rather than continue the primary work.

From Recovery Guilt to Recovery Intelligence

Perhaps the most challenging aspect of implementing effective recovery isn't designing the practices but overcoming the psychological barriers that prevent us from prioritizing restoration.

Recognizing Recovery Resistance

Before you can develop recovery intelligence, you must identify your particular patterns of resistance:

The Achievement Identity

- Self-worth tied primarily to productivity and accomplishment
- Discomfort with periods of non-doing or rest
- Fear that recovery signals weakness or lack of commitment
- Tendency to make even recovery into another achievement task

The Scarcity Mindset

- Belief that time is insufficient for both work and recovery
- Fear that recovery will result in falling behind or missing opportunities
- Anxiety about what others will accomplish during your rest
- Perception of recovery as luxury rather than necessity

I recognized the Achievement Identity in myself long before I had a name for it. During my photography years, I measured my worth by how many shoots I booked, how many images I delivered, how quickly I turned them around. Rest felt like falling behind. Downtime triggered a low hum of anxiety — not about specific deadlines but about some vague sense that I was losing ground. It took burning out completely to see what was driving it: I had fused my identity with my output. Separating the two — learning to see rest as part of the work rather than its opposite — was the deeper recovery that no amount of sleep alone could provide.

This demonstrates the importance of addressing the psychological and identity-based barriers to recovery. Without exploring these deeper patterns, even the best-designed recovery practices often falter against deeply ingrained resistance.

Creating Green Moments Through Recovery

One of the most powerful benefits of effective recovery is its role in creating Green Moments—those experiences of perfect alignment where time seems to expand, presence deepens, and you connect with profound meaning in the present moment.

When your system is depleted, these transcendent moments of flow and presence become increasingly rare. The constant background noise of fatigue, stress, and fragmentation makes it difficult to access the state of clear receptivity where Green Moments emerge naturally.

A dancer described this connection beautifully: "When I'm honoring the recovery phase of my cycle, those 'Green Moments' seem to appear everywhere—not just in performance but in rehearsal, in teaching, even in ordinary daily activities. It's as if recovery cleans the lens through which I perceive life, allowing me to notice the significance and beauty that's always present but not always visible."

This perspective reveals recovery not just as a practical necessity but as a gateway to the most meaningful experiences life offers—a practice that enhances not just performance but presence itself.

~ § ~

REFLECTION PROMPT

Consider your personal relationship with recovery:

• Which phase of the flow cycle do you most commonly skip or shortchange?

• What signs of recovery deficit have you noticed in your work or life?

• Which recovery modalities seem most relevant to your specific patterns?

• When was your last Green Moment, and how might enhanced recovery create more of these experiences?

"You're not lazy for needing rest. You're cyclical for being human."

~ § ~

Flow is not a straight line. It's a spiral. And rest is the turn that brings you back to center.

Yoga Connection: *The yogic concept of "santosha" (contentment) recognizes that constant striving creates suffering, while acceptance of natural rhythms produces ease. Traditional yoga practice includes savasana (corpse pose)—not as an afterthought but as essential integration of the benefits from active practice. Similarly, ancient wisdom traditions across cultures recognized that fallow periods in fields weren't unproductive but necessary for future abundance—a principle equally applicable to human creativity and performance.*

Chapter Thirteen.

The Flow Lifestyle

"Flow isn't just what you feel–it's how you build. Rhythm becomes your architecture."

~ / ~

Y our work feels different from others I've collaborated with," said the project lead sitting across from me. "There's something about it I can't quite put my finger on—it feels more... alive."

I smiled, recognizing the observation beneath the words. It wasn't just about technique or skill but something more fundamental—something that couldn't be achieved through tools or methodologies alone.

"The difference isn't in the approach," I explained. "It's in how I've learned to be present with the process."

What this colleague couldn't see was the comprehensive system supporting that "alive" quality: the morning practices that calibrated my nervous system before creative work, the environmental design of my workspace, the rhythmic alternation between different types of energy, the seasonal cycles of deep work and deliberate recovery, the relationships curated to support authentic expression.

These weren't random habits but a cohesive lifestyle designed around a central question: What conditions consistently allow flow to emerge in all domains of my life and work?

The transformation hadn't happened overnight. It began with small experiments—adjusting my morning routine, restructuring my work schedule, reimagining my environment. Over time, these individual practices evolved into a comprehensive approach to living—one where flow wasn't occasional but foundational to how I navigated my days, weeks, and years.

The results extended far beyond my professional work. Relationships deepened through more consistent presence. Physical health improved as I honored my body's natural rhythms. Financial stress diminished as I made decisions from alignment rather than reactivity. The sense of rushed urgency that had characterized my early career gave way to a paradoxical experience: accomplishing more while striving less, creating higher quality work while experiencing greater ease.

What I had discovered wasn't just a better way to work but a better way to live—a flow lifestyle that transformed not just what I did but how I experienced every aspect of my life.

The Systems Perspective on Flow

A flow lifestyle is fundamentally about systems thinking rather than isolated techniques. Understanding the theoretical principles of complex systems helps explain why integrated approaches produce dramatically different results than fragmented ones.

Emergence and Wholeness

In systems theory, "emergence" describes how complex systems exhibit properties that can't be predicted by understanding their components in isolation.[1] This principle explains why addressing individual flow blocks without changing the overall system rarely creates lasting transformation.

When you adjust one element of your life—say, your morning routine—without considering how it interacts with other elements (relationships, environment, work structure), the change often fails to produce sustainable results. The isolated approach treats symptoms rather than underlying patterns, leading to temporary improvements followed by regression to baseline.

A flow lifestyle, by contrast, recognizes the interdependent nature of different life domains. When you design complementary practices across physical, mental, emotional, and social dimensions, you create what systems theorists call "positive feedback loops"—virtuous cycles where improvements in one area naturally enhance others.[2]

For instance, improved sleep quality increases cognitive function, which enhances work quality, which reduces stress, which further improves sleep quality. These reinforcing loops create exponential rather than linear improvements, explaining why integrated flow approaches often produce results that seem disproportionate to the effort invested.

Coherence vs. Fragmentation

Another key systems concept is "coherence"—the degree to which different components of a system work in harmony rather than opposition. When different aspects of your life operate according to contradictory principles, they create what systems theorists call "structural tension"—a state that requires constant energy to maintain.

For example, if your work environment demands constant reactivity and multitasking while your creative practice requires sustained focus and depth, you experience internal conflict that depletes resources. Even with excellent flow techniques in each domain, the contradiction between domains creates ongoing friction.

A flow lifestyle resolves these contradictions by establishing coherent principles across domains. When your relationship approach, work methodology, creative practice, and self-care all honor similar rhythms and values, they mutually reinforce rather than undermine each other. This coherence creates what systems theorists call "structural alignment"—a state where the system's configuration itself generates energy rather than consuming it.

The most profound shift in my career came when I stopped seeing flow as something to achieve in isolated moments and started seeing it as an outcome of how I structured my entire life. I realized that my flow states weren't just about techniques for entering creative flow as an artist but about how I designed my mornings, handled relationships, structured my environment, and managed energy across the day and season.

This systems perspective explains why small adjustments across multiple domains often create more significant transformation than major changes in just one area. It's not about effort but architecture—designing a coherent system where flow emerges naturally as a property of the whole rather than being forced into individual parts.

What a Flow Lifestyle Looks Like

A flow lifestyle doesn't mean being in flow states constantly—that would be neither possible nor desirable. Rather, it means designing your life to support the natural rhythm between different states of consciousness and energy, creating the conditions where flow can emerge naturally and sustainably.

Beyond Techniques to Systems

Most approaches to flow focus on specific techniques or triggers—how to enter flow in particular situations. A flow lifestyle takes a broader perspective, addressing the entire ecosystem that either supports or inhibits your access to optimal states.

This comprehensive approach involves several key shifts:

From Isolated Practices to Integrated Systems

- Recognizing how different domains of life affect one another
- Designing complementary practices that work together
- Creating coherence across various aspects of daily experience
- Building mutually reinforcing habits rather than conflicting ones

From Occasional States to Baseline Capacity

- ‣ Developing the foundational conditions that make flow more accessible
- ‣ Enhancing your nervous system's baseline regulation
- ‣ Building attention capacity that transfers across activities
- ‣ Creating environmental and relationship support for optimal states

"I'm working too hard at this," I thought to myself one day as I observed and really brought awareness to my list of flow-inducing methods. Flow isn't something you achieve through force. It's what happens naturally when you remove what's in the way.

I then proceeded to design my entire lifestyle around supporting creative flow—from my morning practices to my workspace design, from my project selection to my relationship boundaries, from my daily rhythms to my seasonal patterns. Nothing was left to chance or treated as separate from the whole.

It's not about finding flow in your work. It's about creating a life where flow can find you.

The Five Dimensions of a Flow Lifestyle

A complete flow lifestyle addresses five interconnected dimensions that together create the conditions for sustainable optimal experience:

Internal Architecture: Practices and Patterns

Your internal architecture consists of the regular practices that build your capacity for presence, regulation, and engagement:

DAILY FOUNDATION PRACTICES

- ‣ Morning routines that set nervous system tone
- ‣ Transition rituals between different activities
- ‣ Regular attention training through meditation or focus practices
- ‣ Evening integration and preparation for restorative sleep

I'll be honest: I'm not good at rituals. Elaborate morning routines with multiple timed segments have never stuck for me. What I discovered instead was something simpler—a single practice that accomplishes what all those steps are trying to do.

Nine rounds of Sun Salutations. 108 poses total. Under ten minutes. Ideally outside, facing the sunrise.

The science behind this timing turns out to be profound. Neuroscientist Andrew Huberman has documented that viewing morning sunlight within the first hours of waking triggers a cascade of beneficial effects: morning sunlight increases cortisol levels by about 50%—which is a good thing early in the day because it increases immune function, alertness, and sets a timer for healthy sleep 14-16 hours later. This early light exposure prepares the body for sleep later that night while improving sleep quality, hormones, and overall mood.

What struck me was how this aligns with ancient yogic wisdom. Sun Salutations were designed to be practiced at sunrise—not for mystical reasons, but because something in the tradition understood what neuroscience now confirms: our bodies are meant to greet the light.

When I practice outside, facing east, the experience deepens beyond the physiological. Birds become part of the practice—flocks of geese calling out as they fly overhead, hummingbirds appearing in nearby trees, songbirds providing a morning chorus that grounds me in the natural world. These moments of connection remind me that I'm participating in a rhythm far older than my personal concerns. The sunrise itself becomes a form of intention-setting, an alignment with something larger.

I won't pretend the practice is always easy or inviting. Each morning is different. Some days I feel immediate resistance—my mind generating reasons to skip it, my body stiff and reluctant through the first few rounds. Other mornings surprise me with suppleness and ease from the first forward fold, though that's less common. What I've learned is that resistance isn't a sign something is wrong; it's just part of the practice. I'm nearly always aware of my mind's objections, sometimes my body's too. I move through them anyway.

And here's what I know after years of this: I have never once regretted completing the practice. Not once. The version of me that finishes those nine rounds is always grateful the version of me that started chose to begin.

When I returned to this practice after a long break from yoga, I was surprised to find that my mind needed conditioning as much as my body. Working up to just nine rounds took time—not because of physical limitation but because of mental resistance. This experience led me to develop the progressive conditioning plans in Integration Guide II, designed to meet people where they are.

Beyond this morning anchor, I use movement and breath throughout the day to regulate—but intuitively, not ritually. A few conscious breaths before a challenging conversation. A stretch when I notice tension building. Walking when my thinking gets stuck. These aren't scheduled practices; they're responsive ones. I've learned to notice what my body needs and give it, without elaborate systems.

This is what internal architecture actually looks like for me: one anchoring practice connected to nature and light, plus ongoing responsiveness to my own state.

The impact of this architecture extends far beyond how it feels in the moment. By starting from centered presence rather than reactivity, each day takes on a different quality. Decisions emerge from intention rather than pressure. Challenges become opportunities rather than obstacles. Interactions with colleagues come from grounded presence rather than scattered energy.

External Environment: Spaces and Structures

Your external environment either reinforces or undermines your flow access through its design and structure:

PHYSICAL SPACE DESIGN

- Workspace organization that minimizes friction and distraction
- Environmental elements that trigger desired states
- Multi-sensory cues that support different modes of work
- Transition spaces that facilitate state shifts

The principle is straightforward: different types of work benefit from different spatial cues. If you can, designate distinct zones — even corners of the same room — for different modes. An editing area with controlled light and minimal distraction. A brainstorming space with more visual stimulation and room to move. When the environment itself signals what mode you're in, you spend less mental energy on the transition.

For entrepreneurs and business leaders, this might involve creating different physical or digital environments for strategic thinking versus operational execution. For athletes, it could mean designing specific environmental cues for different training modalities. The principle remains the same: aligning your surroundings with your desired states creates effortless support for flow access.

Temporal Design: Rhythms and Cycles

DAILY RHYTHMS

- Work blocks aligned with natural energy patterns
- Strategic alternation between focus and recovery
- Task batching based on cognitive mode
- Transition buffers between different types of activities

WEEKLY CADENCE

- Clear distinction between different types of days
- Deliberate recovery and integration periods
- Input/output balance across the week
- Social connection strategically positioned

The shift from linear to cyclical time perception transformed how I experienced even challenging periods. Intense work phases became sustainable because they were balanced with appropriate recovery. Difficult projects became manageable because they were positioned within a larger rhythm that included integration and learning. The pressure to be constantly "on" dissolved as I recognized that different phases served different but equally important functions in the overall creative process.

Relational Field: Connections and Community

The people and relationships in your life profoundly impact your flow capacity:

CONNECTION QUALITY

- Relationships that enhance rather than drain energy
- Authentic expression versus performance-based interaction
- Psychological safety that allows creative risk-taking
- Support systems for different aspects of wellbeing

I learned about presence agreements before I had a name for them — on the soccer field, where our best performances came not from individual brilliance but from shared states. We developed pre-game centering rituals without calling them that. We communicated through glances and spacing during play, maintaining a collective flow that didn't survive when even one person checked out mentally.

Years later, I brought the same principle into my personal relationships. I started making explicit what had always been implicit: mutual agreements about when we were fully available to each other and when we needed uninterrupted focus. Not rigid rules — more like a shared understanding that partial presence serves no one. I'd rather give my daughters thirty minutes of undivided attention than two hours of half-listening while checking my phone.

The shift was simple but transformative. By being fully present rather than partially available, connections deepened. By creating explicit agreements rather than unspoken expectations, tensions decreased. The people in my life stopped competing with my work for attention — because attention was no longer something I was rationing. It was something I was giving completely, in designated rhythms.

Purpose Alignment: Meaning and Direction

The deeper "why" behind your activities creates the motivational foundation for flow:

Values Clarity

- Explicit understanding of what matters most to you
- Regular reconnection with core values
- Decision-making filtered through value alignment
- Boundaries based on meaningful priorities rather than just logistics

The most profound shift in many professionals' relationship with flow comes through purpose reconnection. Rather than seeing daily tasks as isolated activities, reconnecting with the deeper significance of your work transforms seemingly mundane responsibilities into meaningful contributions, making flow more accessible even during challenging aspects of the process.

Clarifying your core values — and filtering decisions through them — reduces the decision fatigue that fragments flow. When you know what matters, you stop spending energy on choices that don't.

Daily Flow Design

Your day forms the building block of your flow lifestyle. By designing daily patterns that support optimal states, you create the foundation for sustainable flow access.

Morning: Setting the Foundation

How you begin your day establishes both physiological and psychological conditions that influence your flow access:

THE FIRST HOUR PROTOCOL

- Delay digital engagement to allow internal connection
- Include physical movement to activate energy systems
- Practice conscious breathing to establish autonomic tone
- Set clear intentions that guide attention and decisions

Rather than beginning each day by immediately checking messages, which created a reactive pattern, I developed what I call 'The Creator's Morning.' It's a 30-minute sequence beginning with breath and movement, followed by creative input from inspiring sources, then 10 minutes of focused planning, and concluding with a clear transition ritual before engaging with communication tools.

The impact extended far beyond how I felt in the morning. By starting from clarity and presence rather than reactivity, my entire day took on a different quality. Design decisions emerged from intention rather than pressure. Challenges became opportunities rather than obstacles. Team interactions came from centered presence rather than scattered energy.

Midday: Maintaining Momentum

The middle period of your day often determines whether initial energy translates into sustained flow or deteriorates into fragmentation:

Energy Management vs. Time Management

‣ Schedule tasks based on energy requirements rather than just time[4]
‣ Match activities to your natural alertness patterns
‣ Batch similar types of work to minimize switching costs
‣ Create deliberate oscillation between focus and recovery

This is where the 90-minute focus block system from Chapter 12 becomes practical architecture. I structure my own midday around these pulses—periods of deep concentration followed by genuine recovery, not scrolling-disguised-as-rest. On days when I honor this rhythm, the work that emerges in the afternoon often surprises me. On days when I push through without pause, I can feel the quality thin out by 3 PM, and I end the day having produced more volume but less value.

The principle is simple but counterintuitive: protecting your breaks protects your depth.

Evening: Integration and Preparation

How you end your day affects both your ability to integrate experiences and your preparation for the next cycle:

Work Completion Ritual

‣ Create clear closure for professional activities
‣ Implement a defined "shutdown complete" practice
‣ Capture any open loops for future reference
‣ Express gratitude for the day's accomplishments and learning

Transition Buffer

‣ Establish a boundary between work and personal time
‣ Engage in activities that signal state shift to your system
‣ Allow processing of the day's experiences

> ‣ Create psychological completion rather than lingering preoccupation

Design your evening with the same intention you bring to your morning. A simple integration sequence — reviewing the day's work briefly, a physical unwinding practice, technology disconnection at least an hour before bed, and a short gratitude or journaling practice — transforms evenings from collapse into active recovery. The key insight is that evenings aren't just about rest. They're about integration: processing experiences, consolidating learning, and preparing your system for renewal.

Weekly & Seasonal Flow

Beyond daily patterns, designing your weeks and seasons creates larger rhythms that support sustained flow:

The Ideal Flow Week

Your weekly design creates the container for different types of activities and energy states:

DAY TYPE DIFFERENTIATION

> ‣ Designate different days for different modes of work
> ‣ Create clear boundaries between creation, communication, and administration
> ‣ Design recovery days with the same intention as productive days
> ‣ Balance high-demand activities with restoration across the week

The principle is straightforward: designate different days for different modes of work. Give each day a primary function — creation, communication, administration, learning, restoration — so your brain isn't constantly switching gears. The power isn't in rigidity but in clarity. A baseline rhythm that your nervous system can anticipate makes each mode more accessible and reduces the cognitive tax of perpetual improvisation. Adjust when circumstances demand it, but always return to the rhythm.

The Seasonal Flow Cycle

Larger time horizons allow for deeper rhythms of engagement and recovery:

QUARTERLY THEMES AND FOCUS

- Designate specific development areas for each quarter
- Balance different types of growth across the year
- Create clear completion points and transition rituals
- Design appropriate recovery between intensive periods

I've organized my own year this way for a long time, though it took a while to trust it. Spring and fall for the most outward-facing work — workshops, coaching, active projects. Summer for creation and development. Winter for deep learning, integration, and the quieter work that needs space to unfold. Slower periods aren't gaps in productivity. They're the soil in which the next season's work takes root. When you stop treating the year as a single continuous push and start recognizing the natural rhythm of expansion and contraction, the work that emerges from each season carries more depth than anything sustained pressure alone could produce.

Designing for Resonance

A flow lifestyle isn't just about productivity or performance—it's about creating a life where your actions align with your deeper nature, creating a sense of resonance and integrity.

Alignment vs. Achievement

The shift from conventional success metrics to resonance involves several key distinctions:

FROM EXTERNAL METRICS TO INTERNAL ALIGNMENT

- Prioritizing how activities feel rather than just what they produce
- Valuing the quality of your experience alongside outcomes
- Recognizing that sustained performance requires sustainable states

‣   Making decisions based on resonance rather than just logic or obligation

The shift that matters most is recognizing that your best work rarely emerges from pushing hardest. It emerges from what I call structured flexibility — clear intentions and thorough preparation combined with genuine openness to what wants to emerge in the moment. This isn't passivity. It's a different kind of rigor: the discipline to prepare fully, then the courage to let go of the plan when something more alive presents itself.

Building Your Personal Flow System

Creating a flow lifestyle isn't about adopting someone else's formula but designing systems tailored to your unique patterns and needs:

SELF-OBSERVATION FOUNDATION

‣   Track your natural energy patterns across days and weeks
‣   Note which activities consistently create flow versus fragmentation
‣   Identify your personal barriers to optimal states
‣   Recognize your unique restoration needs and preferences

EXPERIMENTAL APPROACH

‣   Implement small changes rather than complete overhauls
‣   Test specific adjustments and assess their impact
‣   Build on what works rather than forcing idealized systems
‣   Expect iteration rather than immediate perfection

"The biggest revelation was discovering that my flow patterns don't match what I thought they 'should' be," a successful entrepreneur reflected during a business retreat. "I'm not naturally a morning person—my creative energy peaks in the late afternoon and evening. Once I stopped fighting this pattern and designed my schedule around it, everything changed. I now do administrative work in the mornings, client meetings in mid-afternoon when my social energy is highest, and strategic thinking in the evenings when my analytical capabilities are most fluid."

This observation highlights a crucial principle of flow lifestyle design: the goal isn't to conform to someone else's ideal pattern but to discover and honor your own natural rhythms. The most effective system is one aligned with your unique wiring rather than imposed despite it.

Here's what I didn't expect.

When I began designing my life around these principles — not just applying a technique here or there but actually restructuring how I moved through my days — the most surprising change wasn't in my work. It was in the space between my work.

I started noticing Green Moments in places I never had before. Not during peak creative sessions or high-stakes shoots, but in the ordinary seams of a day. Standing in my kitchen waiting for water to boil, suddenly aware of the quality of afternoon light on the counter and the specific weight of the mug in my hand. Walking from my workspace to the mailbox and catching the smell of desert rain before it arrives — that electric, mineral scent that stops me mid-stride every time. Sitting with my daughters and realizing, mid-sentence, that nothing in that moment needed to be different.

These weren't dramatic experiences. They were quiet arrivals — the kind of presence that used to visit me only during flow states now showing up during the pauses. It was as if clearing the static from my daily rhythm had uncovered a signal that was always there, just too faint to catch beneath the noise.

That shift — from chasing peak experiences to noticing the ones already available — may be the deepest thing this practice has given me.

~ § ~

REFLECTION PROMPT

Consider your current approach to life design:

• Where do you already see elements of a flow lifestyle in your current patterns?

• Which dimension (internal practices, environment, time, relationships, or purpose) offers the greatest opportunity for enhancing your flow access?

• What is one daily practice you could implement or refine this week?

- When was your last Green Moment, and what conditions supported its emergence?

> *"Flow isn't just what you feel—it's how you build.*
> *Rhythm becomes your architecture."*

~ § ~

A flow lifestyle doesn't mean constant motion. It means aligned motion. Motion that honors your nature—and expands your capacity to create from the center of who you are.

> **Yoga Connection:** *The yogic tradition of dinacharya—daily routine aligned with natural rhythms—recognizes what modern chronobiology confirms: sustainable energy comes from consistency, not intensity. Rising with the sun, eating at regular intervals, sleeping before the pitta hours of late night—these aren't rigid rules but invitations to harmonize your personal rhythm with the larger rhythms moving through all life. A flow lifestyle isn't built from occasional peak experiences but from the accumulated power of aligned daily choices.*

Chapter Fourteen.

The Flow Manifestation Method

"Manifestation isn't about bending reality to your will. It's about becoming so coherent with what you seek that life reorganizes itself around you."

~ / ~

You know that feeling when you're trying to remember a word and it's right there on the tip of your tongue? You can almost taste it, but the harder you strain for it, the more it slips away. Then the moment you stop trying—boom, there it is. That's manifestation in a nutshell, and if you've ever felt frustrated by the gap between what the manifestation gurus promise and what actually shows up in your bank account, you're about to understand why.

I learned this the hard way while staring at my laptop screen on a rain-soaked Tuesday afternoon, watching my business revenue chart spike and dive like it was tracing my nervous system. There were moments of momentum, followed by sudden drop-offs that left me questioning everything. My work was meaningful, but the income remained elusive—and I carried the kind of low-grade financial anxiety that turns even small expenses into emotional landmines.

I had studied the business playbooks. I'd built sales funnels, tweaked offers, tested copy, even ran ads that seemed promising—but none of it created the stability I needed. Some of it felt forced from the start, like I was trying to wear someone else's strategy. Other parts looked good on paper but drained me in practice. I kept adjusting, hoping to find the missing link—but underneath it all, something deeper was asking for realignment. Not just a better tactic, but a better truth.

The problem wasn't my skills—clients raved about the work. It wasn't my rates—they were competitive. Something more fundamental needed to shift, and I had the sinking suspicion it had less to do with my LinkedIn strategy and more to do with the fact that I was approaching my business like a desperate person trying to remember that word on the tip of their tongue.

Around this time, I stumbled into two completely opposite camps of thinking about success. The manifestation crowd said to visualize, affirm, "raise your vibration", and trust the universe to deliver your dreams (preferably while drinking organic, cold-pressed, green juice). The business strategists said to hustle harder, optimize everything, and track metrics until your eyes bled from spreadsheet strain.

The visualization-heavy path often felt like trying to pay rent with good intentions alone, while the all-strategy approach ignored the energetic shifts I could feel in real time—how my internal state, whether grounded or anxious, seemed to change how others responded to me, even when the words I used were exactly the same.

What if there was a third way? Something that honored both the mysterious and the mechanical—a method that treated consciousness and action not as opposing forces but as dance partners who knew exactly how to move together?

This hunch led me to what I now call the Flow Manifestation Method, an approach I developed through years of study with brilliant mentors like Martha Beck (who taught me that our bodies know things our minds haven't figured out yet) and master life coach Koelle Simpson (who showed me that horses can sense our authentic intentions from across a pasture—and humans aren't that different). Their wisdom was transformative, but I began to notice something troubling in how these teachings were often applied.

Why Most Manifestation Approaches Actually Block Flow

Before we dive into the method itself, we need to address the elephant in the room: much of what passes for manifestation work today actually creates the opposite of flow states. And this isn't just ineffective—it can be harmful.

I've spent years in manifestation communities, training programs, and coaching circles. I've witnessed the profound breakthroughs that happen when people reconnect with their authentic desires and internal wisdom. But I've also seen a shadow side that rarely gets discussed openly: the subtle (and sometimes not-so-subtle) ways that alignment-focused approaches can become a form of spiritual gaslighting.

Here's what I mean. Someone shares a real struggle—maybe they're facing financial stress despite doing everything "right," or dealing with discrimination in their workplace, or struggling with health issues. Instead of acknowledging these legitimate external challenges, the response often becomes some version of: "Well, what is your body telling you about this? You must be attracting this through misalignment. What stories are you telling yourself? Are you really in your essence?"

Sound familiar? This approach, while well-intentioned, bypasses the very real external factors that influence our lives and places all responsibility on the individual's internal state. It's like telling someone stuck in traffic that they just need to align their energy with flowing movement while ignoring the fact that there's an actual accident blocking the road.

The Flow-Blocking Patterns

From a flow science perspective, this approach creates several problems:

- Fragmented Awareness: True flow requires integrated awareness of internal state AND external environment. When we're told to focus only on internal alignment while dismissing external reality, we fragment the very integration that flow depends on. It's like trying to surf while ignoring the actual waves.

▸ Increased Internal Conflict: When someone's lived experience doesn't match what they're "supposed" to be manifesting, and they're told this is evidence of misalignment, it creates internal conflict and self-doubt. This psychological friction is exactly what prevents flow states from emerging.

▸ Bypassing Natural Feedback Loops: Flow involves constant micro- adjustments based on environmental feedback. But when external challenges are dismissed as just "internal work," we lose access to the very feedback that could guide us toward more effective approaches.

▸ Misunderstanding Resistance: In flow, what feels like resistance often contains important information—maybe the timing isn't right, maybe a different approach is needed, maybe there are legitimate external obstacles to address. But in alignment-only approaches, resistance gets pathologized as evidence of misalignment rather than wisdom to be explored.

When "Alignment" Becomes Spiritual Bypassing

I've seen this play out in coaching contexts where people facing real systemic barriers—discrimination, economic instability, health challenges—get told they're "attracting" these experiences through their vibration. Where any criticism of the approach gets labeled as "resistance" or being "stuck in old patterns." Where people get blamed for not being pure enough in their intentions when the method doesn't produce expected results.

This isn't just ineffective—it can be genuinely harmful. It isolates people from community support by suggesting their struggles are self-created. It prevents them from taking practical action by implying that external action isn't necessary if they're truly aligned. It gaslights them into doubting their own experience when something feels off about the approach.

Most insidiously, it creates a hierarchy where those whose lives appear to be "flowing" are seen as more aligned, more evolved, more spiritually advanced— while those facing challenges are subtly positioned as doing something wrong. This completely misses how privilege, systemic factors, and plain old luck influence our external circumstances.

[Note: If you're reading this from a crisis situation—financial instability, unsafe living conditions, or other survival challenges—please see Chapter 14.5: "The Bridge - Manifestation from Crisis" for specific adaptations. The principles here remain true, but the application needs to be bridged differently when manifesting from survival mode.]

A Flow-Based Alternative

The Flow Manifestation Method I'll share with you works because it honors the same principles as flow in every other domain we've explored in this book. It's integrated rather than fragmented. It works WITH reality rather than trying to transcend it. It treats feedback as information rather than evidence of failure. It acknowledges that we're operating within larger systems while still empowering individual agency.

This doesn't mean we ignore the importance of internal state—it's crucial. Our nervous system patterns, our perceptual filters, our emotional coherence all profoundly influence what we create. But we hold this alongside acknowledgment of external factors, systemic influences, and the simple reality that sometimes timing matters, luck happens, and forces beyond our control affect outcomes.

True manifestation, like true flow, emerges from the dynamic interaction between inner state and outer environment, not from trying to control one while ignoring the other. It's about becoming exquisitely responsive to what is while maintaining clear intention about what we're creating.

Their wisdom, combined with emerging neuroscience research and hard-won experience with the limitations of alignment-only approaches, revealed something profound: manifestation isn't about positive thinking or grinding harder. It's about creating coherence between your inner state, outer actions, and environmental realities so complete that opportunities seem to emerge naturally.

Here's what I started doing, and I'll warn you upfront—it's going to sound both ridiculously simple and surprisingly specific. Each morning, I wrote out exactly what I wanted my business to look like: collaborative partnerships with companies whose missions actually excited me, monthly retainers that ended the feast-or-famine cycle, and a calendar that energized rather than drained me. But here's the crucial part—I didn't write it as a wish list. I wrote it like a journalist reporting on something that was already happening.

Then I read this vision aloud every morning, not like I was reciting grocery items but like I was describing my actual life to a friend. I started talking about these emerging realities in conversations with colleagues, using phrases like "I'm in the process of..." instead of "Someday I hope..." And most importantly, I paired all this inner work with aligned outer action—redesigning my portfolio to reflect this vision, reaching out to companies that made my soul sing instead of just anyone with a budget.

The transformation didn't happen overnight (despite what every manifestation Instagram account would have you believe), but over six months, something undeniable shifted. Instead of the revenue roller coaster, I found myself doing work that felt like an extension of my deepest calling—creating spaces for transformation, partnering with people and projects that shared my values, and building momentum for events and offerings that made me feel fully alive.

But here's what really convinced me this wasn't just a lucky streak: my relationship with money completely changed. The constant low-level anxiety about having enough gave way to a quiet confidence in my ability to create value and be compensated for it. It was like I'd finally learned to remember that word on the tip of my tongue—not by straining harder, but by relaxing into a different way of knowing.

Why Your Brain Is Already a Manifestation Machine

Before we dive into the method, let's get clear on what's actually happening when manifestation works (and why it often doesn't). Your brain is already manifesting your reality 24/7—the question is whether you're directing the process consciously or letting it run on autopilot with outdated programming.

Your Personal Reality Filter

Here's something that will either fascinate or terrify you: your brain filters out about 99% of available information every second, deciding what deserves your conscious attention. Right now, you weren't thinking about the temperature of your left foot or the sound of air moving through your space, but the moment I mention them—hello, suddenly you notice.

This filtering system, which neuroscientists call "predictive processing," is constantly making predictions about what you're likely to encounter and then looking for evidence to confirm or deny those predictions.[1] It's like having a personal assistant who's incredibly efficient but also incredibly biased toward whatever you've trained them to notice.

When you consistently focus on specific possibilities through manifestation practice, you're literally reprogramming this filtering system. It's not that opportunities magically appear—it's that you finally start noticing the ones that were always there. Like when you're thinking about buying a red car and suddenly see red cars everywhere. The cars didn't multiply; your brain just got new instructions about what mattered.

Martha Beck calls this "the way of attention"—where you place your focus determines what expands in your experience. It's not mystical; it's neurological. Your brain is designed to find whatever you're genuinely looking for, which explains why pessimists consistently find evidence that the world is falling apart while optimists keep stumbling into serendipitous connections.

Your Nervous System Is Broadcasting

Here's where it gets really interesting. Your internal state—whether you're operating from anxiety or confidence, scarcity or abundance—creates distinct patterns in your nervous system that other people unconsciously detect and respond to. It's like you're constantly broadcasting a radio signal, and others are tuning in whether they realize it or not.

Research on mirror neurons shows that we automatically mimic the emotional states of people around us.[2] When you walk into a room feeling genuinely confident about your value, others' nervous systems literally start resonating with that confidence. When you approach networking from desperation, people can sense it before you even open your mouth—not because they're psychic, but because their mirror neuron systems are picking up on subtle cues in your posture, tone, and energy.

The HeartMath Institute has measured actual electromagnetic field patterns that extend several feet beyond our bodies, changing based on our emotional states.[3] When you're in coherent emotional states like appreciation or calm confidence, you generate field patterns that others unconsciously find attractive and trustworthy.

This explains why the same elevator pitch delivered from two different internal states can produce completely different responses. It's not just about your words or body language—there's actual nervous system communication happening below the threshold of conscious awareness. You're not attracting opportunities through cosmic ordering; you're influencing how others perceive and respond to you through biological signaling systems that evolved over millions of years.

The Dance Between Being and Doing

Here's where most manifestation approaches go wrong: they treat consciousness and action as separate phases. First visualize, then act. First get clear on what you want, then figure out how to get it. This artificial separation misses the most important part—they're actually one integrated process.

When you truly embody the state of being aligned with your vision, different actions naturally emerge. You find yourself making different choices, having different conversations, noticing different possibilities—not because you're forcing yourself to act differently, but because the actions feel natural from this new internal state.

Think of it like learning to dance. At first, you have to think about each step separately: foot here, turn there, don't step on your partner. But once you really get it, the movements flow naturally from the music. You're not thinking your way through each motion; you're responding from a place of embodied knowing.

Conversely, when you take actions aligned with your vision (even when you don't quite feel ready), these actions start to shift your internal state. Each time you reach out to a values-aligned potential client instead of accepting misaligned work, each time you speak about your vision as emerging reality rather than distant hope, you're strengthening the neural pathways that support this new identity.

This creates what systems theorists call a "virtuous cycle"—each element reinforces the other, building momentum over time. But you have to engage both elements. Visualization without aligned action creates internal conflict. Action without aligned consciousness produces results that don't match your deeper intentions. Only when both dimensions dance together does manifestation feel effortless and powerful.

The Flow Manifestation Method: Your Four-Step Dance with Reality

Now that you understand the mechanics, let's get practical. This method integrates everything we know about how consciousness shapes reality into a simple, repeatable process that anyone can use.

STEP 1: WRITE IT
Compose an embodied declaration

STEP 2: READ IT
Review the declaration daily

STEP 3: SPEAK IT
Share aspects of your vision

STEP 4: ACT IT
Take inspired steps forward

Step 1: Write It

(Like a Journalist from the Future)

Most people write their goals like they're composing a letter to Santa. "I want this, I hope for that, maybe someday I'll have…" This approach automatically puts you in the energy of lack—focusing on what you don't have rather than what you're creating.

Instead, write your vision like you're a journalist reporting on something that's already unfolding. Use present tense: "I am collaborating with…" not "I will find…" Describe both what's happening and how it feels to be living it. Include enough sensory detail that your nervous system can't tell the difference between the vision and reality.

Here's the key principle: your brain responds similarly to vividly imagined experiences and actual experiences.[4] When you write with present-tense embodiment, you're creating neural pathways that support this reality before it shows up in your external world. You're giving your predictive processing system new instructions about what to notice and expect.

But—and this is crucial—focus on the essence of what you want, not just the external form. Instead of "I have exactly $10,000 in monthly revenue," try "I am consistently creating value that people are excited to pay for, and money flows to me in a way that feels both abundant and sustainable." The first locks you into a specific number; the second opens space for your vision to manifest in ways that might be even better than what you originally imagined.

My mentor Martha Beck taught me to always check whether your vision creates expansion or contraction in your body. If writing about your future makes you feel tight, anxious, or effortful, you're probably trying to manifest from ego rather than essence. Real vision feels like coming home to yourself.

Step 2: Read It
(With Feeling, Not Just Thinking)

This isn't about mindlessly repeating affirmations while your brain scrolls through your to-do list. Reading your vision should be like spending time with your favorite person—present, engaged, and genuinely enjoyable.

Read aloud every morning, ideally at the same time to establish neural consistency. Your brain loves patterns, and this repetition strengthens the predictive models you're creating. But here's what most people miss: read with full emotional engagement. Feel the satisfaction of the collaborations described. Sense the relief of consistent income. Experience the energy of meaningful work.

This emotional engagement is crucial because emotion is what consolidates memory and motivates action.[5] When you feel the reality of your vision, not just think about it, you're programming both your conscious and unconscious mind to recognize and move toward aligned opportunities.

Pay attention to which phrases or images create what I call "sparkle moments"—those little hits of recognition where something lights up inside you. These moments often point toward the most authentic aspects of your vision. They're your nervous system saying "Yes, this is true for me" rather than "This sounds nice."

And here's something beautiful: this practice often becomes a highlight of your day. Instead of forcing yourself through another self-improvement exercise, you start looking forward to this time of connecting with your emerging reality. It becomes less like homework and more like checking in with an exciting life that's waiting for you to step into it.

Step 3: Speak It
(The Art of Strategic Sharing)

This step is where many people either overshare with everyone they meet (and wonder why they get weird looks) or undershare because they're afraid people will think they're delusional. The key is strategic sharing—talking about your vision with the right people in the right way.

Start with people who are naturally supportive of your growth. You know who they are—the friends who get excited about your dreams rather than immediately listing all the reasons they won't work. Share aspects of your vision as emerging reality, not distant hopes.

Instead of "Someday I hope to work with companies I actually care about," try "I'm in the process of transitioning my client base toward more values-aligned partnerships." It's the difference between asking for permission and sharing a progression.

Notice how different phrases feel in your body as you say them. "I'm hoping to..." usually feels small and tentative. "I'm in the process of..." feels like movement and momentum. "I'm excited about how..." feels like enthusiasm and confidence. Your word choices aren't just semantic—they're neurological instructions to both yourself and others about how to respond to your vision.

This isn't about fake-it-till-you-make-it energy. It's about speaking from the part of you that already knows this vision is possible. Koelle Simpson taught me that horses can instantly detect the difference between authentic confidence and bravado—and humans have the same ability, even if they don't consciously realize it. Speak from genuine excitement about what you're creating, not from trying to convince anyone (including yourself) that it's going to happen.

Step 4: Align Action
(Following the Path of Resonance)

Here's where manifestation gets practical. All the vision and speaking in the world won't pay your bills if you don't take aligned action in the physical world. But aligned action feels different from forcing or grinding.

Learn to distinguish between inspired action and effortful action. Inspired action often feels like following a breadcrumb trail—you take one step, which reveals the next step, which opens a door you couldn't see before. Effortful action feels like pushing a boulder uphill while someone throws rocks at you.

This doesn't mean aligned action is always easy or comfortable. Sometimes the most aligned step is having a difficult conversation or putting yourself in an unfamiliar situation. But there's a quality of rightness to it, even when it's challenging. Your nervous system recognizes the difference between good discomfort (growth) and bad discomfort (forcing something that isn't meant to happen).

If inspired action feels impossible because you're in survival mode, start with protective action—any step that increases your safety or stability, however small. Sometimes the most aligned action is simply securing your basic needs first. Building a foundation of safety IS manifestation work.

Start with minimum viable steps—what's the smallest action that moves you toward your vision without overwhelming your system? Maybe it's updating one page of your website to reflect your new direction. Maybe it's reaching out to one person whose work aligns with your values. Maybe it's saying no to one project that doesn't fit your vision so you create space for something better.

Martha Beck calls this "following your internal compass"—that felt sense of what expands versus contracts your energy. When you're taking aligned action, even challenging steps tend to create energy rather than deplete it. You might feel nervous, but underneath the nerves is a sense of rightness, of moving toward something that matters.

Important: If you're attempting to manifest from a place of genuine crisis—financial emergency, unsafe living situation, health challenges, or trauma—please read Chapter 14.5 before proceeding. The practices there are specifically designed for building a bridge from difficult circumstances, honoring where you are while moving toward where you want to be.

Course Correction: The ALIGN Method for When Reality Gets Messy

Here's what no one tells you about manifestation: it rarely unfolds in a straight line. Sometimes what you think you want isn't actually what's best for you.

Sometimes the timing is off. Sometimes your vision needs to evolve as you do. **The ALIGN Method** helps you navigate these inevitabilities with grace instead of giving up entirely.

A: Acknowledge Current Reality - Get honest about where things stand without making it mean anything about your worth or the validity of your vision. Maybe the specific clients you wanted didn't materialize, but you got different opportunities that actually fit better. Maybe your timeline was overly optimistic. Maybe your nervous system needed more time to integrate new possibilities.

L: Listen for Deeper Intelligence - Approach gaps and delays as information rather than failure. What might your current circumstances be trying to tell you? Sometimes what looks like a setback is actually a redirection toward something better aligned. Sometimes delays indicate you need to develop certain capacities first, or that your vision needs refinement.

I: Integrate New Understanding - Adjust your vision based on what you've learned, while maintaining its essential spirit. This might mean tweaking timelines, refining specific outcomes, or addressing internal blocks that the manifestation process revealed. The goal isn't to lower your standards but to increase your alignment.

G: Generate New Evidence - Take small actions that reflect your updated understanding. If you realized you need certain skills first, take steps toward developing them. If timing seems off, create smaller versions of your vision that can manifest more immediately. Build proof that this new direction is viable.

N: Notice Response and Repeat - Pay attention to how your adjustments affect both your internal state and external results. Manifestation becomes an iterative process of increasing precision and alignment rather than a one-time goal-setting exercise.

This method transforms obstacles from evidence that manifestation doesn't work into valuable feedback that makes it work better. It's like having GPS that recalculates your route when you hit traffic, always finding the most efficient path to your destination.

Modern neuroscience increasingly supports what ancient teachers intuited: the brain is not a passive recorder of events but an active **prediction engine.** Each moment, it generates a model based on sensory feedback. When your inner model of the world stabilizes around a coherent vision, your perceptions, decisions, and even micro-movements begin aligning to confirm that model—a process cognitive scientists call *predictive coding*. In practice, this means the clearer and more emotionally resonant your inner vision, the more your nervous system automatically organizes behavior to make it real. Manifestation, from this lens, isn't mystical; it's a natural expression of how perception, emotion, and action co-create experience.

When Manifestation Serves Something Bigger

Here's what I've learned after years of experimentation: it becomes most powerful when your vision serves something larger than personal gain. This isn't about being selfless or spiritual—it's about **practical effectiveness.**

When your manifestation practice serves others or contributes to positive change, it aligns with what many wisdom traditions call "dharmic action"— action that supports the larger flow of life rather than fighting against it. Paradoxically, this shift toward service often **accelerates material results while creating deeper fulfillment.**

Instead of manifesting *just* more money, consider manifesting work that creates value for others in ways that happen to be financially rewarding. Instead of attracting "any" romantic partner, consider attracting someone with whom you can create a relationship that serves both your growth and theirs. Instead of manifesting success that only boosts your ego, imagine manifesting opportunities to share your unique gifts in ways the world actually needs.

This evolution typically happens naturally. You start small with personal goals and build trust in the process; then you **expand your vision** to include how your success can serve something meaningful beyond yourself.

The Consciousness Question: Three Models

Here's where we venture into territory that makes materialist scientists uncomfortable but contemplatives take for granted: What if the relationship between intention and outcome isn't just behavioral—what if consciousness interfaces with probability at fundamental levels?

The Three Possible Models

When you set clear intentions from coherent states and desired outcomes occur, what actually happened?

Model 1: Precognition (Seeing Future Probabilities)

You didn't create the outcome—you perceived what was already emerging. Time is less linear than we assume. In coherent states, you briefly accessed information about future probabilities, allowing you to position yourself optimally. The event was always going to happen; you just saw it early enough to participate effectively.

This model suggests consciousness can extend forward in time, perceiving probable futures before they actualize in the present.

Model 2: Manifestation (Consciousness Creating Outcomes)

Your intention and coherent state actively caused the outcome. Consciousness has causal power over physical reality, not just your behavior. The alignment between your inner state and outer action created conditions that literally shaped what occurred.

This model suggests consciousness is primary—not emergent from matter, but fundamental to reality's structure.

Model 3: Probability Selection (Navigating Quantum Possibilities)

Neither precognition nor manifestation fully captures what's happening. Quantum mechanics tells us particles exist in superposition—all possibilities simultaneously present until observation collapses the wave function into a single outcome. String theory suggests multiple dimensions beyond our typical four, possibly representing different probability frequencies.

What if coherent states don't let you see fixed futures or force specific outcomes, but rather tune your consciousness to particular probability frequencies? Like a radio dial selecting which station to receive from many broadcasting simultaneously, your coherence selects which quantum possibilities become your experienced reality.

You're not seeing the future (precognition) or creating outcomes (manifestation)—you're navigating which timeline you inhabit.

What My Observations Suggest

I don't know which model is correct. The mechanism remains genuinely mysterious. But patterns across three decades of direct observation suggest something:

It doesn't always work. If this were pure manifestation, success rate should approach 100% with sufficient coherence and belief. It doesn't. Success rate is perhaps 60-70% in optimal states—better than chance, but far from certainty. This suggests influence over probabilities, not control of outcomes.

It only works in coherent states. If this were precognition of fixed futures, accuracy should be independent of my emotional or physiological state. But it isn't. The "knowing" only emerges when I'm in what this book calls Green

Moments—heart coherent, breath regulated, attention focused. This suggests the state matters for accessing the information or affecting the probabilities.

It feels like tuning, not forcing. The experience isn't one of pushing reality to conform to my will. It's more like adjusting an internal dial until signal clarity improves—finding the frequency where desired outcomes become more probable. Less like manifestation through force, more like navigation through coherence.

Timing involves both discrete moments and continuous fields. It's not a single instant of knowing (though those occur). It's more like sustained coherence creates a field that biases which quantum moments collapse in preferred directions. Continuous influence producing discrete outcomes.

The 50/50 balance matters. Quantum superposition suggests equal probability for opposing outcomes—50/50 before collapse. Coherence seems to tip this to 60/40 or 70/30, but never to 100/0. Other variables—other people's intentions, environmental factors, chance—affect which probabilities actualize. You're participating in probability collapse, not determining it.

It works at the edge of chaos and structure. Pure randomness offers nothing to navigate. Pure determinism offers no choice. But at the boundary—where enough structure exists for patterns yet enough chaos permits possibility—coherent states seem to increase influence over which patterns emerge. This matches complexity science's "edge of chaos" where emergence happens.

The Research Context

This isn't just mystical speculation. Research exists, though controversial:

Dean Radin's meta-analyses of random number generator studies show small but statistically significant effects of intention on quantum randomness. The Global Consciousness Project documented random systems showing non-random patterns during major world events. Presentiment studies from HeartMath Institute and others show measurable physiological responses before random stimuli occur—bodies "knowing" what's coming.

The double-slit experiment in quantum mechanics demonstrates observation affecting particle behavior—though whether "observation" requires consciousness remains debated. Daryl Bem's precognition studies suggest future events affecting past responses, though replication has been inconsistent.

Patanjali's *Yoga Sutras* describe *siddhis*—abilities emerging from sustained concentration—including knowledge of past and future, awareness of subtle realms, and influence over physical matter. Yogananda taught that deep meditation reveals the "eternal now" where all moments exist simultaneously, accessible to expanded consciousness.

The effect sizes are small. The mechanisms are unknown. The philosophical implications are profound.

Where I Stand

I'm trained as a scientist. I track both successes and failures. I remain appropriately skeptical of my own observations. But intellectual honesty requires admitting: something interesting happens at the intersection of coherent states and experienced reality that materialist neuroscience doesn't fully explain.

I can't prove causation. I acknowledge the possibility of confirmation bias and enhanced pattern recognition explaining everything. But I've observed patterns—synchronicities clustering, knowing emerging, probabilities shifting—with sufficient consistency to warrant continued investigation.

The practices in this chapter work whether consciousness affects reality or simply changes your behavior. Use what works. Remain intellectually honest. Track both successes and failures.

For those experiencing the mysterious—manifestations too precise to dismiss, synchronicities clustering around coherence, moments of knowing that transcend logic—you're not alone. The phenomenon is documented across cultures and research traditions. The mechanism remains mysterious. The investigation continues.

For now: **Practice. Observe. Record.** Stay honest. And remain open to the possibility that consciousness is far more interesting than we currently understand—that coherent states might be gateways not just to optimal performance, but to fundamental participation in how reality unfolds.

Green Moments: When Everything Clicks

Throughout this practice, pay attention to what I call **Green Moments**—those experiences where time seems to expand, presence deepens, and you feel yourself participating in something larger than your individual effort. These moments often indicate when your practice is connecting with authentic possibility rather than just mental construction. They have a distinctive quality: it feels less like trying to *make* something happen and more like recognizing something that already exists at some level of reality–something simply waiting for you to align with it. In these moments, you sense that you're not forcing an outcome but allowing it to unfold.

These might arise during your morning reading when certain phrases create a sense of déjà vu, as if you're remembering rather than imagining. They might happen during aligned action when you feel yourself acting from the future reality rather than toward it. They might occur during course correction when honest assessment reveals patterns or timing that feel intuitively perfect rather than mentally constructed.

Emerging research on **group coherence** offers a modern counterpart to these experiences. When people share a common intention–whether through meditation, synchronized movement, or collective focus–their heart rhythms and brain waves begin to synchronize.[b] Studies of "team flow" show overlapping neural signatures and hormonal patterns among collaborators fully absorbed in a shared goal.[c] It's as if the boundaries between individual nervous systems become more porous, allowing creativity and timing to emerge from a unified field. Those spontaneous Green Moments you feel may in fact be micro-instances of this larger synchrony: a brief tuning-in to the same frequency of coherence that connects all living systems.

> *"Green Moments are the universe's subtle nods that you're moving in harmony with its rhythm."*

Learn to recognize and trust these moments. They're often your nervous system's way of signaling when you're aligned with authentic possibility versus trying to manifest from ego or fear. The more you attune to these experiences, the more your entire practice becomes a process of discovery rather than construction.

Living the Method

After practicing this approach for several years now, I've noticed that the most profound shifts happen not during the formal practices but in the countless **micro-moments** when you find yourself naturally operating from your vision rather than your old patterns.

You catch yourself making decisions from abundance rather than scarcity. Physiology mirrors his shift. Research on **heart-brain coherence** demonstrates that when intention and emotion harmonize, the heart's electromagnetic field becomes measurably more ordered.[d] This coherent state improves cognitive function, emotional regulation, and interpersonal resonance–the very ingredients of what yogis would call *pranic flow*.

Likewise, **visualization and verbal rehearsal** engage the same neural circuits used in real-world execution.[e] Each time you *write, read, or speak* your intention with genuine feeling, you prime motor and emotional networks that later enact those possibilities almost automatically. Even belief alone can trigger measurable biochemical cascades: placebo research shows shifts in dopamine, endorphins, and immune markers simply through expectancy.[f]

Manifestation, then, becomes less about forcing outcomes and more about **training your physiology to recognize success as familiar.**

You notice yourself speaking about your work from excitement rather than out of obligation. You approach challenges with curiosity rather than anxiety. These small course-corrections compound over time, creating what feels less like "achieving goals" and more like **becoming the person for whom these results are natural.**

The external changes—increased income, better relationships, more meaningful work—become byproducts of internal transformation rather than the primary focus. It's like the difference between chasing happiness and becoming the kind of person who naturally experiences joy. One approach is effortful and elusive; the other is organic and sustainable.

*(Important note: These methods work best from a baseline of safety. If you're not there yet, be compassionate with yourself and remember that **building that foundation is manifestation work right now**. Your vision isn't wrong—it might just need a bridge.)*

Your Turn

Here are my questions for you:

What have you been trying to remember that's right there on the tip of your tongue?

What vision has been calling to you that you've been approaching with either too much force or not enough focus?

~ § ~

To consider:

• What would you write if you approached your vision like a journalist reporting on emerging reality rather than a child writing to Santa?

• Which people in your life feel safe to share authentic dreams with, and which ones consistently deflate your enthusiasm? (Hint: spend more time with the first group.)

• What's one minimum viable action you could take this week that would move you toward your vision without overwhelming your system?

• When was the last time you experienced a Green Moment related to creating something meaningful, and what conditions supported its emergence?

"Manifestation isn't about bending reality to your will. It's about becoming so coherent with what you seek that life reorganizes itself around you."

~ § ~

Yoga Connection: *The yogic concept of "sankalpa" (heartfelt intention) recognizes that transformation begins with aligning consciousness before action.[6] Similarly, Buddhist "bhavana" (creative visualization) isn't about merely picturing desired outcomes but cultivating the precise feeling states that draw those experiences closer.[7]*

Neuroscience now gives language to what the sages described. Coherence between heart, brain, and behavior is measurable; collective intention registers statistically across random-event systems; visualization activates neural templates for action. Yet the ancients taught the same principles through sankalpa and bhavana: align the feeling, the word, and the act. Both paths converge on one truth–when inner order meets outer purpose, manifestation is simply life flowing through a prepared channel.

Chapter Fourteen-Point-Five.

The Bridge - Manifestation from Crisis

"You can't manifest abundance from scarcity by pretending the scarcity doesn't exist. You build a bridge, plank by plank, from where you are to where you're going."

~ / ~

If you've just read Chapter 14 and felt a knot in your stomach because you're trying to manifest from a crisis situation, this chapter is for you. If you're reading this from an unsafe living situation, with a negative bank balance, or while dealing with trauma that makes "feeling abundant" feel like a cruel joke, I see you. And more importantly, neuroscience sees you too.

The truth that often gets buried under manifestation teachings is this: your brain in crisis works differently than your brain in safety. This isn't a spiritual failing or a lack of alignment. It's biology. And once you understand the science, you can work with your biology instead of against it.

The Neuroscience of Manifestation from Crisis

In 2013, researchers Sendhil Mullainathan and Eldar Shafir published groundbreaking research showing that poverty and crisis create what they call a "bandwidth tax" on cognitive function.[1] People dealing with financial scarcity showed a reduction in cognitive performance equivalent to losing 13 IQ points—similar to the effect of going without sleep for 24 hours.

This means when you're in crisis, your brain literally cannot access the same visualization and creative capacities as someone manifesting from safety. The prefrontal cortex—responsible for imagination, planning, and possibility thinking—goes offline when the amygdala detects threat.[2] You're not "bad at manifesting." Your brain is doing exactly what it evolved to do: prioritize immediate survival over future dreams.

Dr. Stephen Porges' Polyvagal Theory explains why.[3] When we're in chronic stress or unsafe environments, our nervous system shifts into dorsal vagal (freeze) or sympathetic (fight/flight) states. From these states, the very neurological pathways needed for manifestation—connection, creativity, and expanded awareness—are physiologically unavailable.

This is why someone in an abusive living situation can't simply "vibrate higher" their way to safety. It's like asking someone to solve calculus problems while running from a bear. The brain doesn't work that way.

The Bridge Vision Method

So how do we manifest from crisis? We build bridges.

A bridge vision isn't about pretending you're already where you want to be. It's about creating neurologically achievable stepping stones from your current reality to increasing levels of safety and possibility. Each step must be close enough to your current reality that your nervous system believes it's possible, while far enough to create forward momentum.

Here's how it works:

Step 1: Map Your Minimum Viable Safety (MVS)

Before any manifestation can occur, your nervous system needs to believe safety is possible. Your MVS is the absolute minimum change that would allow your nervous system to downshift from survival mode.

Write this in present tense, but make it specific and achievable:

- "I have $2,000 in a bank account only I can access"
- "I sleep in a room with a door that locks"
- "I go 24 hours without anyone yelling at me"
- "I eat three meals without commentary or judgment"

Dr. Judith Herman's research on trauma recovery shows that safety must be established before any other healing or growth can occur.[4] This isn't spiritual bypassing—it's neurological necessity.

Step 2: Create Implementation Anchors

Peter Gollwitzer's research on implementation intentions shows that "if-then" planning increases goal achievement by 200-300%.[5] Instead of vague intentions, create specific neural pathways:

- "When I receive any money, I immediately transfer 50% to my escape fund"
- "When I feel the desperation rising, I do 5 push-ups and send one professional email"
- "When someone offers me less than my worth, I say 'I'll need to think about that' and walk away"

These aren't affirmations—they're neural programming that works even when your prefrontal cortex is offline.

Step 3: Build Evidence Chains

Your brain in crisis has been trained to notice danger and scarcity. We need to retrain it to notice progress and possibility—but in a way it can believe.

Create a simple evidence journal:

- Day 1: Saved $10. Sent one email. Survived.
- Day 2: Saved $5. Got one response. Still here.
- Day 3: Saved $20. Booked one small gig. I'm doing this.

Dr. Martin Seligman's research on learned optimism shows that documenting small wins literally rewires neural pathways from helplessness to agency.[6]

Step 4: Use Somatic Manifestation

When your thinking brain is compromised by crisis, your body brain (somatic nervous system) becomes your manifestation ally. This isn't woo-woo—it's based on Dr. Bessel van der Kolk's trauma research showing the body keeps the score and can also change the score.[7]

Before any visualization:

- Do 2 minutes of bilateral movement (marching, tapping alternate knees)
- Hum for 30 seconds (activates vagus nerve)
- Hold a power pose for 60 seconds (changes hormonal state)

Then do your manifestation work. Your body has now created the neurological conditions for possibility thinking.

~ § ~

THE CRISIS MANIFESTATION PROTOCOL

Here's the daily protocol that works when you're manifesting from crisis:

Morning (5 minutes):

Bilateral movement (1 minute)

Read your MVS vision (2 minutes)

Write one implementation intention for today (1 minute)

Choose one micro-action (1 minute)

Midday Check-in (2 minutes):

Have I taken my micro-action?

What evidence of progress can I document?

What's one thing I can do this afternoon?

Evening (3 minutes):

Document any evidence of progress (even tiny)

Transfer any money to escape fund

Write tomorrow's one micro-action

Total time: 10 minutes. Because in crisis, you don't have bandwidth for 2-hour manifestation rituals.

The Frequency Ladder

The original chapter mentions manifesting by frequency, not force. In crisis, you can't jump from despair to joy. But you can climb what I call the Frequency Ladder, based on Dr. David Hawkins' Scale of Consciousness:[8]

1. **Shame/Despair** → Move to Anger
   "This is unfair and I deserve better"
2. **Anger** → Move to Pride
   "I've survived this long. I'm stronger than I thought"
3. **Pride** → Move to Courage
   "I can take one small step today"
4. **Courage** → Move to Acceptance
   "This is where I am, and I'm moving forward"
5. **Acceptance** → Move to Willingness
   "I'm open to unexpected help and opportunities"

Each rung is neurologically achievable from the previous one. You can't leap from shame to willingness, but you can climb from shame to anger—and anger has more energy for change than despair.

When Manifestation Meets Reality

Let me be crystal clear about something the original chapter touched on but didn't fully address: Sometimes external reality is the problem, not your vibration.

If you're facing:
- Systemic discrimination

- Economic exploitation
- Abusive situations
- Health crises
- Generational poverty

These are not "manifestation failures." They're real external challenges that require both inner work AND outer action, sometimes including:

- Legal intervention
- Community organizing
- Medical treatment
- Political engagement
- Systemic change

Dr. Shawn Ginwright's research on healing-centered engagement shows that individual healing and systemic change must happen together.[9] You're not spiritually bypassing when you acknowledge that sometimes the system is broken, not your frequency.

The Three Pillars of Crisis Manifestation

Based on research and lived experience, sustainable manifestation from crisis rests on three pillars:

Pillar 1: Radical Self-Compassion

Dr. Kristin Neff's research shows self-compassion is more motivating than self-criticism.[10] In crisis, this means:
- Acknowledging how hard this is
- Celebrating micro-wins
- Forgiving yourself for not manifesting "perfectly"
- Recognizing your courage in continuing

Pillar 2: Strategic Compartmentalization

Sometimes you need to psychologically separate your current reality from your emerging reality. This isn't denial—it's survival. Research on resilience shows that the ability to maintain hope while acknowledging difficulty is key to overcoming crisis.[11]

Create separate mental/physical spaces:
- Current reality: What you must deal with now
- Bridge work: Your daily manifestation practice
- Future vision: What you're building toward

Pillar 3: Community Reality

Dr. Nicholas Christakis' research on social networks shows we literally share neural patterns with those around us.[12] In crisis, finding even one person who believes in your bridge vision can change your neurological capacity to achieve it.

This might be:
- An online community of others building bridges
- One friend who sees your potential
- A therapist who holds hope when you can't
- A mentor who's crossed similar bridges

Integration: Adjusting Chapter 14

The original Chapter 14 contains valuable truths about manifestation. For those manifesting from crisis, these adjustments make it more accessible:

1. **Add Safety First**: Before any four-step process, establish minimum viable safety
2. **Acknowledge Reality**: External circumstances matter. Address them while building internal state
3. **Scale Expectations**: In crisis, micro-wins are massive victories
4. **Bridge Don't Leap**: Create stepping stones between current and desired reality
5. **Body Before Mind**: Use somatic practices to create conditions for visualization

Your Bridge Starts Here

If you're reading this from crisis, know this: Your bridge is already beginning. The fact that you're seeking ways forward, despite everything, is evidence of the incredible resilience of your spirit.

Start with one micro-action today. Document one tiny piece of evidence. Take one step on your bridge. You don't need to see the other side clearly. You just need to lay the next plank.

As poet Rainer Maria Rilke wrote, "Perhaps all the dragons in our lives are princesses who are only waiting to see us act, just once, with beauty and courage."[13]

Your dragons are real. Your crisis is valid. And your bridge is possible.

The universe doesn't require you to pretend everything is fine. It only asks that you take the next smallest step from where you actually are.

> **Yoga Connection:** *The Yoga Sutras acknowledge that practice looks different depending on circumstance. Patanjali distinguishes between those who can practice with full intensity (tivra samveganam) and those whose path must be gentler (mrdu madhya). There is no hierarchy—only honest acknowledgment of where you are. The practices in this chapter honor the mrdu path: small steps, realistic expectations, building capacity slowly. This too is yoga.*

Chapter Fifteen.

Living a Flow-Based Life

"You're not starting over. You're returning with rhythm."

~ / ~

I was waiting near the stage at WPPI in Las Vegas, listening to Kevin Kubota introduce the next speaker.

The event was Photographers Ignite — Kubota's closing-day program where twenty speakers, selected from hundreds of submissions, each had exactly five minutes onstage. Two massive screens flanked the podium so the back of the conference hall could see. The lineup included names that had headlined WPPI keynotes — Jerry Ghionis brought the house down with a wedding photographer's rendition of "I Will Survive." Most of the talks were entertaining, high-energy, crowd-pleasers. Mine was different. I was the newcomer: one slot had been reserved for a promising idea from someone who hadn't cycled through the keynote circuit, and I'd applied for it.

A thousand photographers filled that room. People I admired, people I'd learned from, people who — like me — had built careers around the ability to be fully present in unrepeatable moments.

My talk was called "Living Legacy." The idea was that we were missing something as photographers — that we captured the present moment beautifully but rarely preserved the stories behind the people in our images. A bride who'd lost both parents within a year. My own grandmother, still running a carpet installation business into her eighties — the woman who had given me my first camera before that trip to Scandinavia and later my first SLR, the equipment that made a photography career possible in the first place. I'd interviewed my grandfather for a high school history assignment and discovered he'd once tipped over an outhouse with a woman inside and managed to get a horse into the back of a car. Without their stories, our most beautiful images would become, within a generation or two, just photos of people nobody remembered. I was asking a room full of visual artists to become storytellers — to see their clients more fully and to preserve what a photograph alone couldn't capture.

I didn't know it at the time, but I was circling something that would take me another fifteen years to articulate. The deeper seeing I was talking about — really being present with people, attending to the whole person rather than just the surface — that was flow. The integration of skills and stories and presence I was advocating was what I'd later come to understand as the foundation of a sustainable creative life.

What I didn't say in those five minutes — what I couldn't yet say — was how. How do you sustain that quality of presence across a career without burning out? How do you protect your capacity for depth when everything in modern life fragments your attention? How do you build a life that supports the kind of seeing your best work demands?

I'm still learning.

That's what this chapter is actually about — not a formula I've perfected but a practice I'm still inside of. The principles work. When I get them right, relationships deepen through more consistent presence. Health improves as I honor natural rhythms rather than override them. Creative work carries more depth when it emerges from alignment rather than pressure. I find myself accomplishing more while striving less.

But I want to be honest: I don't always get them right. The financial stability I once had didn't survive the crisis years I described in Chapter 14.5, and rebuilding it has been slower and harder than any framework can account for. There are days when the gap between what I know about flow and what my life actually looks like feels uncomfortably wide. This book is part of what I'm building toward — not a report from the summit but a map I'm drawing as I climb.

What I can tell you with certainty is this: the fragmentation I once accepted as the price of a creative life has been replaced by something real — a sense that my work, my relationships, my health, and my creative practice aren't separate compartments competing for limited resources but expressions of the same underlying rhythm. That integration is genuine, even when the external results haven't caught up yet. And it's the foundation everything else is being built on.

The Philosophy of Integration: Beyond Productivity

While integration has practical benefits, its deeper significance extends beyond performance enhancement. Understanding the philosophical dimensions of integration reveals why it creates not just better results but greater meaning and fulfillment.

Integration as Fundamental Human Need

Philosophers and psychologists from diverse traditions have recognized integration as a core human need rather than merely a productivity strategy. From Carl Jung's concept of "individuation" (the integration of conscious and unconscious aspects of the psyche) to Abraham Maslow's "self-actualization" (the integration of potential into expression), mature human development inherently involves bringing fragmented aspects of self into coherent wholeness.[1]

Developmental psychologist Robert Kegan describes integration as progress along a continuum from "subject" (what we're embedded in and can't see) to "object" (what we can observe and work with).[2] As we develop, previously unconscious patterns become conscious, allowing greater choice and coherence. This process doesn't just improve performance but fundamentally transforms our relationship with life itself.[2]

Neuroscientist Dan Siegel defines integration as "the linkage of differentiated elements of a system."[3] In healthy development, different aspects of experience become both more distinct (differentiation) and more connected (linkage). Without differentiation, we experience fusion and rigidity. Without linkage, we experience fragmentation and chaos. Only with both do we experience the flexible, adaptive coherence that characterizes both psychological health and optimal performance.[3]

This theoretical understanding explains why integration feels subjectively different from mere efficiency. When we experience integration, we don't just accomplish more; we experience a sense of rightness, authenticity, and meaning that transcends practical outcomes.[4]

The Ecology of Time

Another philosophical dimension of flow-based living involves reconceptualizing our relationship with time. Modern culture primarily treats time as a linear resource to be managed, controlled, and maximized. This view creates what philosopher Byung-Chul Han calls "the burnout society"—a culture where time becomes an enemy to conquer rather than a medium to inhabit.[5]

A flow-based life embodies an ecological rather than mechanical relationship with time. Like natural ecosystems, human life involves cycles, seasons, and rhythms that can't be reduced to uniform units without significant loss. Just as sustainable agriculture works with natural cycles rather than against them, sustainable creativity honors the inherent rhythms of human energy and attention.

This ecological perspective aligns with philosopher Henri Bergson's concept of "duration" (durée)—the understanding that lived time is qualitatively different from clock time.[6] In durée, time is experienced as continuous, heterogeneous flow rather than homogeneous units. Some moments are naturally expansive while others are naturally contracted, with the quality of experience mattering as much as quantity.[6]

The most fundamental shift in my creative practice came from adopting an ecological time perspective—though I didn't always call it that. For years, I thought I had a procrastination problem. I'd delay, circle around projects, let deadlines loom before finally diving in with intense focus.

Then I noticed something: the work that emerged from those compressed final pushes was often my best. What looked like avoidance was actually incubation. My unconscious was processing, gathering, connecting—and the deadline provided the container that finally allowed it to pour out.

This pattern carried me through earning two bachelor's degrees in five years while conducting field research in Africa, studying Spanish immersion in Guatemala, completing an honors thesis, playing on a traveling lacrosse team, and serving as president of a service and leadership honorary. It wasn't efficient by conventional standards. But it worked—because I was unknowingly honoring my natural creative rhythm.

I stopped viewing productivity as uniform output and began recognizing the rhythm of my creative process: periods of gathering, germination, focused creation, and integration. By working with these rhythms rather than fighting them, my work deepened while my experience of creating it transformed from struggle to alignment.

By designing your life around natural rhythms rather than arbitrary schedules, you're not just being more efficient; you're aligning with a fundamentally different philosophy of time—one that honors its ecological rather than mechanical nature. This alignment reduces the existential friction that arises when lived experience conflicts with conceptual frameworks, creating not just better results but deeper congruence between how life is and how we think it should be.[4]

Flow as a Lifelong Practice

Living a flow-based life isn't about perfecting a technique or reaching a destination. It's about embracing a continuous practice that evolves as you do.

From Techniques to Lifestyle

The journey toward a flow-based life typically unfolds through several stages:

Stage 1: Discovering Flow

- First conscious experiences of flow states
- Recognition of their distinctive qualities
- Initial experiments with triggers and conditions
- Primarily accidental or sporadic access

Stage 2: Cultivating Flow

- Deliberate practice of specific techniques
- Strategic application in particular contexts
- Developing baseline skills and awareness
- Increasing frequency and duration of states

Stage 3: Designing for Flow

- Creating environmental and lifestyle supports
- Implementing systematic approaches across domains
- Integrating complementary practices and systems
- Developing consistent access in multiple contexts

Stage 4: Living Flow

- Flow principles become fundamental operating system
- Intuitive navigation of conditions and states
- Natural integration across life domains
- Evolution beyond techniques to embodied wisdom

My own journey through these stages spans more than two decades, and it didn't unfold in the tidy order you might expect.

Stage 1 was pure instinct, long before I had any language for what was happening. At thirteen, sprinting across that Norwegian field, something opened — a state where I could sense the whole game without thinking about it. I found it again in high school art classes, in the absorption of writing, in the yoga practice I taught myself from a dog-eared book in my bedroom. I didn't know the word flow. I just knew certain activities made the world go quiet and sharp at the same time.

In college, the thread continued — not as something I studied on purpose, but as something I kept gravitating toward. Working in Dr. Pepperberg's cognition lab, watching Alex demonstrate intelligence that challenged every assumption about consciousness, I was learning to observe states of deep engagement across species without realizing I was building a framework for my own. The biopsychology coursework, the field research in Cameroon's rainforests, the self-help books I consumed on the side — all of it was circling the same question, even if I couldn't have articulated it yet: What makes a mind come fully alive?

Stage 2 arrived at ALCOA, though I wouldn't have called it that at the time. As a health and safety manager across two 24/7 aerospace facilities, I was redesigning shift schedules, work environments, and operational rhythms — and discovering that when conditions honored how humans actually function, something shifted in performance and presence that went beyond compliance. I was applying flow principles before I knew they had a name, watching what happened when people's environments worked with their biology instead of against it.

Stage 3 began when I left the industrial world and became a photographer. Under Phyllis Lane, Jesh de Rox, Rassouli, and others, I learned to deliberately create flow conditions — not just for myself but for the people in front of my camera. This was the phase of conscious study and experimentation: workshops, yoga teacher training, immersion in the science of attention and the ancient traditions that had mapped this territory for centuries. Martha Beck taught me that our bodies know things our minds haven't figured out yet. Koelle Simpson showed me that horses can read our authentic state from across a pasture. I was weaving together threads from athletics, neuroscience, industrial design, contemplative practice, and creative work — and for the first time, I could see they were all part of the same fabric.

Then I lost it.

There was a period — I won't go into detail — when my circumstances became genuinely unsafe. The threats were more real than imagined. And everything I thought I knew about flow and alignment was tested against conditions where my nervous system was operating in survival mode more days than not. The practices that had worked from a foundation of safety became almost inaccessible. I had to learn something harder: how to find rhythm when the ground itself was unstable. How to rebuild flow access plank by plank, from the body up, through nervous system regulation and radical honesty about where I actually was — not where I wished I were.

That period is why Chapter 14.5 exists. It's not theoretical.

Stage 4 is where I am now, and it's less a destination than an ongoing negotiation. Flow principles have become the foundation for how I approach not just work but relationships, health, learning, and the daily texture of being alive. The nine rounds of Sun Salutations at sunrise. The seasonal rhythms. The way I navigate creative blocks, make decisions, and recover from intensity. But I hold it all more lightly than I used to — knowing the spiral will take me through territory I've visited before, at new depths, and that losing access is sometimes part of the practice rather than a failure of it.

The progression wasn't linear. It was a spiral — and the turn through crisis, the part I would never have chosen, may have been the one that made the rest of it real.

What holds all of this together — the stages, the spiral, the losses and returns — comes down to four shifts that happen so gradually you barely notice them.

You stop thinking in straight lines and start thinking in rhythms. You stop compartmentalizing your life and start seeing how its parts feed each other. You stop postponing presence until conditions are right and start engaging fully with what's here. And you stop forcing outcomes and start creating conditions — trusting that what needs to emerge will emerge when the ground is prepared.

These aren't techniques. They're what's left after the techniques become unnecessary.

Perhaps the most significant shift in flow-based living comes through embracing rhythm rather than relentless forward motion. When we begin seeing creative cycles, energy fluctuations, and even emotional variations as natural patterns to work with rather than obstacles to overcome, everything changes. Productivity paradoxically increases while struggle decreases. Results improve as forcing diminishes.[7]

If you track your energy and focus across a typical week — not your calendar, your actual alertness and creative sharpness — you'll likely find patterns you've been ignoring. Morning strength for one type of work, afternoon precision for another, evening openness for a third. Most people design their schedules around external demands and then wonder why they feel misaligned. Design around your rhythms first, then fit the demands in.[7]

Green Moments in Everyday Life

The ultimate expression of a flow-based life is the increased frequency and depth of Green Moments—those experiences of perfect alignment where time seems to expand, presence deepens, and you connect with the profound significance available in ordinary experience.[9]

While these moments often emerge during peak creative or athletic experiences, a flow-based life creates the conditions for them to appear throughout your everyday activities:

▸ In Routine Activities: Something as simple as preparing a meal, commuting to work, or organizing your space can become a portal to presence when approached with the rhythmic attention of flow-based living. These ordinary activities become opportunities for alignment rather than just tasks to complete.[9]

▸ During Transitions: The spaces between activities—often rushed through or filled with distraction—become especially fertile ground for Green Moments when given conscious attention. A deliberate breath between meetings, a moment of awareness when arriving home, or the pause before beginning creative work can open into experiences of expanded time and deepened presence.

▸ In Relationship: Perhaps the most meaningful Green Moments emerge in connections with others. A flow-based life creates the conditions for more frequent experiences of perfect attunement—those conversations where time seems suspended, the boundary between self and other softens, and communication flows with effortless precision and depth.[10]

In Nature: The natural world provides especially reliable access to Green Moments when approached with the receptive presence cultivated through flow-based living. Even brief encounters with plants, animals, weather patterns, or landscapes can open into experiences of profound connection and expanded awareness.[9]

The Flow Block Recovery System

Even with optimal practices, challenges inevitably arise. A sustainable flow- based life includes effective systems for addressing these disruptions:

The RESET Protocol

When flow becomes consistently blocked, this structured approach helps restore optimal conditions:

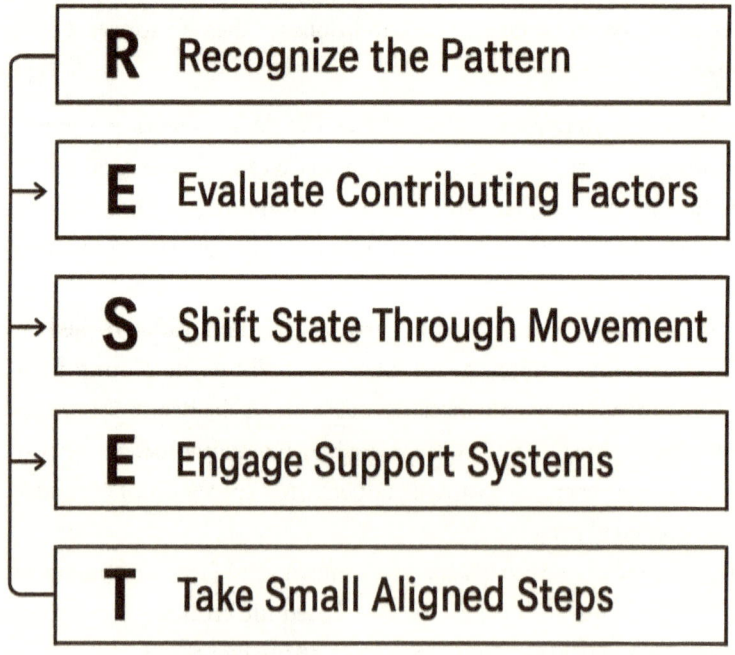

R Recognize the Pattern

E Evaluate Contributing Factors

S Shift State Through Movement

E Engage Support Systems

T Take Small Aligned Steps

R: Recognize the Pattern

- Identify specific symptoms of block or fragmentation
- Notice when and where disruption typically occurs
- Observe both external circumstances and internal states
- Acknowledge the block without judgment or resistance

E: Evaluate Contributing Factors

- Assess physical factors (sleep, nutrition, movement)
- Consider emotional and psychological elements
- Examine environmental influences
- Identify relationship dynamics that may contribute

S: Shift State Through Movement

- Engage in physical activity that changes energetic state
- Use movement patterns that address specific block types
- Implement breath practices that regulate nervous system
- Create kinesthetic patterns that interrupt mental loops

E: Engage Support Systems

- Activate appropriate resources and connections
- Communicate needs clearly to relevant others
- Implement systems designed for specific challenges
- Recognize when external perspective is needed

T: Take Small Aligned Steps

- Identify the minimum viable action that creates momentum
- Focus on process rather than outcome
- Create evidence of capability through completion
- Build progressive momentum through successive steps

The protocol works in practice because it addresses multiple dimensions simultaneously. During a challenging creative period, one practitioner identified the specific pattern (perfectionism triggering procrastination), addressed the amplifying factor (inadequate sleep), shifted state through daily movement, engaged a trusted collaborator for perspective, and took small daily steps focused on process over outcome. Flow access returned within two weeks — whereas previous attempts to simply push through had only deepened the block.[4]

Integration Is the Work

The ultimate goal of a flow-based life isn't periodic peak experiences but sustainable integration—where the principles of flow infuse every aspect of your life and work.

From Fragmentation to Wholeness

Integration represents a fundamental shift in how you experience your life:

▸ From Compartmentalization to Coherence
▸ From Time Management to Energy Architecture
▸ From External Metrics to Internal Alignment

Perhaps the most profound shift in a flow-based life comes through recognizing that integration itself is the work—not just another item on the task list but the fundamental task of a well-lived life.[10] When we begin seeing our professional work, creative expression, relationships, and self-care not as competing demands but as different expressions of the same core values and purpose, everything changes. The constant sense of being pulled in multiple directions gives way to a feeling of coherent unfolding across all domains.

I've come to see it this way: the flow-based life isn't about perfect balance or constant peak experiences. It's about recognizing that your work, relationships, creativity, and health all emerge from the same source. When you design your life to support that core — rather than trying to manage separate compartments — the fragmentation dissolves on its own. You discover you were never juggling multiple lives. You were living one life through different expressions.

This integration manifests in practical ways. Rather than maintaining rigid boundaries between "work time" and "personal time," many practitioners design days that intentionally combine different elements in complementary patterns—perhaps a morning creative session followed by collaborative work, afternoon physical training, and evening family time. This integrated approach often enhances both professional quality and relationship depth by matching activities to natural energy rhythms rather than arbitrary divisions.

Similarly, many stop seeing creative exploration and professional development as separate activities with competing priorities. The most innovative professional contributions often emerge directly from periods of personal creative exploration, while professional challenges frequently spark new directions for personal growth. By recognizing the generative relationship between these seemingly different domains, practitioners create virtuous cycles where each aspect enhances the others rather than competing for limited resources.[10]

~ / ~

The Daily Integration Practice

While comprehensive integration develops over time, this daily practice accelerates the process:

MORNING CONNECTION

+ Begin each day by reconnecting with your whole self
+ Acknowledge all aspects of your life and roles
+ Set intentions that honor various dimensions
+ Create a centering practice that grounds you in core values

TRANSITION AWARENESS

+ Notice how you move between different activities and contexts
+ Create intentional shifts rather than unconscious splits
+ Develop rituals that maintain continuity of presence
+ Design bridges between seemingly separate domains

EVENING REVIEW

+ Reflect on how different life aspects influenced each other
+ Acknowledge moments of alignment and fragmentation
+ Celebrate instances of coherence and flow
+ Set intentions for greater integration tomorrow

~ / ~

I use a version of this myself — what I think of as the Integration Minute. At transition points throughout the day, I pause for three conscious breaths, acknowledge what I'm moving from and toward, and briefly reset my intention. It takes less than sixty seconds. The effect is disproportionate: instead of carrying the residue of one context into the next — the energy of a difficult conversation into a creative session, the intensity of focused work into family time — the pause creates a clean threshold. You arrive where you actually are rather than dragging where you've been.

~ § ~

REFLECTION PROMPT

Consider your journey toward a flow-based life:

• Which elements of flow-based living are already present in your current patterns?

• What area offers the greatest opportunity for enhancing integration and alignment?

• What single practice from this book would create the most significant positive impact if fully implemented?

• When was your last Green Moment, and what conditions might have supported more of these experiences in your daily life?

"You're not starting over. You're returning with rhythm."

~ § ~

A flow-based life is not the absence of challenge. It's the refusal to let challenge destroy your rhythm. You will lose it. That's not failure — that's being human. The practice is the return. And every return makes the next one faster, closer, more natural — until returning is the rhythm.

> **Yoga Connection:** *The Sanskrit concept of "purnatva" (completeness or wholeness) recognizes that true fulfillment comes not from perfecting individual aspects of life but from harmonizing them into an integrated whole. Traditional Tantric philosophy didn't separate spiritual practice from daily life but sought to transform ordinary experience into expressions of the sacred.[11] Similarly, a flow-based life doesn't compartmentalize peak experiences but integrates their principles into the full spectrum of human experience.*

For centuries, practices like yoga trained steadiness in the midst of movement — not as escape, but as preparation. The pose was never the point. The breath was never the point. The stillness was never the point.

The point was the return.

Not once. Not perfectly. But repeatedly.

A flow-based life is not the absence of resistance. It is the discipline of return.

You will lose rhythm. That is human.

You will face disruption, fatigue, uncertainty. That is life.

The practice is coming back — again and again — until returning is no longer effort.

It is identity.

And when return becomes identity, flow is no longer something you chase.

It is how you live.

Epilogue.

The Green Moment

"Flow isn't something you force. It's something you allow."

~ / ~

You've felt it before.

That breathless moment where everything aligns. The way light hits the room. The quiet certainty of being exactly where you're meant to be.

That's the Green Moment.

It doesn't always announce itself. Sometimes it arrives in silence. In stillness. In a subtle shift of presence.

I felt it recently while observing a family in their home. Nothing extraordinary was happening—just parents and children in their living room, engaged in the simple act of being together. As I observed, time seemed to suspend. The ordinary scene before me suddenly appeared extraordinary in its perfect ordinariness. The quality of light through the window, the unconscious way the mother's hand rested on her child's shoulder, the father's expression of quiet contentment—all of it revealed itself as infinitely precious.

In that moment, I wasn't thinking about techniques or strategies. I wasn't planning the next step or evaluating the last one. I was simply there, completely present to the unfolding reality before me. And in that presence, something deeper than the scene itself became visible—the love connecting these people, the significance of everyday moments, the extraordinary gift of ordinary time.

This is what I've come to call a Green Moment—that point of perfect alignment when your heart opens to the present with such clarity that time seems to expand, significance deepens, and you recognize the profound value of exactly what is.

The "green" refers not just to the heart chakra in yogic tradition, where compassion and connection reside, but to the vibrant aliveness that such moments contain—like the fresh green of spring emerging after winter, signaling renewal and possibility.

These moments aren't reserved for dramatic occasions or peak experiences. They can arrive in the simplest circumstances—while washing dishes as sunlight patterns the water, during a conversation when you suddenly feel deeply heard, or in the midst of creative work when effort gives way to flow and you become a channel for something larger than yourself.

What makes a Green Moment isn't its external circumstances but the quality of awareness you bring to it—a presence so complete that the boundary between observer and observed softens, revealing the inherent value and beauty of whatever stands before you.

This book has been a map—not to something new, but to something ancient inside you. A rhythm you've always known. A frequency that was never lost, only muffled beneath the noise of modern life.

The journey through flow states, creative processes, relationship dynamics, and lifestyle design all points toward this essential truth: that our deepest fulfillment doesn't come from extraordinary achievements or rare peak experiences, but from bringing extraordinary presence to the ordinary moments that make up our lives.

The practices and principles we've explored aren't ultimately about optimizing performance or enhancing productivity, though they certainly support those outcomes. They're about remembering how to be fully alive in each moment—how to return to the natural rhythm that is your birthright and your home.

Now, as you close these pages and continue your journey, I invite you to carry one simple question into your days: Where is the Green Moment available to me right now?

It might be in the cup of coffee warming your hands. In the face of the person sitting across from you. In the challenge that's asking for your best response. In the quiet space between thoughts.

The next time you feel scattered or stuck, pause. Close your eyes. Breathe. Ask yourself: Where is my rhythm now? What is one small thing I can do to return to it? And then begin again—from that place.

You don't need to force anything. You only need to remember. The moment is already here. It always was.

You access it not by striving but by returning. Not by adding something new but by removing what blocks your natural awareness. Not by becoming someone else but by remembering who you already are.

In the end, flow isn't about peak performance or rare experiences. It's about returning to the rhythm that runs through all things—including you. It's about recognizing that presence isn't something you achieve but something you allow.

The Green Moment is always available—in your breath, in your body, in the quality of your attention, in your connection with others, in the simplest experiences of your everyday life.

Every time you consciously breathe, you're practicing. Every time you fully engage with what's before you, you're practicing. Every time you notice when you've lost presence and gently return, you're practicing.

This is the work of a lifetime—not a linear path to some distant achievement but a spiral journey of continuous return. Each time you come back to presence, the return becomes more familiar. Each time you recognize a Green Moment, your capacity to notice the next one expands.

So I leave you with this invitation: Look for the Green Moments in your days. Create the conditions that allow them to emerge more frequently. And when you inevitably lose touch with this awareness—as all of us do—know that the way back is always available through the simplest of practices: one conscious breath, one moment of full presence, one deliberate return to the rhythm that has always been your home.

Welcome back.

And for those who sense there may be something more—doorways that flow opens to territories beyond performance—the Afterword awaits.

Afterword.

Flow as Gateway

For readers who have finished the book and find themselves curious about what lies beyond.

~ / ~

This book provides evidence-based frameworks for accessing flow states consistently. The practices work regardless of your beliefs about consciousness—the neuroscience is sound, the methods are tested, the results are measurable.

But if you've experienced flow deeply, you may have noticed phenomena the performance literature rarely acknowledges:

Time doesn't just speed up or slow down—it feels non-linear, as if past, present, and future are somehow accessible simultaneously.

Meaningful coincidences cluster around coherent states with frequency that strains statistical probability. Creative solutions emerge from sources you can't identify—as if you're accessing information beyond your conscious knowledge. You know things before you logically should, positioning yourself for moments before they unfold. The boundary between self and environment becomes permeable, creating a felt sense of connection that transcends ordinary perception.

These aren't metaphors. They're direct observations from practitioners across traditions and domains.

Ancient Maps of This Territory

Contemplatives have mapped this territory for millennia. Patanjali's Yoga Sutras describe how sustained concentration develops not just mastery but expanded perception—what he called prajna, or direct knowing. Yogananda taught that deep practice reveals the "eternal now" where linear time dissolves into simultaneous awareness. These weren't abstract philosophies— they were reporting observations from sustained investigation.

The Japanese concept of mushin, the Taoist wu-wei, the Sufi fana—across cultures, practitioners describe states where ordinary boundaries dissolve and something larger becomes accessible.

Modern Research

Modern consciousness researchers are beginning to validate these reports. Studies on presentiment show physiological responses occurring before random stimuli—suggesting access to information about future events. Research on intention affecting random number generators hints at consciousness interfacing with probability at quantum scales. The Global Consciousness Project documented random systems showing non-random patterns during major world events.

The mechanisms remain mysterious. We don't know if these experiences represent:
- Enhanced perception revealing patterns that were always present
- Access to non-linear time allowing glimpses of future probabilities
- Consciousness affecting which possibilities actualize
- Navigation between parallel probability streams
- Something else entirely that our current frameworks can't describe

The Invitation

What we do know: coherent states—what this book calls Green Moments—create conditions where these phenomena occur more frequently. The practices that cultivate flow also seem to open doorways to expanded awareness.

Whether you interpret these experiences as neurological quirks, quantum effects, or genuine perception beyond ordinary consciousness is yours to determine. The frameworks work regardless. The transformation happens. The results are measurable.

But for those experiencing the mysterious aspects—the synchronicities, the knowing, the sense that consciousness extends beyond your skull, the feeling that you're participating in something larger than individual performance—you'll find acknowledgment here. Not dogma, not certainty, but honest recognition that something interesting happens at the intersection of coherent states and experienced reality.

The practices are practical. The mystery remains... inviting.

Throughout this book, you've found frameworks grounded in neuroscience and proven through organizational application. You can use them purely for performance optimization, creative excellence, or sustainable achievement. They work.

But know that some practitioners report accessing something more—threshold experiences where flow becomes gateway. I'm one of them. I don't claim to understand the mechanism, but I have observed patterns across three decades that warrant investigation.

This book establishes the foundation. The deeper exploration continues.

If the territory explored in this afterword resonates with your experience, I'd love to hear from you. These observations deserve further investigation, and your experiences contribute to our collective understanding.

Connect at: carolynbentleywells.com

Integration Guide I.

The RHYTHM Framework

"Flow isn't a destination you reach once. It's a relationship you cultivate daily—a conversation between who you are and what you do, between your energy and your environment, between your focus and your freedom."

~ / ~

The RHYTHM Framework integrates all the core principles from this book into a comprehensive system for sustainable flow. Each letter represents a key dimension of flow mastery, creating a complete approach to presence, performance, and fulfillment.

Use this guide as a reference to understand and implement the complete framework in your life. For each component, you'll find the core concept, key practices, implementation strategies, and common obstacles to navigate.

Living Flow as a Way of Being

The question came during a Q&A session after I'd spoken about flow principles to a group of executives: "This all sounds wonderful in theory, but how do you actually live this way? How do you integrate everything you've shared into real life with real pressures and real constraints?"

I paused, recognizing the genuine frustration behind the question. I'd been there myself—inspired by concepts and techniques but struggling to weave them into a coherent approach that could withstand the complexity of daily life.

"That's exactly why I developed the RHYTHM Framework," I replied. "Not as another system to learn, but as a way of being that becomes as natural as breathing."

Over the years of working with flow principles across different domains—from high-pressure creative deadlines to parenting challenges, from athletic performance to relationship dynamics—I'd noticed that sustainable transformation required more than isolated techniques. It demanded an integrated approach that could adapt to any situation while maintaining its essential nature.

The RHYTHM Framework emerged from this need. It's not just a collection of practices but a comprehensive way of engaging with life that makes flow states not just possible but inevitable. When you understand and embody these six dimensions, flow stops being something you chase and becomes something you inhabit.

The Dance of Integration

RHYTHM works because it mirrors how life actually unfolds—not in linear steps but in dynamic, interconnected patterns. Like a jazz musician who has mastered the fundamentals so thoroughly that improvisation becomes natural, when you embody the RHYTHM Framework, responding to life's complexities with flow becomes your default mode.

Each letter represents both a practice and a way of being:

THE RHYTHM FRAMEWORK

The RHYTHM Framework integrates all the core principles from this book into a comprehensive system for sustainable flow. Each letter represents a key dimension of flow mastery, creating a complete approach to presence, performance, and fulfillment.

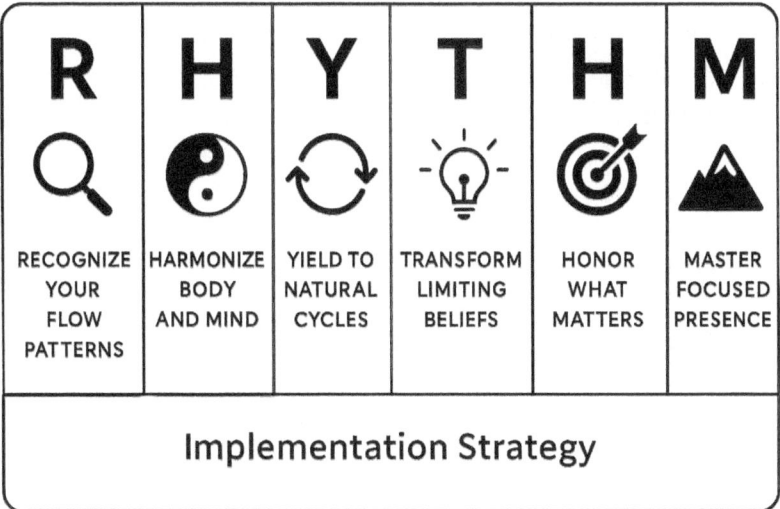

R	H	Y	T	H	M
RECOGNIZE YOUR FLOW PATTERNS	HARMONIZE BODY AND MIND	YIELD TO NATURAL CYCLES	TRANSFORM LIMITING BELIEFS	HONOR WHAT MATTERS	MASTER FOCUSED PRESENCE

Implementation Strategy

R - Recognize your natural patterns and current state

H - Harmonize your body and mind into coherence

Y - Yield to the natural cycles of energy and attention

T - Tune your environment to support optimal states

H - Heighten challenge and meaning in your activities

M - Master the art of focused presence

But RHYTHM is more than an acronym—it's a living system where each element reinforces and enhances the others. When you recognize your patterns, you naturally harmonize your internal state. When you harmonize, you're better able to yield to natural cycles. When you yield, you can more skillfully tune your environment, and so on.

Let's explore how each dimension transforms not just what you do, but how you experience life itself.

R: RECOGNIZE Your Flow Patterns

"Awareness is the first step in any transformation, but awareness without judgment is the first step in lasting transformation."

Recognition goes far deeper than simply noticing when you're in flow. Building on the flow markers and characteristics we identified in Chapter 1, this dimension develops what I call "state literacy"—the capacity to read the subtle signals that indicate where you are in your natural rhythm and what you need to return to optimal states.

This includes refining your ability to recognize the personal flow signatures discussed in Chapter 3's Flow Profile Assessment, while developing moment-to-moment awareness of your internal landscape.

The Art of Flow Awareness

Most people experience flow accidentally—those magical moments when everything clicks, but they can't explain how it happened or how to make it happen again. Flow masters, however, develop what I call "state literacy"—the ability to recognize their internal landscape with the same precision a musician recognizes pitch.

This begins with understanding your personal flow signatures. While the general characteristics of flow remain consistent across individuals, how they manifest for you is as unique as your fingerprint.

Your Flow Markers: Perhaps your flow states are marked by a particular quality of breathing—deeper and more rhythmic than usual. Maybe you notice a specific type of alertness, simultaneously relaxed and focused. Some people feel flow as a physical sensation—warmth in the chest, tingling in the hands, or a sense of expansion through the torso.

Your Block Signals: Equally important are your early warning systems. Maybe tension gathers in your jaw when you're forcing rather than flowing. Perhaps you notice scattered thinking or a compulsive need to check your phone when you're avoiding something important. Learning to recognize these signals before they become entrenched patterns is crucial for maintaining consistent access to flow.

Your Energy Rhythms: Beyond moment-to-moment states, recognition includes understanding your larger patterns. Are you naturally sharper in the morning or evening? Do you have 90-minute cycles of high focus followed by natural dips? How do seasons affect your creative output? Do you work best in sustained periods or short bursts?

Implementation: The Flow Journal Method

For two weeks, keep what I call a "Flow Journal"—not a detailed diary, but a simple tracking system:

Daily Flow Check: Each evening, note:

‣ When you experienced flow (time, duration, activity)
‣ The conditions present (environment, energy level, challenges, people involved)
‣ The transitions in and out of the state
‣ Any blocks or disruptions you noticed

Weekly Pattern Audit: At week's end, ask:

‣ When was flow most accessible this week?
‣ What consistently supported or disrupted flow?
‣ What patterns am I noticing across different activities?

This isn't about perfecting your states but about developing intimate familiarity with your unique flow fingerprint. The goal is recognition without judgment—simply seeing what is, which creates the foundation for skillful response.

H: HARMONIZE Body and Mind

> *"The body and mind aren't separate systems that sometimes cooperate. They're one integrated intelligence expressing itself through different channels."*

Harmonization addresses a fundamental misunderstanding in our culture: the belief that mental performance and physical state are separate. Flow emerges from the dynamic alignment of your nervous system, physical presence, and mental focus. When these systems work in harmony, optimal states become naturally accessible.

Building on Coherence

As we explored in Chapter 2, physiological coherence—the synchronized communication between heart, brain, and nervous system—forms the foundation for flow states.[1] The heart rate variability patterns and optimal breathing we discussed create the neurobiological conditions that support sustained flow.[2]

Building on these earlier insights, RHYTHM's harmonization dimension focuses on making this coherence accessible in daily life rather than just during dedicated practice periods.

Deepening Nervous System Mastery

The polyvagal theory and nervous system regulation techniques we explored in Chapter 9 provide the foundation for RHYTHM's harmonization practices.[3] Rather than viewing these as separate techniques, harmonization integrates nervous system awareness into moment-to-moment living.

Your autonomic nervous system's continuous assessment of safety, as we discussed earlier, directly influences your capacity for flow. The "calm alertness" state that supports optimal performance requires what Stephen Porges identified as social nervous system engagement—parasympathetic activation combined with appropriate sympathetic tone.[4]

The Integration Breath: Building on the breathing techniques introduced in Chapter 12, this practice synthesizes coherence breathing with embodied awareness:

- Breathe rhythmically (5 counts in, 5 counts out) as established in earlier chapters
- Place attention on your heart area to activate coherence patterns[5]
- Simultaneously scan your body for areas of tension or holding
- Continue for 3-5 minutes, allowing both physiological coherence and embodied presence

Embodied Presence

Harmonization also means treating your body as a source of intelligence rather than just a vehicle for your mind. Your body holds wisdom about what's working and what isn't, what's aligned and what's forced.

The Body Check: Before any important activity, spend 30 seconds scanning your body:

- Where do you hold tension?
- What does your energy level feel like?
- What does your body need right now—movement, stillness, nourishment, rest?

This isn't self-indulgence but practical intelligence. When you honor your body's feedback, you create conditions where flow can emerge naturally rather than forcing it through will alone.

Daily Harmonization Practices

Morning Coherence (5 minutes):

- 3 minutes of rhythmic breathing with heart focus
- Brief body scan to release any held tension
- Set an embodied intention for the day (feeling it in your body, not just thinking it)

Transition Harmonization (30 seconds):

- Between activities, take three conscious breaths
- Move your body briefly to shift energy
- Set a clear intention for the next engagement

Evening Integration (5 minutes):

- Gentle movement to release the day's accumulated tension
- Breathing practice to downregulate your nervous system
- Brief appreciation for your body's service

Y: YIELD to Natural Cycles

"Resistance to natural rhythms creates the friction that blocks flow. Yielding to them creates the conditions where flow becomes inevitable."

Perhaps the most radical aspect of the RHYTHM Framework is its recognition that sustainable high performance comes not from constant effort but from understanding and honoring natural cycles. In a culture obsessed with linear productivity, yielding to cycles feels counterintuitive, but it's the secret to long-term effectiveness and wellbeing.

Integrating Flow Cycle Wisdom

As we explored comprehensively in Chapter 12, sustainable flow emerges from understanding and honoring natural cycles rather than forcing continuous peak performance.[6] The four-phase flow cycle—Struggle, Release, Flow, Recovery—provides the rhythm that RHYTHM's yielding dimension builds upon.

The neurobiological research we examined earlier reveals why each phase serves an essential function: struggle phase activates learning networks, release phase enables unconscious processing, flow phase optimizes performance networks, and recovery phase consolidates gains while restoring resources.[7] RHYTHM's yielding dimension makes this cycle wisdom practical for daily implementation.

Deepening Biorhythm Alignment

The ultradian rhythms discussed in Chapter 12—your natural 90-120 minute cycles of high focus and recovery need—form the foundation for RHYTHM's approach to sustainable performance.[8] Rather than fighting these biological patterns, yielding works with them strategically.

Implementation: Rhythm-Based Design

Daily Rhythm Blocks:

Structure your day around 90-minute "rhythm blocks" with intentional recovery periods:

- 90 minutes of focused engagement
- 20-30 minutes of genuine rest (not just switching tasks)
- Track which blocks naturally align with your energy peaks
- Honor the need for recovery even when you feel like you could push through

Weekly Rhythm Design:
Instead of treating every day the same, create different themes:

- Deep work days for sustained focus
- Collaborative days for meetings and teamwork
- Administrative days for planning and organization
- Integration days for reflection and strategic thinking
- Recovery days for genuine rest and inspiration

Flow Cycle Navigation:
Develop specific approaches for each phase:

- **Struggle:** Research, skill building, problem definition
- **Release:** Walking, shower thinking, unrelated activities
- **Flow:** Distraction-free engagement with optimal challenges
- **Recovery:** Integration, reflection, celebration, physical restoration

The key insight is that recovery isn't a luxury—it's a biological necessity that makes the next flow cycle possible. When you honor this, your overall productivity increases while your stress decreases.

T: TUNE Your Environment

"Your environment isn't just where you work—it's a co-creator of your internal state."

Most people underestimate the profound impact of environment on their capacity for flow. Your surroundings continuously influence your nervous system, attention, and energy levels. Strategic environment tuning can eliminate barriers to flow and create consistent triggers for optimal states.

Advancing Environment Design

Building on the environmental optimization principles we explored in earlier chapters, RHYTHM's tuning dimension transforms environmental awareness from occasional consideration to continuous practice. The research on environmental psychology showing how surroundings affect nervous system states, attention capacity, and creative thinking becomes a lived practice through systematic tuning.[16]

Rather than simply creating pleasant spaces, tuning involves designing environments that actively support your specific flow patterns and remove friction from accessing optimal states.[17]

Physical Environment Optimization

Dedicated Flow Spaces: Create specific areas associated with different types of flow:

- Deep work space with minimal distractions
- Creative space with inspiring elements
- Movement space for physical flow practices
- Recovery space for restoration and integration

Sensory Design: Optimize the sensory elements that most affect your flow:

- **Lighting:** Natural light when possible, adjustable intensity for different activities
- **Sound:** Understand what audio environments work for different types of flow
- **Temperature:** Most people focus better in slightly cool environments
- **Scent:** Certain aromas can trigger state changes and enhance memory
- **Texture:** The materials you interact with affect your nervous system

Flow Triggers: Create environmental cues that consistently signal flow time:

- Specific music that accompanies deep work
- Lighting changes that indicate focus periods
- Objects or images that inspire optimal states
- Physical rituals that prepare your space for flow

Digital Environment Mastery

Your digital environment may be even more important than your physical one, given how much time you spend interacting with screens and devices.

Attention Architecture: Design your digital spaces to support rather than fragment attention:

- Separate devices or profiles for different types of work
- Eliminate notifications during flow periods
- Use apps and tools that minimize rather than increase cognitive load
- Create visual simplicity in your digital interfaces

Flow-Friendly Technology: Choose tools that enhance rather than complicate your optimal states:

- Focus apps that block distractions during flow periods
- Environment apps that adjust lighting and sound automatically
- Task managers that support natural rhythms rather than forcing linear productivity

Implementation: Environmental Audit

Weekly Environment Review:

- Which spaces most reliably support your flow states?
- What environmental factors consistently disrupt your focus?
- How can you modify your surroundings to better support optimal states?

Environmental Experiments:

- Try working in different locations and notice how they affect your state

- Experiment with different sensory elements (music, lighting, scents)
- Test various arrangements of your workspace

The goal isn't to create perfect environments but to understand how your surroundings affect your internal state, then make strategic adjustments that support consistent access to flow.

H: HEIGHTEN Challenge and Meaning

"Flow emerges at the intersection of what challenges you and what matters to you."

The second H in RHYTHM addresses a crucial element often missing from productivity discussions: the need for meaningful challenge. Flow doesn't emerge from easy tasks or arbitrary difficulties, but from the sweet spot where your skills meet challenges that matter to you.

Expanding on Challenge-Skill Dynamics

The challenge-skill balance, which we identified in Chapter 2 as fundamental to flow states, becomes a living practice through RHYTHM's heightening dimension.[9] Csikszentmihalyi's research showing flow emerges when challenges slightly stretch current capabilities—that optimal 4% beyond your skill level—provides the foundation for conscious challenge design.[10]

The flow triggers we explored in Chapter 8—clear goals, immediate feedback, and meaningful engagement—transform from concepts into daily practices through heightening.[11] This isn't about making everything harder, but about making everything appropriately challenging and deeply meaningful.

Meaningful Engagement

Beyond the right level of difficulty, flow requires that you care about what you're doing. This doesn't mean every task must be your life's passion, but it does mean finding authentic connection to your activities.

Values Alignment: Regularly examine how your activities connect to what you truly value. Even routine tasks can become more engaging when you understand their connection to larger purposes.

Autonomy and Mastery: Flow increases when you have some degree of choice in how you approach challenges and when you can see your skills developing over time.

Service Orientation: Some of the deepest flow states emerge when your challenges involve serving something larger than yourself—whether that's other people, a cause you believe in, or the expression of your highest capabilities.

Implementation: Challenge Design

Daily Challenge Calibration:

Before starting any significant activity, ask:

- Is this challenge appropriately difficult for my current skill level?
- Do I understand exactly what I'm trying to accomplish?
- How will I know if I'm succeeding?
- Why does this matter to me?

Skill Development Planning:

- Identify the skills most relevant to your important challenges
- Create deliberate practice routines that build these capabilities
- Seek feedback from people whose opinions you respect
- Regularly reassess your skill level and adjust challenges accordingly

Meaning Connection:

- Regularly reflect on how your activities connect to your deeper values
- Look for ways to frame routine tasks as contributions to larger purposes
- Seek challenges that allow you to use your strongest talents
- Consider how your work serves others or contributes to something you believe in

The key is becoming an active architect of your own challenges rather than passively accepting whatever difficulties arise.

M: MASTER Focus

"Attention is the currency of consciousness. How you spend it determines the quality of your experience."

The final element of RHYTHM is perhaps the most foundational: developing mastery over your own attention. In our distraction-rich environment, the ability to direct and sustain focus has become a superpower that creates the foundation for all other flow practices.

Advanced Attention Integration

The attention training principles we explored in Chapter 12—developing sustained focus capacity while managing modern distraction challenges—form the foundation of RHYTHM's mastery dimension.[12] The transient hypofrontality we discussed in Chapter 2, where the analytical mind quiets during flow, occurs most readily when attention skills are well-developed.[13]

Building on the focused attention and mindfulness practices already introduced, mastery emphasizes integration: making these attention skills seamless parts of daily engagement rather than separate meditation practices.

The "effortless attention" characteristic of flow states emerges not from forcing focus but from developing what we might call "attention fitness"—the capacity to direct and sustain awareness without strain.[14] This builds on the neuroplasticity principles we discussed earlier, where consistent practice literally reshapes the brain's attention networks.[15]

Deepening Attention Training

Enhanced Concentration Practice: Building on the basic attention training introduced earlier:

‣ Extend your single-pointed focus capacity systematically (begin where the earlier practices left off)
‣ Integrate the body awareness techniques from Chapter 6 with sustained attention

- Notice the specific patterns that disrupt your focus (building on your Flow Journal insights)
- Practice returning attention without the self-judgment that can compound distraction

Integrative Mindfulness Practice: Advancing beyond basic mindfulness to flow-specific awareness:

- Develop continuous background awareness of your flow state throughout activities
- Practice recognizing the early stages of flow emergence (building on recognition skills)
- Learn to maintain spacious awareness during intense focus (paradox of effortless attention)

Flow Entry Protocols: Advanced Integration

Building on the basic transition rituals discussed earlier, advanced flow entry protocols integrate all RHYTHM dimensions:

Pre-Flow Rituals: Develop consistent practices that signal to your brain it's time for deep focus:

- Clear your physical and digital environment of distractions
- Set a specific intention for your focus session
- Use breathing or movement practices to optimize your internal state
- Create consistent external cues (music, lighting, location)

Attention Anchors: Develop the skill of using specific focus points to maintain flow:

- In creative work, this might be the emerging vision of what you're creating
- In physical activities, it could be the sensation of movement or breath
- In analytical work, it might be the specific problem you're solving
- In interpersonal flow, it's often the quality of presence and connection

Managing Modern Attention Challenges

Digital Discipline: Create clear boundaries around technology use:

- Designated phone-free periods for deep work
- Separate devices for different types of activities
- Notification management that preserves focus rather than fragmenting it
- Regular digital detox periods to restore attention capacity

Environment Design: Create physical and digital spaces that support rather than undermine attention:

- Remove visual clutter and distracting elements
- Use tools that simplify rather than complicate focus
- Design workflows that minimize task switching
- Create dedicated spaces for different types of attention

Implementation: Attention Development

Daily Attention Practice:

- Begin each day with 5-10 minutes of focused attention training
- Throughout the day, practice brief attention checks: "Where is my focus right now?"
- End each day by reflecting on your attention patterns and planning improvements

Weekly Attention Review:

- What consistently supports your ability to focus?
- What most frequently fragments your attention?
- How can you modify your environment or habits to better support sustained focus?

The mastery of attention is perhaps the most transferable skill you can develop—it enhances every other area of your life while creating the foundation for consistent access to flow states.

Integrating the RHYTHM Framework

While each element of RHYTHM can be practiced individually, the true power emerges from their integration. When recognition, harmonization, yielding, tuning, heightening, and mastery work together, they create a self-reinforcing system that makes flow not just accessible but inevitable.

The Implementation Sequence

For those new to flow-based living, I recommend this progression:

Week 1-2: Recognition (R) - Build awareness through flow journaling and pattern observation

Week 3-4: Harmonization (H) - Establish daily coherence and embodied presence practices

Week 5-6: Tuning (T) - Optimize your environments for consistent flow access

Week 7-8: Yielding (Y) - Redesign your schedule around natural rhythms and cycles

Week 9-10: Heightening (H) - Calibrate your challenges and deepen meaningful engagement

Week 11-12: Mastery (M) - Develop advanced attention skills and focus protocols

This sequence allows each element to build on the previous ones, creating a solid foundation for sustainable transformation.

Daily RHYTHM Integration

Once you've developed familiarity with each element, a comprehensive daily practice might include:

Morning RHYTHM (10 minutes):

- **Recognition:** Brief check-in with your current state and energy
- **Harmonization:** Coherence breathing and body awareness
- **Heightening:** Review your meaningful challenges and intentions

Throughout the Day:

- **Yielding:** Honor your 90-minute work cycles with genuine recovery
- **Tuning:** Maintain environments optimized for your current activities
- **Mastery:** Implement focus protocols for deep work periods

Evening RHYTHM (5 minutes):

- **Recognition:** Reflect on your flow moments and challenges
- **Harmonization:** Nervous system downregulation through breath and movement
- **Yielding:** Intentional recovery and integration activities

Weekly RHYTHM Reset

Each week, conduct a brief review and optimization:

- Review your Flow Journal for emerging patterns
- Adjust your environments based on what you're learning
- Redesign challenges for the coming week based on your developing skills
- Identify one aspect of the framework to strengthen
- Plan recovery and integration time

The beauty of RHYTHM is that it becomes increasingly automatic. What initially requires conscious attention gradually becomes your natural way of engaging with life. You stop thinking about flow techniques and start living from flow intelligence.

The Ripple Effects

When you embody the RHYTHM Framework, the effects extend far beyond individual performance. You begin to influence the people and systems around you, creating expanding circles of coherence and optimal experience.

In Relationships: Your increased presence and emotional coherence make you a more reliable source of support and inspiration for others. Conversations become more meaningful, conflicts resolve more easily, and shared activities naturally move toward flow states.

In Work: Your enhanced focus and sustainable high performance inspire colleagues while your understanding of natural rhythms helps you design more effective and humane ways of working together.

In Community: Your embodied understanding of flow principles makes you a natural facilitator of group flow experiences, whether in families, teams, or larger communities.

In the World: Perhaps most importantly, living from RHYTHM contributes to a larger transformation—away from the burnout culture of constant striving toward a more sustainable and fulfilling way of being human.

Beyond Technique to Way of Being

The ultimate goal of the RHYTHM Framework isn't to become better at applying flow techniques. It's to transform flow from something you do into something you are. When this happens, optimal experience becomes your baseline rather than your peak.

You stop asking "How do I get into flow?" and start asking "How do I live from flow?" The answer isn't found in any single practice but in the dynamic integration of all these elements into a coherent way of engaging with whatever life presents.

This is what it means to live a flow-based life—not the absence of challenge or the presence of constant peak experiences, but the embodied knowledge that you can meet whatever arises with presence, skill, and authentic engagement. It's the deep confidence that comes from knowing you can always return to your center, always access your optimal states, always contribute your best to whatever situation you encounter.

The RHYTHM Framework provides the map, but the journey is uniquely yours. Each person's expression of these principles will be different, adapted to their circumstances, temperament, and calling. What remains constant is the invitation to remember what you've always known: that your natural state is one of dynamic, responsive presence, capable of meeting life with both effectiveness and joy.

As you continue to embody these practices, you may notice something remarkable: flow stops being something special that occasionally happens and starts becoming the ground from which you meet each moment. Problems become puzzles, challenges become opportunities for growth, and ordinary activities reveal their extraordinary potential.

This is what the masters of flow understand—that these states aren't reserved for elite performers or special circumstances. They're your birthright, accessible in this moment through the simple act of returning to your natural rhythm. The techniques fade into the background, and what remains is the dance itself—the eternal flow of consciousness meeting life with full presence, appropriate response, and authentic expression.

You're not learning to become someone different. You're remembering who you've always been beneath the noise and rush of modern life. You're returning to the rhythm that has always been your home.

The practices and principles we've explored aren't ultimately about optimizing performance or enhancing productivity, though they certainly support those outcomes. They're about remembering how to be fully alive in each moment— how to return to the natural rhythm that is your birthright and your home.

Integration Guide II.

The Seasonal Flow - 108 Practice Guide

"The seasons are nature's perfect demonstration of flow—the eternal rhythm of expansion and contraction, peak and valley, action and rest. At each turning point, we find a mirror for our own creative cycles and an invitation to align with the deeper rhythm that moves through all things."

~ / ~

Throughout human history, the four cardinal points of the solar year—the two solstices and two equinoxes—have been recognized as natural gateways to heightened states of consciousness. These astronomical events create optimal conditions for accessing flow states, offering us four annual opportunities to realign with our deepest rhythms and highest potential.

The Sacred Architecture of Seasonal Flow

Each seasonal turning point carries distinct energetic qualities that can be harnessed for specific aspects of flow development:

- **Spring Equinox (Vernal Equinox):** New beginnings, creative emergence, fresh energy
- **Summer Solstice:** Peak expression, manifestation, full flowering
- **Autumn Equinox (Autumnal Equinox):** Harvest wisdom, integration, gratitude
- **Winter Solstice:** Deep rest, inner knowing, contemplative renewal

The Significance of 108

In creating this practice guide, I've chosen to center it around the number 108—a figure that holds profound significance across numerous traditions and connects beautifully to the principles of flow we've explored throughout this book.

The Mathematics of Harmony

108 isn't arbitrary—it's mathematically significant:

- The sun's diameter is approximately 108 times the Earth's diameter
- The sun's average distance from the Earth is approximately 108 times the sun's diameter
- The moon's average distance from the Earth is approximately 108 times the moon's diameter

These cosmic proportions speak to natural harmony and proportion—the very foundations of rhythm and flow in our universe.

Cross-Cultural Significance

The number 108 appears with remarkable consistency across diverse traditions:

- **In yoga:** Traditional malas (meditation beads) contain 108 beads
- **In Buddhism:** There are said to be 108 earthly desires and 108 feelings
- **In Ayurveda:** There are 108 marma points (energy centers) in the body
- **In astronomy:** The five planets visible to the naked eye, plus the sun and moon, each have 108 significant distances
- **In mathematics:** $1^1 \times 2^2 \times 3^3 = 108$, a rare numerical harmony

This convergence across disciplines suggests something fundamental about this number—a natural harmonic that aligns with flow states.

Connection to Flow States

The significance of 108 to flow isn't just symbolic. The number represents:

Completion and Cyclical Return

108 represents a full cycle—like the cycle of seasons, the flow cycle, or the creative process from inception to completion.

Balance of Effort and Surrender

In the digits, we can see 1 (beginning/action), 0 (emptiness/potential), and 8 (infinity/continuation)—mirroring the balance of action and surrender essential to flow.

Multiple Pathways to Presence

With so many cultural and mathematical connections, 108 reminds us that flow can be accessed through diverse practices—physical, creative, intellectual, or contemplative.

Sun and Moon Salutations: The Foundation Practices

Before exploring the seasonal 108 events, it's essential to understand the foundational movement sequences that create reliable gateways to flow states. The Sun and Moon Salutations from yoga tradition offer particularly powerful case studies in ritualized movement for state transformation.

The Structure of Ritualized Movement

What makes these sequences so effective for inducing flow states?

Established Patterns

- Clear sequence eliminates decision fatigue
- Familiar progression allows focus on experience, not choreography
- Recognizable structure creates security for exploration
- Repeated practice builds neural pathways for the sequence

Breath-Movement Integration

- Each movement links directly to breath
- Established breath patterns regulate nervous system
- Breath serves as continuous attention anchor
- Rhythm of breath creates natural timing for movement

Full-Body Engagement

- Sequences activate all major muscle groups
- Alternating between different movement patterns
- Engaging both strength and flexibility
- Creating balance between effort and release

Symbolic Meaning

▸ Movements connect to archetypal meanings
▸ Sequence tells a coherent "story" through the body
▸ Practice becomes both physical and metaphorical
▸ Meaning dimension adds depth to the experience

Sun Salutations (Surya Namaskar): Activating Flow

The Sun Salutation serves as an activating sequence that can prepare your system for energetic engagement:

Physiological Effects

▸ Increases heart rate and circulation
▸ Stimulates sympathetic nervous system (appropriately)
▸ Enhances oxygen delivery to tissues
▸ Releases energy-promoting neurochemicals

Attentional Effects

▸ Creates focused attention through movement complexity
▸ Establishes rhythmic pattern that calms mental chatter
▸ Builds heat that anchors awareness in physical sensation
▸ Generates momentum that carries through subsequent activities

The Classical Sun Salutation Sequence (12 Poses)

Begin the sequence moving through the flow outlined below first to the right, stepping back and then forward with the right leg, then repeating on the left side for the second set. This completes one round. Two sets, first with the right leg leading into the pose and then with the left leg, equals one round for a balanced practice. As outlined below, this Sun Salutation sequence has a count of 12 poses.

Position 1 - Prayer Pose (*Pranamasana*)

▸ Stand tall with feet hip-width apart
▸ Palms together at heart center
▸ Breath: Exhale completely, centering in Prayer pose
▸ Focus: Grounding and intention setting

Position 2 - Raised Hands (*Hasta Uttanasana*)

▸ Inhale, sweep arms overhead
▸ Slight backbend if comfortable
▸ Breath: Deep, expansive inhale
▸ Focus: Opening and expanding upward

Position 3 - Standing Forward Bend (*Hastapadasana*)

▸ Exhale, hinge at hips, fold forward
▸ Hands toward floor or on legs
▸ Breath: Full, releasing exhale
▸ Focus: Surrender and grounding

Position 4 - High Lunge (*Ashwa Sanchalanasana*)

▸ Inhale, step right leg back into lunge
▸ Left knee over ankle, hands to floor or on left leg
▸ Breath: Steady inhale
▸ Focus: Strength and balance

Position 5 - Plank Pose (*Phalakasana*)

▸ Exhale, step left foot back to plank
▸ Strong straight line from head to heels
▸ Breath: Controlled exhale
▸ Focus: Core strength and stability

Position 6 - Eight Limbed Pose (*Ashtanga Namaskara*)

▸ Lower knees, chest, and chin to floor
▸ Keep hips lifted
▸ Breath: Controlled exhale
▸ Focus: Humility and strength

Position 7 - Cobra Pose (*Bhujangasana*)

- Inhale, slide forward and lift chest
- Arms straight or bent, heart opening
- Breath: Expansive inhale
- Focus: Heart opening and courage

Position 8 - Downward-Facing Dog (*Adho Mukha Svanasana*)

- Exhale, tuck toes, lift hips up
- Form inverted V shape
- Breath: Grounding exhale
- Focus: Strength and perspective

Position 9 - High Lunge (*Ashwa Sanchalanasana*)

- Inhale, step right foot forward to lunge
- Same as position 4
- Focus: Balance and strength

Position 10 - Standing Forward Bend (*Hastapadasana*)

- Exhale, step left foot forward, fold
- Same as position 3
- Focus: Integration

Position 11 - Raised Hands (*Hasta Uttanasana*)

- - Inhale, rise up with arms overhead
- - Same as position 2
- - Focus: Rising energy

Position 12 - Prayer Pose (*Pranamasana*)

- Exhale, hands to heart center
- Same as position 1
- Focus: Integration and completion

Repeat the sequence stepping back with the left leg first to complete one balanced round.

Recommended Application

▸ Use before activities requiring energy and focus
▸ Practice as a transition from rest to activity
▸ Perform to overcome inertia or resistance
▸ Adapt speed and intensity to specific needs

Whether approached as a traditional yoga practice or simply as a movement sequence, Sun Salutations offer a reliable way to shift into a more energized, focused state conducive to active flow.

Moon Salutations (Chandra Namaskar): Receptive Flow

The less well-known Moon Salutation creates a different quality of flow oriented toward receptivity and integration:

Physiological Effects

▸ Activates the parasympathetic nervous system
▸ Creates side-to-side balance through lateral movements
▸ Opens areas often held tight (hips, side body)
▸ Establishes a slower, more fluid rhythm

Attentional Effects

▸ Promotes receptive rather than directive awareness
▸ Encourages inward attention without withdrawal
▸ Creates space for insight and integration
▸ Balances doing-mode with being-mode

The Classical Moon Salutation Sequence (14 Poses)

Begin the sequence moving through the flow outlined below first to the left, circling around to the right from the low lunge back to standing center, completing the first set, then repeat moving first to the right, circling down and around back up. This completes one round. Two sets, first to the left and then to the right, equals one round for a balanced practice. This Moon Salutation sequence has a count of 14 poses, with one round totaling 28 poses, similar to the moon's 27-28 day cycle.

(For a 12-pose Moon Salutation sequence, remove Mountain pose and begin/end in Palm Tree pose. 9 sets of 12 poses equals 108 poses.)

Position 1 - Mountain Pose (*Tadasana*)

▸ Stand tall with feet hip-width apart
▸ Arms at sides, palms facing forward
▸ Breath: Exhale, centering and grounding
▸ Focus: Root and sacral chakras

Position 2 - Palm Tree Pose (*Talasana*)

▸ Inhale, reach arms overhead
▸ Stretch to the side, beginning the sequence to the left
▸ Breath: Side-body expansion inhale
▸ Focus: Heart chakra, stretching to begin the sequence

Position 3 - Goddess Pose (*Utkata Konasana*)

▸ Exhale, step feet wide, bend knees deeply
▸ Arms in cactus shape or prayer at heart
▸ Breath: Empowering exhale
▸ Focus: Root, sacral, and solar plexus chakras

Position 4 - Extended Triangle Pose (*Utthita Trikonasana*)

▸ Inhale, straighten legs, reach left hand down
▸ Right arm extends up, creating triangle shape
▸ Breath: Expanding inhale
▸ Focus: Root, sacral, and heart chakras

Position 5 - Intense Side Stretch (*Parsvottanasana*)

▸ Exhale, hands to floor or blocks, fold over left leg
▸ Side intense stretch pose
▸ Breath: Releasing exhale
▸ Focus: Root, sacral, solar plexus, throat, and crown chakras

Position 6 - Crescent Low Lunge (*Anjaneyasana*)

▸ Inhale, bend left knee deeply, hands to floor
▸ Low lunge position
▸ Breath: Grounding inhale
▸ Focus: Root, sacral, and solar plexus chakras

Position 7 - Side Lunge Pose (*Skandasana*)

▸ Exhale, shift weight to left leg, extend right leg
▸ Attacking warrior pose, side lunge
▸ Breath: Shifting exhale
▸ Focus: Root and sacral chakras

The sequence continues in reverse, moving slowly through center and returning to standing. Each movement is performed with conscious breath and attention to the opening and closing of energy centers.

Integration Focus:

The Moon Salutation emphasizes the receptive qualities of lunar energy, promoting introspection, intuition, and the integration of experiences. Unlike the linear, heating quality of Sun Salutations, Moon Salutations move in curves and circles, honoring the cyclical nature of lunar energy.

Recommended Application

▸ Use to transition from active to receptive states
▸ Practice before creative activities requiring openness
▸ Perform between intense focus periods
▸ Adapt to facilitate integration after learning

The Moon Salutation offers a valuable counterbalance to our culture's emphasis on active, directive energy—creating space for the receptive dimension of flow.

Designing Your Own Movement Ritual

While traditional sequences offer valuable starting points, creating personalized movement rituals can be even more effective for your specific needs:

Personal Ritual Design Elements

- ‣ Identify the specific state shift you're targeting
- ‣ Include movements that reliably produce that shift for you
- ‣ Create a clear beginning, middle, and end
- ‣ Integrate breath patterns that support the desired state
- ‣ Keep it simple enough to memorize completely

Implementation Approach

- ‣ Practice daily until the sequence becomes automatic
- ‣ Use consistently in similar contexts to strengthen association
- ‣ Adapt subtly based on what your body needs each time
- ‣ Maintain the core structure while allowing organic variation

The Four Seasonal 108 Practices

Each seasonal turning point offers unique opportunities for flow cultivation. The following practices are designed to align with the specific energetic qualities of each season while maintaining the powerful 108 framework.

Spring Equinox: The 108 of New Beginnings

"Spring arrives not as a gradual warming but as a sudden recognition— the moment when possibility becomes visible and the world remembers how to grow."

The Energy of Spring Equinox

The spring equinox represents perfect balance between day and night, winter and summer, rest and action. It's nature's invitation to emerge from contemplative winter energy into creative expansion.

Astronomical Significance:

- Day and night are exactly equal length
- Sun crosses the celestial equator moving northward
- Light begins to dominate darkness in the northern hemisphere
- Natural world awakens from winter dormancy

Psychological Significance:

‣   Increased energy and optimism
‣   Natural impulse toward new projects and growth
‣   Enhanced creativity and inspiration
‣   Desire for fresh starts and renewal

Flow Applications:

‣   Initiating new creative projects
‣   Breaking through stuck patterns
‣   Energizing stagnant areas of life
‣   Planting seeds for future manifestation

21-Day Spring Preparation Practice

Week One: Awakening (Days 1-7)

Gentle emergence from winter patterns
Daily Core Practice: The Spring Awakening Sequence

‣   **Earth Connection (1 minute):** Stand barefoot if possible, feeling ground beneath feet
‣   **Gentle Activation (2 minutes):** Light movement to awaken the body—stretching, bouncing, shaking
‣   **Breath of Renewal (2 minutes):** 4-count inhale, 6-count exhale, visualizing fresh energy entering

Focus Area: Physical space clearing and organization
Reflection Prompt: What wants to be born in my life this season? What old patterns am I ready to release?

Week Two: Sprouting (Days 8-14)

Building energy and momentum
Daily Core Practice: Growth Breathing

- **Rhythmic Breathing (3 minutes):** 6-count inhale, 4-count exhale (energizing pattern)
- **Movement Flow (2 minutes):** Sun salutation or personal morning sequence
- **Intention Setting (1 minute):** Visualize your spring projects taking root and growing

Focus Area: Creative project initiation
Reflection Prompt: What creative projects excite me most? How can I take small daily actions toward these goals?

Week Three: Blooming (Days 15-21)

Full engagement with spring energy

Daily Core Practice: Creative Activation

- **Dynamic Breathing (2 minutes):** Breath of fire or energizing pranayama
- **Creative Movement (3 minutes):** Dance, free-form movement, or martial arts
- **Visioning (1 minute):** See yourself fully expressing your creative potential

Focus Area: Community connection and collaboration
Reflection Prompt: How can I share my growing energy with others? What collaborations want to emerge?

The Spring Equinox 108 Event

Option 1: Movement-Based Spring Awakening

- 108 Sun Salutations divided into 4 sets of 27
- Each set represents an element awakening: Earth (grounding), Water (flow), Fire (energy), Air (inspiration)
- Focus: Building energy progressively from gentle to dynamic

Option 2: Breath-Centered New Beginnings

108 breath cycles alternating between three patterns:

- 36 Balanced breaths (4-4 pattern) for equilibrium
- 36 Energizing breaths (6-4 pattern) for activation
- 36 Creative breaths (visualization with each cycle)

Option 3: Multi-Modal Spring Practice

- 36 movements (Spring-modified Sun Salutations)
- 36 creative visualizations (see new projects manifesting)
- 36 gratitude acknowledgments (for winter's rest and spring's arrival)

Integration Focus:

- Planting literal or metaphorical seeds
- Creating vision boards or goal maps
- Sharing spring intentions with community
- Establishing new creative routines

Summer Solstice:
The 108 of Peak Expression

"The summer solstice is nature's perfect demonstration of flow—the sun reaching its fullest expression, the year at its brightest point, the rhythm of

the seasons in perfect equilibrium before beginning its next phase. In this moment of culmination, we find a mirror for our own creative cycles."

The Energy of Summer Solstice

The summer solstice represents maximum light and energy in the annual cycle. It's nature's demonstration of full potential realized—the culmination of spring's growth into mature expression.

Astronomical Significance:

- Longest day and shortest night of the year
- Sun reaches its highest point in the sky
- Maximum solar energy available
- Peak of the light half of the year

Psychological Significance:

- Natural energy levels at their highest
- Increased confidence and extroversion
- Peak creativity and productivity potential
- Abundance mindset and generous spirit

Flow Applications:

- Bringing projects to completion
- Peak performance in chosen areas
- Sharing gifts with larger communities
- Celebrating achievements and growth

21-Day Summer Preparation Practice

Week One: Building (Days 1-7)

Gathering energy for peak expression

DAILY CORE PRACTICE: SOLAR CHARGING

- **Sun Gazing (1 minute):** Safe morning or evening sun exposure with gratitude
- **Heat Building (3 minutes):** Vigorous movement to build internal fire
- **Power Breathing (2 minutes):** Strong, rhythmic breathing to charge the system

FOCUS AREA: Identifying your peak gifts and talents

REFLECTION PROMPT: What are my unique gifts that are ready for full expression? How can I prepare to share them boldly?

Week Two: Intensifying (Days 8-14)

Increasing capacity for sustained peak performance

DAILY CORE PRACTICE: PEAK STATE TRAINING

- **Challenge Selection:** Identify one area for peak performance focus
- **Intensity Practice (4 minutes):** Sustained effort in chosen area
- **Recovery Integration (2 minutes):** Conscious rest and appreciation

FOCUS AREA: Peak performance preparation

REFLECTION PROMPT: What does my highest expression look like? What support do I need to sustain peak performance?

Week Three: Culminating (Days 15-21)

Preparing for full radiance

DAILY CORE PRACTICE: RADIANCE CULTIVATION

- **Heart Opening (2 minutes):** Physical and energetic chest expansion
- **Generous Giving (3 minutes):** Offer your gifts freely—create, serve, express

‣ **Celebration (1 minute):** Acknowledge your readiness for peak expression

FOCUS AREA: Community and sharing preparation

REFLECTION PROMPT: How do I want to celebrate and share my peak expression? Who do I want to serve with my gifts?

The Summer Solstice 108 Event

Option 1: Solar Power Movement Practice

‣ 108 Sun Salutations performed at peak intensity
‣ Divided into 6 sets of 18 (representing the hours of daylight)
‣ Each set builds in intensity, peaking at midpoint, then integrates
‣ **Focus:** Sustained high-energy flow with rhythmic intensity

Option 2: Peak Expression Breath Work

‣ 108 power breaths building to maximum intensity
‣ **Pattern:** 27 building breaths + 54 peak breaths + 27 integration breaths
‣ **Visualization:** Your light radiating out to serve the world
‣ **Focus:** Internal solar energy cultivation and generous sharing

Option 3: Community Celebration Practice

‣ 36 movements honoring personal peak expression
‣ 36 offerings of gratitude for growth and abundance
‣ 36 intentions for serving others with your gifts

Integration Focus:

‣ Peak performance in a chosen area
‣ Community celebration and sharing
‣ Creating something beautiful to offer the world
‣ Honoring the balance between achievement and humility

Autumn Equinox:
The 108 of Harvest Wisdom

"Autumn teaches the beauty of letting go—not as loss but as generous offering, making space for what wants to emerge next."

The Energy of Autumn Equinox

The autumn equinox marks the return to balance after summer's peak, the beginning of the journey inward, and the time of harvest—both literal and metaphorical.

Astronomical Significance:

- Day and night return to equal length
- Sun crosses celestial equator moving southward
- Darkness begins to lengthen
- Natural world prepares for winter rest

Psychological Significance:

- Natural desire for reflection and evaluation
- Increased appreciation for what has been accomplished
- Wisdom and maturity themes emerge
- Preparation for introspective winter phase

Flow Applications:

- Harvesting insights from the year's experiences
- Integrating lessons learned
- Expressing gratitude for growth and abundance
- Preparing foundations for future development

21-Day Autumn Preparation Practice

Week One: Gathering (Days 1-7)

Collecting the harvest of experience
DAILY CORE PRACTICE: WISDOM GATHERING

1. **Gratitude Scanning (2 minutes):** Review recent growth and accomplishments
2. **Lesson Harvesting (3 minutes):** Identify key insights from recent experiences
3. **Integration Breathing (1 minute):** Deep, slow breaths to embody wisdom gained

FOCUS AREA: Life review and lesson identification
REFLECTION PROMPT: What have I learned this year? What insights want to be integrated and shared?

Week Two: Processing (Days 8-14)

Transforming experience into wisdom
DAILY CORE PRACTICE: TRANSFORMATION RITUAL

1. **Story Review (2 minutes):** Reflect on a significant recent experience
2. **Meaning Making (3 minutes):** Extract the wisdom or teaching from the experience
3. **Embodiment (1 minute):** Feel how this wisdom lives in your body

FOCUS AREA: Creative expression of insights
REFLECTION PROMPT: How can I express or share the wisdom I've gained? What wants to be created from my experience?

Week Three: Preparing (Days 15-21)

Creating foundation for winter's introspection
DAILY CORE PRACTICE: FOUNDATION SETTING

1. **Appreciation Practice (2 minutes):** Honor all that has supported your growth

2. **Release Ritual (3 minutes):** Let go of what no longer serves

3. **Foundation Strengthening (1 minute):** Connect with your core values and strengths

FOCUS AREA: Home and sanctuary preparation

REFLECTION PROMPT: How do I want to spend the introspective season ahead? What environment will best support my inner work?

The Autumn Equinox 108 Event

Option 1: Gratitude Flow Movement

- 108 Moon Salutations performed with deep appreciation
- Each movement becomes a gesture of thanks
- Focus: Fluid, graceful movement honoring all that has been received

Option 2: Wisdom Harvest Meditation

- 108 conscious breaths, each connected to a specific gratitude
- Review the year's gifts, lessons, and growth moments
- Focus: Deep appreciation and integration of life's teachings

Option 3: Community Thanksgiving Practice

- 36 expressions of personal gratitude
- 36 acknowledgments of others' contributions to your growth
- 36 offerings of your own gifts and service to community

Integration Focus:

- Creating gratitude journals or appreciation art
- Sharing appreciation with important people in your life
- Establishing foundations for winter's introspective phase

‣ Community feast or celebration of collective harvest

Winter Solstice: The 108 of Deep Renewal

"In the heart of winter's darkness, we find the first spark of returning light—reminding us that even in the depths of rest, new life is stirring."

The Energy of Winter Solstice

The winter solstice represents the deepest point of introspection in the annual cycle, the longest night, and paradoxically, the return of the light.

Astronomical Significance:

‣ Longest night and shortest day of the year
‣ Sun reaches its lowest point in the sky
‣ Beginning of the return journey toward longer days
‣ Deep winter energy at its peak

Psychological Significance:

‣ Natural inclination toward introspection and contemplation
‣ Opportunity for profound inner work and healing
‣ Connection with deeper wisdom and intuition
‣ Preparation for the gradual return to active expression

Flow Applications:

‣ Deep contemplative practices and inner work
‣ Connecting with intuitive wisdom and inner knowing
‣ Healing and integration work
‣ Visioning and dreaming for the coming cycle

21-Day Winter Preparation Practice

Week One: Deepening (Days 1-7)

Moving into contemplative space
DAILY CORE PRACTICE: INWARD JOURNEY

1. **Settling (2 minutes):** Gradual slowing and centering
2. **Inner Listening (3 minutes):** Quiet meditation or contemplation
3. **Deep Rest (1 minute):** Complete relaxation and receptivity
FOCUS AREA: Creating contemplative environment
REFLECTION PROMPT: What do I need for deep inner work? How can I honor my need for introspection?

Week Two: Exploring (Days 8-14)

Diving deeper into inner wisdom
DAILY CORE PRACTICE: WISDOM SEEKING

1. **Question Holding (2 minutes):** Pose a meaningful life question
2. **Silent Listening (3 minutes):** Wait receptively for inner guidance
3. **Insight Receiving (1 minute):** Notice and honor whatever emerges
FOCUS AREA: Inner guidance and intuitive development
REFLECTION PROMPT: What is my inner wisdom trying to tell me? What guidance wants to emerge from the quiet?

Week Three: Visioning (Days 15-21)

Seeing the seeds of new possibilities
DAILY CORE PRACTICE: FUTURE DREAMING

1. **Present Appreciation (1 minute):** Honor where you are now
2. **Possibility Sensing (3 minutes):** Feel into emerging potentials
3. **Vision Planting (2 minutes):** Plant seeds of intention for the coming cycle
FOCUS AREA: Vision and intention for the coming year

REFLECTION PROMPT: What wants to be born through me in the coming cycle? What vision is stirring in the depths?

The Winter Solstice 108 Event

Option 1: Contemplative Movement

‣ 108 slow, meditative movements
‣ Each movement becomes a prayer or meditation
‣ Focus: Deep inner listening while moving
‣ Style: Tai chi, qigong, or slow yoga flow

Option 2: Silent Meditation with Light

‣ 108 minutes of silent contemplation (broken into comfortable segments)
‣ Focus on inner light and returning solar energy
‣ Use of candles or other light sources for symbolism
‣ Focus: Deep inner journey and visioning

Option 3: Wisdom Council Practice

‣ 36 minutes of personal contemplation
‣ 36 minutes of sharing wisdom and insights with others
‣ 36 minutes of silent integration of collective wisdom

Integration Focus:

‣ Deep journaling and inner exploration
‣ Vision creation for the coming year
‣ Community gathering for shared contemplation
‣ Light ceremonies honoring the return of longer days

Connecting the Seasonal Cycle

The four seasonal practices create a complete cycle of flow development:

Spring → Summer → Autumn → Winter → Spring...

Emergence → Expression → Integration → Contemplation → Emergence...

The Seasonal Flow Rhythm

Spring (Emergence): New ideas and projects are born
Summer (Expression): Ideas reach full manifestation and are shared
Autumn (Integration): Experiences are transformed into wisdom
Winter (Contemplation): Deep wisdom informs new visions

Annual Practice Suggestions

For Beginners

▸ Participate in one seasonal 108 practice per year to start
▸ Focus on the season that most resonates with your current life phase
▸ Use the 21-day preparation practices throughout the year

For Experienced Practitioners

▸ Engage with all four seasonal practices
▸ Create personal variations that honor your unique path
▸ Lead community events and share the practices with others

For Community Leaders

▸ Organize seasonal gatherings in your area

‣   Create local adaptations that honor regional seasonal variations
‣   Develop ongoing support groups for seasonal flow practitioners

Personalizing Your Seasonal Practice

Finding Your Seasonal Affinity

While all four seasons offer valuable gifts, you may find particular resonance with one or two:

Spring People: Natural initiators, love new beginnings, energized by possibility

Summer People: Peak performers, love to shine and serve, energized by expression

Autumn People: Wisdom keepers, love integration and teaching, energized by harvest

Winter People: Deep contemplatives, love inner work, energized by stillness

Adapting to Your Climate

If you live in a climate without distinct seasons:

‣   Use astronomical dates rather than weather patterns
‣   Create artificial seasonal markers (decorations, foods, activities)
‣   Travel to seasonal locations for practice if possible
‣   Focus on internal seasonal rhythms regardless of external weather

Creating Your Personal Seasonal Calendar

Design your year around the seasonal flow principles:

‣   **Plan major creative projects** to align with seasonal energies
‣   **Schedule rest and retreat** during your less energized seasons
‣   **Time important life decisions** with appropriate seasonal support
‣   **Create traditions and celebrations** that honor each seasonal transition

The Transformative Power
of Seasonal Flow

The Seasonal Flow practice embodies the core principles explored throughout this book:

Rhythm Recognition: Aligning with the master rhythm of the earth's journey around the sun

Harmonized Body-Mind: Using integrated practices that honor both physical and mental/spiritual development

Yielding to Cycles: Honoring the natural pattern of expansion and contraction, peak and rest

Tuned Environment: Creating optimal conditions for different types of inner work

Heightened Meaning: Connecting personal growth to cosmic cycles and universal principles

Mastered Focus: Using ritual and repetition to deepen attention and presence

By participating in the Seasonal 108 practices, you're not just doing techniques—you're joining an ancient rhythm, connecting with the fundamental flow that moves through the natural world, and aligning your personal development with the wisdom of the cosmos.

The Invitation

The seasons remind us that flow isn't something we create—it's something we join, a rhythm already moving through the natural world that we can choose to align with. In this alignment, we find our truest expression and our deepest fulfillment.

Each seasonal turning point offers us the same invitation: to release what no longer serves, to embrace what wants to emerge, and to trust the natural rhythm that knows exactly how to carry us forward.

The solstices and equinoxes teach us that even at moments of greatest peak, we begin the journey toward rest. Even in the depths of rest, we begin the return to expression. This is not loss—it's rhythm, the eternal flow that connects us to everything.

Getting Started: Your First Seasonal 108 Practice

Choose the seasonal event closest to when you're reading this:

▸ **Read the specific seasonal section** that corresponds to your chosen practice
▸ **Begin the 21-day preparation** three weeks before the astronomical date
▸ **Gather any needed materials** (yoga mat, candles, journal, etc.)
▸ **Decide on your format:** individual practice or community gathering
▸ **Mark the date** and treat it as a sacred appointment with yourself
▸ **Follow up with integration practices** to embed the experience

Remember: The goal isn't perfection but presence. Whether you complete all 108 repetitions or find your own authentic expression within the framework, the power lies in your sincere engagement with the seasonal rhythm and your commitment to honoring these natural turning points as opportunities for growth and alignment.

The seasons are waiting to teach you. The rhythm is already there. All that's required is your willing participation in the eternal flow that connects you to everything.

~ / ~

May your practice be a bridge between ancient wisdom and modern life, between your individual journey and the cosmic dance, between who you are and who you are becoming.

Acknowledgments

This book would not exist without the moments of resonance, courage, and clarity that showed up in the middle of chaos. Thank you to everyone who reminded me—through presence or pause—that flow is always available when we choose to return.

To my early readers and supporters—your insights, encouragement, and reflections give this work shape, soul, and strength.

To the teachers, mentors, friends, and unexpected mirrors along the way— you helped restore rhythm to my life.

To Dr. Irene Pepperberg—thank you for welcoming my curiosity into your lab and into the wild intelligence of the parrots we both adored. You showed me what it meant to follow truth with both heart and hypothesis.

And to you, dear reader—thank you for choosing to engage deeply, to pause, to reflect, and to honor your own Green Moments.

Endnotes by Chapter

Endnotes for the Introduction

1. Norway Cup. *About the Norway Cup*. Accessed July 16, 2025.
2. Mihaly Csikszentmihalyi. *Flow: The Psychology of Optimal Experience*. New York: Harper & Row, 1990.
3. Steven Kotler. *The Rise of Superman: Decoding the Science of Ultimate Human Performance*. New York: New Harvest, 2014.
4. Arne Dietrich. "Neurocognitive mechanisms underlying the experience of flow." *Consciousness and Cognition* 13, no. 4 (2004): 746–761.
5. "Workplace Email Statistics 2025: Usage, Productivity, Trends." *cloudHQ*, April 22, 2025.
6. Microsoft. "New Microsoft study reveals the rise of the 'infinite workday.'" June 17, 2025.
7. "User attention span: The biggest challenge for marketers." *Devrix*, September 18, 2024.
8. "Average human attention span statistics & facts." *Samba Recovery*, June 25, 2025.
9. "Average human attention span (statistics)." *Golden Steps ABA*, March 4, 2025.
10. "Attention spans are dropping, research shows: how to focus." *New York Post*, May 17, 2025.
11. "Executive burnout statistics 2025: A look into the leadership crisis." *Superhuman Blog*, June 11, 2025.
12. *The Rooted Way*. "Executive burnout in 2025: A comprehensive analysis." April 8, 2025.
13. Bryan Robinson. "Job burnout at 66% in 2025, new study shows." *Forbes*, February 8, 2025.
14. "Anxiety statistics in the United States in 2025." *LAOP Center*, May 20, 2025.
15. *TherapyRoute.com*. "Anxiety: 2025 statistics." June 27, 2025.
16. World Health Organization. "COVID-19 pandemic triggers 25% increase in prevalence of anxiety and depression worldwide." March 2, 2022.
17. "Anxiety statistics 2025." *SingleCare*, January 24, 2025.
18. Christina Maslach, Michael Leiter, and Wilmar Schaufeli. "Measuring burnout." *Annual Review of Psychology* 52 (2001): 397–422.
19. Jonathan Malesic. *The End of Burnout: Why Work Drains Us and How to Build Better Lives*. Oakland: University of California Press, 2022.

Endnotes for Chapter 1

1. Mihaly Csikszentmihalyi, *Flow: The Psychology of Optimal Experience* (New York: Harper & Row, 1990).
2. Mihaly Csikszentmihalyi, *Flow: The Psychology of Optimal Experience* (New York: Harper & Row, 1990).
3. Mihaly Csikszentmihalyi, Finding *Flow: The Psychology of Engagement with Everyday Life* (New York: Basic Books, 1997).
4. Mihaly Csikszentmihalyi, *Flow*, 3.
5. Mihaly Csikszentmihalyi, *Finding Flow*.

6. Jeanne Nakamura and Mihaly Csikszentmihalyi, "The concept of flow," in *Handbook of Positive Psychology*, ed. C. R. Snyder and S. J. Lopez (Oxford: Oxford University Press, 2002), 89–105.
7. Mihaly Csikszentmihalyi, *Flow*.
8. Mihaly Csikszentmihalyi, *Finding Flow*.
9. Mihaly Csikszentmihalyi, *Flow*.
10. Mihaly Csikszentmihalyi, *Flow*.
11. Mihaly Csikszentmihalyi, *Finding Flow*.
12. Mihaly Csikszentmihalyi, *Flow*.
13. Jeanne Nakamura and Mihaly Csikszentmihalyi, "The concept of flow," in *Handbook of Positive Psychology*, ed. C. R. Snyder and S. J. Lopez (Oxford: Oxford University Press, 2002), 89–105.
14. Mihaly Csikszentmihalyi, *Flow*.
15. Angela Duckworth, Grit: *The Power of Passion and Perseverance* (New York: Scribner, 2016), 57–62; Steven Kotler and Jamie Wheal, *Stealing Fire: How Silicon Valley, the Navy SEALs, and Maverick Scientists Are Revolutionizing the Way We Live and Work* (New York: Dey Street Books, 2017), 79–86.
16. Mihaly Csikszentmihalyi, *Flow*.
17. Steven Kotler, *The Rise of Superman: Decoding the Science of Ultimate Human Performance* (Boston: Houghton Mifflin Harcourt, 2014), 130–146.
18. Arne Dietrich, "Neurocognitive mechanisms underlying the experience of flow," *Consciousness and Cognition* 13, no. 4 (2004): 746–761.
19. László Harmat, Örjan de Manzano, Töres Theorell, and Fredrik Ullén, "Physiological correlates of the flow experience during computer game playing," *International Journal of Psychophysiology* 97, no. 1 (2015): 1–7.
20. Steven Kotler, *The Rise of Superman*; Arne Dietrich, "Neurocognitive mechanisms underlying the experience of flow," *Consciousness and Cognition* 13, no. 4 (2004): 746–761.
21. Arne Dietrich, "Neurocognitive mechanisms underlying the experience of flow," *Consciousness and Cognition* 13, no. 4 (2004): 746–761.
22. Shunryu Suzuki, Zen *Mind, Beginner's Mind* (New York: Weatherhill, 1970).
23. Laozi, Tao Te Ching, trans. D. C. Lau (London: Penguin Classics, 1997). (Original work published ca. 6th century BCE.)
24. Annemarie Schimmel, *Mystical Dimensions of Islam* (Chapel Hill: University of North Carolina Press, 1975), 306–312.
25. Vine Deloria Jr., *God Is Red: A Native View of Religion* (Golden, CO: Fulcrum Publishing, 1994), 160, 210–211.
26. Patañjali, Yoga Sūtras 1.2 and 3.3; see Edwin Bryant, *The Yoga Sūtras of Patañjali* (New York: North Point Press, 2009), 15, 298–306.
27. Paramahansa Yogananda, *Autobiography of a Yogi* (Los Angeles: Self-Realization Fellowship, 1946), ch. 26.
28. W. H. McNeill, *The Pursuit of Power: Technology, Armed Force, and Society since A.D. 1000* (Chicago: University of Chicago Press, 1996); on kairos and Greek time, see esp. 69–70.
29. Mihaly Csikszentmihalyi, *Good Business: Leadership, Flow, and the Making of Meaning* (New York: Viking, 2003), 45–54.
30. G. Wilson, *The Infomania Study* (Commissioned by Hewlett-Packard, 2010).

31. Gloria Mark, Daniela Gudith, and Ulrich Klocke, "The cost of interrupted work: More speed and stress," in *Proceedings of the SIGCHI Conference on Human Factors in Computing Systems* (New York: ACM, 2008), 107–110.
32. Joshua S. Rubinstein, David E. Meyer, and Jeffrey E. Evans, "Executive control of cognitive processes in task switching," *Journal of Experimental Psychology: Human Perception and Performance* 27, no. 4 (2001): 763–797.
33. Mihaly Csikszentmihalyi, *Finding Flow*.
34. Mihaly Csikszentmihalyi, *Flow*.
35. Steven Kotler, *The Rise of Superman*, 122–138.
36. Steven Kotler and Jamie Wheal, *Stealing Fire*, 116–122.
37. Roy F. Baumeister and John Tierney, *Willpower: Rediscovering the Greatest Human Strength* (New York: Penguin Press, 2011), 238–257.
38. Mihaly Csikszentmihalyi, *Finding Flow*.
39. Mihaly Csikszentmihalyi, *Flow*.
40. Steven Kotler, *The Rise of Superman*, 141–147.
41. Roy F. Baumeister and John Tierney, *Willpower*, 44–55.
42. Mihaly Csikszentmihalyi, *Finding Flow*.
43. Mihaly Csikszentmihalyi, *Flow*; Steven Kotler, *The Rise of Superman*.
44. Jeanne Nakamura and Mihaly Csikszentmihalyi, "The concept of flow," in *Handbook of Positive Psychology*, ed. C. R. Snyder and S. J. Lopez (Oxford: Oxford University Press, 2002), 89–105; Steven Kotler, *The Rise of Superman*, 86–97.
45. Mihaly Csikszentmihalyi, *Finding Flow*.
46. Mihaly Csikszentmihalyi, *Flow*, 213–218.
47. Mihaly Csikszentmihalyi, *Flow: The Psychology of Optimal Experience* (New York: Harper & Row, 1990).

Endnotes for Chapter 2

1. Dietrich, A. (2004). Neurocognitive mechanisms underlying the experience of flow. *Consciousness and Cognition*, 13(4), 746–761. https://doi.org/10.1016/j.concog.2004.07.001
2. Harris, R. J., O'Boyle, M. W., & Sutton, K. C. (2017). The neural basis of flow experience. *Neuroscience and Biobehavioral Reviews*, 75, 559–568. https://doi.org/10.1016/j.neubiorev.2017.01.025
3. Dietrich, A. (2004).
4. Kotler, S. (2014). *The Rise of Superman: Decoding the Science of Ultimate Human Performance*. Houghton Mifflin Harcourt.
5. Csikszentmihalyi, M. (1990). *Flow: The Psychology of Optimal Experience*. Harper & Row.
6. Nakamura, J., & Csikszentmihalyi, M. (2014). The concept of flow. In M. Csikszentmihalyi (Ed.), *Flow and the Foundations of Positive Psychology* (pp. 239–263). Springer.
7. Hebb, D. O. (1949). *The Organization of Behavior: A Neuropsychological Theory*. Wiley.
8. Nakamura & Csikszentmihalyi (2014).
9. Csikszentmihalyi, M. (1990).
10. Dietrich, A. (2004).
11. Csikszentmihalyi, M. (1990).

12. Mauri, M., et al. (2011). Why is Facebook so successful? Psychophysiological measures describe a core flow state while using Facebook. *Cyberpsychology, Behavior, and Social Networking*, 14(10), 577–583. https://doi.org/10.1089/cyber.2010.0250

13. Lehrer, J. (2012). *Imagine: How Creativity Works*. Houghton Mifflin Harcourt.

14. Csikszentmihalyi, M. (1990).

15. Csikszentmihalyi, M. (1997). *Finding Flow: The Psychology of Engagement with Everyday Life*. Basic Books.

16. Lehrer, P. M., Vaschillo, E., & Vaschillo, B. (2000). Resonant frequency biofeedback training to increase cardiac variability: Rationale and manual for training. *Applied Psychophysiology and Biofeedback*, 25(3), 177-191.

17. McCraty, R., & Childre, D. (2010). Coherence: Bridging personal, social, and global health. *Alternative Therapies in Health and Medicine*, 16(4), 10-24.

18. Nakamura, J., & Csikszentmihalyi, M. (2009). Flow theory and research. In C. R. Snyder & S. J. Lopez (Eds.), *Oxford Handbook of Positive Psychology* (pp. 195-206). Oxford University Press.

Endnotes for Chapter 3

1. Mihaly Csikszentmihalyi, *Flow: The Psychology of Optimal Experience* (New York: Harper & Row, 1990).

2. Jeanne Nakamura and Mihaly Csikszentmihalyi, "The Concept of Flow," in *Handbook of Positive Psychology*, ed. C. R. Snyder and Shane J. Lopez (New York: Oxford University Press, 2002), 89–105.

3. Gloria Mark, *Attention Span: A Groundbreaking Way to Restore Balance, Happiness and Productivity* (Hanover Square Press, 2023).

4. Steven Kotler, *The Rise of Superman: Decoding the Science of Ultimate Human Performance* (New York: Houghton Mifflin Harcourt, 2014).

5. Keith Sawyer, *Group Genius: The Creative Power of Collaboration*, 2nd ed. (New York: Basic Books, 2017).

6. Cal Newport, *Deep Work: Rules for Focused Success in a Distracted World* (New York: Grand Central, 2016).

7. Adam Grant, *Think Again: The Power of Knowing What You Don't Know* (New York: Viking, 2021).

8. Susan Cain, *Quiet: The Power of Introverts in a World That Can't Stop Talking* (New York: Crown, 2012).

9. Andrew Huberman, "How to Optimize Your Work and Rest Cycles," *The Huberman Lab Podcast*, 2022.

Endnotes for Chapter 4

1. O'Neill, P., & Bowen, H. K. (1994). *Alcoa's Transformation: Leadership Through Crisis*. Harvard Business School Case Study.

2. Csikszentmihalyi, M. (1990). *Flow: The Psychology of Optimal Experience*. Harper & Row.

3. McKinsey Global Institute. (2012). *The social economy: Unlocking value and productivity through social technologies*.

4. Newport, C. (2016). *Deep Work: Rules for Focused Success in a Distracted World*. Grand Central Publishing.
5. Walker, M. (2017). *Why We Sleep: Unlocking the Power of Sleep and Dreams*. Scribner.
6. Rossi, E. (1991). *Ultradian Rhythms in Life Processes: An Introduction to Chronobiology*. Springer.
7. Baumeister, R. F., & Tierney, J. (2011). *Willpower: Rediscovering the Greatest Human Strength*. Penguin Press.
8. Kaplan, S. (1995). "The restorative benefits of nature." *Journal of Environmental Psychology*, 15, 169-182.
9. Fredrickson, B. L., (2004). "The broaden-and-build theory of positive emotions." *Philosophical Transactions of the Royal Society B*, 359(1449), 1367-1377.
10. Sawyer, R. K. (2007). *Group Genius: The Creative Power of Collaboration*. Basic Books.

Endnotes for Chapter 5

1. Wallas, G. (1926). The Art of Thought. Harcourt, Brace and Company.
2. Dietrich, A. (2004). Neurocognitive mechanisms underlying the experience of flow. Consciousness and Cognition, 13(4), 746–761. https://doi.org/10.1016/j.concog.2004.07.001
3. Beaty, R. E., Benedek, M., Silvia, P. J., & Schacter, D. L. (2016). Creative cognition and brain network dynamics. Trends in Cognitive Sciences, 20(2), 87–95. https://doi.org/10.1016/j.tics.2015.10.004
4. Kounios, J., & Beeman, M. (2015). The Eureka Factor: Aha Moments, Creative Insight, and the Brain. Random House.
5. Oppezzo, M., & Schwartz, D. L. (2014). Give your ideas some legs: The positive effect of walking on creative thinking. Journal of Experimental Psychology: Learning, Memory, and Cognition, 40(4), 1142–1152. https://doi.org/10.1037/a0036577
6. Csikszentmihalyi, M. (1996). Creativity: Flow and the Psychology of Discovery and Invention. HarperCollins.
7. Sawyer, R. K. (2007). Group Genius: The Creative Power of Collaboration. Basic Books.
8. Kaufman, S. B. (2013). Ungifted: Intelligence Redefined. Basic Books.
9. Lehrer, J. (2012). Imagine: How Creativity Works. Houghton Mifflin Harcourt.
10. Stokes, P. D. (2006). Creativity from Constraints. Psychology of Aesthetics, Creativity, and the Arts, 2(3), 167–172.

Endnotes for Chapter 6

1. Varela F. J., Thompson E., & Rosch E. (1991). *The Embodied Mind: Cognitive Science and Human Experience*. MIT Press.
2. Damasio A. (1999). *The Feeling of What Happens: Body and Emotion in the Making of Consciousness*. Harcourt Brace.
3. Gallese V., & Lakoff G. (2005). "The Brain's Concepts: The Role of the Sensory-Motor System in Conceptual Knowledge." *Cognitive Neuropsychology*, 22(3-4), 455-479.

4. Clark A. (2008). *Supersizing the Mind: Embodiment, Action, and Cognitive Extension.* Oxford University Press.
5. Fox K. C. R. et al. (2015). "The Human Default Network: A Review and Synthesis." *NeuroImage,* 102, 1-15.
6. Thaut M. H. (2005). *Rhythm, Music, and the Brain.* Routledge.
7. Csikszentmihalyi M. (1990). *Flow: The Psychology of Optimal Experience.* Harper & Row.
8. Oppezzo M., & Schwartz D. L. (2014). "Give Your Ideas Some Legs: The Positive Effect of Walking on Creative Thinking." *Journal of Experimental Psychology: Learning, Memory, and Cognition,* 40(4), 1142-1152.
9. Swann C., Keegan R. J., Piggott D., & Schweickle M. J. (2017). "The Zones: A Systematic Review of Qualitative Studies on Flow and Clutch States in Sport." *Sport, Exercise, and Performance Psychology,* 6(4), 372-392.
10. Beilock S. L., & Carr T. H. (2001). "On the Fragility of Skilled Performance." *Journal of Experimental Psychology:* General, 130(4), 701-725.
11. Taylor J. (1995). "A Conceptual Model for Integrating Athletes' Needs and Sports Psychology Interventions." *The Sport Psychologist,* 9(3), 339-357.
12. Dietrich A. (2004). "Neurocognitive Mechanisms Underlying the Experience of Flow." *Consciousness and Cognition,* 13(4), 746-761.
13. Berka C., Levendowski D. J. et al. (2007). "EEG Correlates of Task Engagement and Mental Workload." *Aviation, Space, and Environmental Medicine,* 78(5), B231-B244.
14. Iyengar B. K. S. (1979). *Light on Yoga.* Schocken Books.

Endnotes for Chapter 7

1. Porges, S. W. (2011). *The polyvagal theory: Neurophysiological foundations of emotions, attachment, communication, and self-regulation.* W. W. Norton & Company.
2. Iacoboni, M. (2008). Mirroring people: *The new science of how we connect with others.* Farrar, Straus and Giroux.
3. Hasson, U., Ghazanfar, A. A., Galantucci, B., Garrod, S., & Keysers, C. (2012). Brain-to-brain coupling: A mechanism for creating and sharing a social world. *Trends in Cognitive Sciences,* 16(2), 114-121.
4. Brown, B. (2018). *Dare to lead: Brave work, tough conversations, whole hearts.* Random House.
5. Edmondson, A. (2019). *The fearless organization: Creating psychological safety for learning, innovation, and growth.* Wiley.
6. Woolley, A. W., Chabris, C. F., Pentland, A., Hashmi, N., & Malone, T. W. (2010). Evidence for a collective intelligence factor in the performance of human groups. *Science,* 330(6004), 686-688.

Endnotes for Chapter 8

1. Nakamura, J., & Csikszentmihalyi, M. (2002). The concept of flow. In C. R. Snyder & S. J. Lopez (Eds.), *Handbook of positive psychology* (pp. 89-105). Oxford University Press.
2. Dietrich, A. (2004). Neurocognitive mechanisms underlying the experience of flow. *Consciousness and Cognition,* 13(4), 746-761.

3. Kounios, J., & Beeman, M. (2015). *The eureka factor: Aha moments, creative insight, and the brain*. Random House.
4. Stokes, P. D. (2006). *Creativity from constraints: The psychology of breakthrough thinking*. Springer Publishing Company.
5. Dweck, C. S. (2006). Mindset: *The new psychology of success*. Random House.
6. Brown, S., & Vaughan, C. (2009). *Play: How it shapes the brain, opens the imagination, and invigorates the soul*. Avery.
7. Kabat-Zinn, J. (2013). *Full catastrophe living: Using the wisdom of your body and mind to face stress, pain, and illness*. Bantam Books.
8. Feuerstein, G. (2008). *The yoga tradition: Its history, literature, philosophy and practice*. Hohm Press.
9. Landhäußer, A., & Keller, J. (2012). Flow and its affective, cognitive, and performance-related consequences. In S. Engeser (Ed.), Advances in Flow Research (pp. 65-85). Springer.
10. Moneta, G. B., & Csikszentmihalyi, M. (1996). The effect of perceived challenges and skills on the quality of subjective experience. Journal of Personality, 64(2), 275-310.
11. Schaffer, O. (2013). Crafting fun user experiences: A method to facilitate flow. Human Factors International White Paper.

Endnotes for Chapter 9

1. Thayer, J. F., Hansen, A. L., Saus-Rose, E., & Johnsen, B. H. "Heart rate variability, prefrontal neural function, and cognitive performance: The neurovisceral integration perspective on self- regulation, adaptation, and health." Annals of Behavioral Medicine, 37(2), 2009: 141-153.
2. Flowly. "Relaxing in Flow State: how flow can regulate your nervous system."
3. Porges, S. W. "The polyvagal theory: Neurophysiological foundations of emotions, attachment, communication, and self- regulation." W.W. Norton & Company, 2011; Polyvagal Institute, "What is Polyvagal Theory?"
4. Frontiers in Integrative Neuroscience. "Polyvagal Theory: A Science of Safety."
5. Brown, R. P., & Gerbarg, P. L. "The healing power of the breath: Simple techniques to reduce stress and anxiety, enhance concentration, and balance your emotions." Shambhala Publications, 2012.
6. Aria Integrative Medicine. "Breathing and the Nervous System."
7. PMC6070065. "The Influence of Breathing on the Central Nervous System."
8. Kellie Okonek. "Flow triggers: deep embodiment."
9. Mindful Ecotourism. "Deep Embodiment and the Flow of Embodied Awareness."
10. Critchley, H. D., & Garfinkel, S. N. "Interoception and emotion." Current Opinion in Psychology, 17, 2017: 7-14; Nature, "Enhancing interoceptive sensibility through exteroceptive techniques."
11. Farb, N., Daubenmier, J., Price, C. J., Gard, T., Kerr, C., et al. "Interoception, contemplative practice, and health." Frontiers in Psychology, 6, 763, 2015.
12. Damasio, A. R. "Descartes' error: Emotion, reason, and the human brain." G.P. Putnam, 1994.
13. Villemure, C., & Bushnell, M.C. "Neurophysiological and neurocognitive mechanisms underlying the effects of yoga-based practices." PMC4424840; PMC7780231. "The Emerging Science of Interoception: Sensing, Integrating ..."

14. Kellie Okonek, "Flow triggers: deep embodiment"; Mindful Ecotourism, "Deep Embodiment..."
15. PMC6968164. "Flow as an Embodied State. Informed Awareness of Slackline Walking."
16. Villemure, C., & Bushnell, M.C. "Neurophysiological and neurocognitive mechanisms underlying the effects of yoga-based practices." PMC4424840.

Endnotes for Chapter 10

1. Kaufman, S. B., & Gregoire, C. (2016). Wired to create: Unraveling the mysteries of the creative mind. Perigee Books.
2. Dietrich, A. (2004). Neurocognitive mechanisms underlying the experience of flow. Consciousness and Cognition, 13(4), 746–761.
3. Botvinick, M. M., Cohen, J. D., & Carter, C. S. (2004). Conflict monitoring and anterior cingulate cortex: An update. Trends in Cognitive Sciences, 8(12), 539–546.
4. Beaty, R. E., et al. (2015). Creativity and the default network: A functional connectivity analysis of the creative brain at rest. Neuropsychologia, 64, 92–98.
5. Shafran, R., Cooper, Z., & Fairburn, C. G. (2002). Clinical perfectionism: A cognitive-behavioural analysis. Behaviour Research and Therapy, 40(7), 773–791.
6. Oppezzo, M., & Schwartz, D. L. (2014). Give your ideas some legs: The positive effect of walking on creative thinking. Journal of Experimental Psychology: Learning, Memory, and Cognition, 40(4), 1142–1152.
7. Kleitman, N. (1963). Sleep and wakefulness. University of Chicago Press.
8. Schippers, M. C., Homan, A. C., & van Knippenberg, D. (2020). To reflect or not to reflect: Prior team performance as a boundary condition of the effects of reflexivity on learning and final team performance. European Journal of Work and Organizational Psychology, 29(2), 218–234.
9. Adams, J. L. (2001). Conceptual Blockbusting: A Guide to Better Ideas (4th ed.). Perseus Books.

Endnotes for Chapter 11

1. Jerath, R., Edry, J. W., Barnes, V. A., & Jerath, V. (2006). Physiology of long pranayamic breathing: Neural respiratory elements may provide a mechanism that explains how slow deep breathing shifts the autonomic nervous system. Medical Hypotheses, 67(3), 566–571.
2. Brown, R. P., & Gerbarg, P. L. (2005). Sudarshan Kriya yogic breathing in the treatment of stress, anxiety, and depression. Journal of Alternative & Complementary Medicine, 11(4), 711–717.
3. Lehrer, P. M., Vaschillo, E., & Vaschillo, B. (2000). Resonant frequency biofeedback training to increase cardiac variability:
4. Rationale and manual for training. Applied Psychophysiology and Bioeedback, 25(3), 177–191.
5. Tang, Y. Y., Hölzel, B. K., & Posner, M. I. (2015). The neuroscience of mindfulness meditation. Nature Reviews Neuroscience, 16(4), 213–225.

6. Lazar, S. W., et al. (2005). Meditation experience is associated with increased cortical thickness. NeuroReport, 16(17), 1893–1897.
7. Zeidan, F., et al. (2010). Mindfulness meditation improves cognition: Evidence of brief mental training. Consciousness and Cognition, 19(2), 597–605.
8. Brewer, J. A., et al. (2011). Meditation experience is associated with differences in default mode network activity and connectivity. Proceedings of the National Academy of Sciences, 108(50), 20254– 20259.
9. Tang, Y. Y., Ma, Y., Wang, J., Fan, Y., Feng, S., Lu, Q., ... & Posner,
10. M. I. (2007). Short-term meditation training improves attention and self-regulation. Proceedings of the National Academy of Sciences, 104(43), 17152–17156.
11. Goyal, M., et al. (2014). Meditation programs for psychological stress and well-being: A systematic review and meta-analysis. JAMA Internal Medicine, 174(3), 357–368.
12. Elliott, S., & Edmonson, D. (2005). The New Science of Breath. Coherence Press.
13. Hölzel, B. K., Carmody, J., Vangel, M., et al. (2011). Mindfulness practice leads to increases in regional brain gray matter density. Psychiatry Research: Neuroimaging, 191(1), 36-43.

Endnotes for Chapter 12

1. Kahneman, D. (1973). Attention and Effort. Prentice Hall.
2. Kleitman, N. (1982). Sleep and Wakefulness (2nd ed.). University of Chicago Press.
3. Dietrich, A. (2004). Neurocognitive mechanisms underlying the experience of flow. Consciousness and Cognition, 13(4), 746-761. https://doi.org/10.1016/j.concog.2004.07002
4. Patanjali. (circa 400 CE). Yoga Sutras of Patanjali. (Translated by various authors).
5. Maquet, P., Smith, C., & Stickgold, R. (2005). Sleep and brain plasticity. Oxford University Press.
6. Dupuy, O., et al. (2018). An evidence-based approach for choosing post-exercise recovery techniques to reduce markers of muscle damage, soreness, fatigue, and inflammation. Frontiers in Physiology, 9, 403.
7. Kleitman, N. (1982). Basic rest-activity cycle—22 years later. Sleep, 5(4), 311-317.
8. Kotler, S. (2014). The Rise of Superman. Houghton Mifflin Harcourt.

Endnotes for Chapter 13

1. Rheinberg, F., Engeser, S., & Vollmeyer, R. (2022). A scoping review of flow research. Frontiers in Psychology, 13, Article 815665. https://doi.org/10.3389/fpsyg.2022.815665
2. Ulrich, M., Keller, J., & Grön, G. (2020). Go with the flow: A neuroscientific view on being fully engaged. Psychological Research, 85(6), 1471–1487. https://doi.org/10.1007/s00426-020-01359-8
3. Dietrich, A. (2004). Neurocognitive mechanisms underlying the experience of flow. Consciousness and Cognition, 13(4), 746–761. https://doi.org/10.1016/j.concog.2004.07.002
4. Rosen, D., Kounios, J., & Beaty, R. E. (2024). Creative flow as optimized processing: Evidence from brain network dynamics. Neuropsychologia, 190, Article 108582. https://doi.org/10.1016/j. neuropsychologia.2024.108582

5. Van der Linden, D., et al. (2021). The neuroscience of the flow state: Involvement of the locus coeruleus-norepinephrine system. Frontiers in Psychology, 12, Article 645498. https://doi.org/ 10.3389/fpsyg.2021.645498
6. Nakamura, J., & Csikszentmihalyi, M. (2002). The concept of flow. In C. R. Snyder & S. J. Lopez (Eds.), Handbook of Positive Psychology (pp. 89–105). Oxford University Press.
7. Lally, P., et al. (2010). How are habits formed: Modelling habit formation in the real world. European Journal of Social Psychology, 40(6), 998-1009.
8. Huberman, Andrew. "Using Light for Health." Huberman Lab Newsletter, February 2025. https://www.hubermanlab.com/newsletter/using-light-for-health. See also Huberman Lab Podcast episodes on circadian rhythm and light exposure.

Endnotes for Chapter 14

1. Clark, Andy. Surfing Uncertainty: Prediction, Action, and the Embodied Mind (New York: Oxford University Press, 2016), 45-67; Hohwy, Jakob. The Predictive Mind (New York: Oxford University Press, 2013), 89-112.
2. Iacoboni, Marco. Mirroring People: The New Science of How We Connect with Others (New York: Farrar, Straus and Giroux, 2008), 134-156; Keysers, Christian and Valeria Gazzola. "Social Neuroscience: Mirror Neurons Recorded in Humans," Current Biology 20, no. 8 (2010): R353-R354.
3. McCraty, Rollin. "The Energetic Heart: Bioelectromagnetic Interactions Within and Between People," HeartMath Research Center Publication No. 03-015 (2003): 1-22; Glen Rein et al., "Effects of Coherent Heart Rhythms on Long-term DNA Winding," Journal of Biological Physics 21, no. 3 (1995): 151-160.
4. Kosslyn, Stephen M., et al. "Neural Foundations of Imagery," Nature Reviews Neuroscience 2, no. 9 (2001): 635-642; Decety, Jean. "The Neurophysiological Basis of Motor Imagery," Behavioural Brain Research 77, no. 1-2 (1996): 45-52.
5. LeDoux, Joseph. The Emotional Brain: The Mysterious Underpinnings of Emotional Life (New York: Simon & Schuster, 1996), 178-201; McGaugh, James L. "The Amygdala Modulates the Consolidation of Memories of Emotionally Arousing Experiences," Annual Review of Neuroscience 27 (2004): 1-28.
6. Feuerstein, Georg. The Yoga Tradition: Its History, Literature, Philosophy and Practice (Prescott: Hohm Press, 2008), 445-467; Rama, Swami. Choosing a Path (Honesdale: Himalayan Institute Press, 1982), 78-92.
7. Gethin, Rupert. The Buddhist Path to Awakening (Boston: Brill Academic Publishers, 1992), 156-178; Bhikkhu, Thanissaro. The Wings to Awakening: An Anthology from the Pali Canon (Barre: Dhamma Dana Publications, 1996), 203-225.

Endnotes for Chapter 14.5

1. Mullainathan, Sendhil and Eldar Shafir. Scarcity: Why Having Too Little Means So Much (New York: Times Books, 2013), 47-68.
2. Arnsten, Amy F.T. "Stress Signalling Pathways That Impair Prefrontal Cortex Structure and Function," Nature Reviews Neuroscience 10, no. 6 (2009): 410-422.

3.   Porges, Stephen W. *The Polyvagal Theory: Neurophysiological Foundations of Emotions, Attachment, Communication, and Self-regulation* (New York: Norton, 2011), 123-145.

4.   Herman, Judith. *Trauma and Recovery: The Aftermath of Violence* (New York: Basic Books, 1992), 155-174.

5.   Gollwitzer, Peter M. and Paschal Sheeran. "Implementation Intentions and Goal Achievement: A Meta-analysis of Effects and Processes," *Advances in Experimental Social Psychology* 38 (2006): 69-119.

6.   Seligman, Martin E.P. *Learned Optimism: How to Change Your Mind and Your Life* (New York: Vintage Books, 2006), 89-112.

7.   Van der Kolk, Bessel. *The Body Keeps the Score: Brain, Mind, and Body in the Healing of Trauma* (New York: Viking, 2014), 203-227.

8.   Hawkins, David R. *Power vs. Force: The Hidden Determinants of Human Behavior* (Carlsbad: Hay House, 2002), 68-89.

9.   Ginwright, Shawn. "The Future of Healing: Shifting From Trauma Informed Care to Healing Centered Engagement," *Medium*, May 31, 2018.

10. Neff, Kristin. "Self-Compassion: An Alternative Conceptualization of a Healthy Attitude Toward Oneself," *Self and Identity* 2, no. 2 (2003): 85-101.

11. Bonanno, George A. "Resilience in the Face of Potential Trauma," *Current Directions in Psychological Science* 14, no. 3 (2005): 135-138.

12. Christakis, Nicholas A. and James H. Fowler. *Connected: The Surprising Power of Our Social Networks* (New York: Little, Brown, 2009), 145-167.

13. Rilke, Rainer Maria. *Letters to a Young Poet*, trans. Stephen Mitchell (New York: Modern Library, 2001), 92.

Endnotes for Chapter 15

1.   C. G. Jung, *The Archetypes and the Collective Unconscious* (London: Routledge, 1959); A. H. Maslow, "A Theory of Human Motivation," *Psychological Review* 50, no. 4 (1943): 370–396.

2.   Robert Kegan, *In Over Our Heads: The Mental Demands of Modern Life* (Cambridge, MA: Harvard University Press, 1994).

3.   Daniel J. Siegel, *The Developing Mind: How Relationships and the Brain Interact to Shape Who We Are* (New York: Guilford Press, 2012), 71–77.

4.   Steger, M. F., Frazier, P., Oishi, S., & Kaler, M. (2006). "The Meaning in Life Questionnaire: Assessing the Presence of and Search for Meaning in Life." *Journal of Counseling Psychology* 53, no. 1 (2006): 80–93.

5.   Byung-Chul Han, *The Burnout Society* (Stanford, CA: Stanford University Press, 2015).

6.   Henri Bergson, *Time and Free Will: An Essay on the Immediate Data of Consciousness* (London: George Allen & Unwin, 1910).

7.   Salanova, M., et al. "Perceived Collective Efficacy, Subjective Well- Being and Task Performance among Electronic Work Groups." *Small Group Research* 37, no. 3 (2006): 299–320.

8.   Ibid.

9.   Ibid.

10. Steger, M. F., Frazier, P., Oishi, S., & Kaler, M. (2006). "The Meaning in Life Question-naire: Assessing the Presence of and Search for Meaning in Life." *Journal of Counseling Psychology* 53, no. 1 (2006): 80–93.

11. Georg Feuerstein, *The Yoga Tradition: Its History, Literature, Philosophy and Practice* (Prescott, AZ: Hohm Press, 2001), 369– 376.

Endnotes for Integration Guide I

1. Thayer, J. F., Hansen, A. L., Saus-Rose, E., & Johnsen, B. H. (2009). Heart rate variabil-ity, prefrontal neural function, and cognitive performance: The neurovisceral integration perspective on self-regulation, adaptation, and health. *Annals of Behavioral Medicine*, 37(2), 141-153.

2. McCraty, R., & Shaffer, F. (2015). Heart rate variability: New perspectives on physiolog-ical mechanisms, assessment of self-regulatory capacity, and health risk. *Global Advances in Health and Medicine*, 4(1), 46-61.

3. Porges, S. W. (2011). *The Polyvagal Theory: Neurophysiological foundations of emotions, attachment, communication, and self-regulation*. W.W. Norton & Company.

4. Porges, S. W. (2009). The polyvagal theory: New insights into adaptive reactions of the autonomic nervous system. *Cleveland Clinic Journal of Medicine*, 76(Suppl 2), S86-S90.

5. McCraty, R., & Atkinson, M. (2012). Resilience training program reduces physiological and psychological stress in police officers. *Global Advances in Health and Medicine*, 1(5), 44-66.

6. Csikszentmihalyi, M., & LeFevre, J. (1989). Optimal experience in work and leisure. *Jour-nal of Personality and Social Psychology*, 56(5), 815-822.

7. Dietrich, A. (2004). Neurocognitive mechanisms underlying the experience of flow. *Con-sciousness and Cognition*, 13(4), 746-761.

8. Rossi, E. L. (1991). *The 20-minute break: Using the new science of ultradian rhythms*. Jeremy P. Tarcher.

9. Nakamura, J., & Csikszentmihalyi, M. (2009). Flow theory and research. In C. R. Snyder & S. J. Lopez (Eds.), *Oxford Handbook of Positive Psychology* (pp. 195-206). Oxford Uni-versity Press.

10. Csikszentmihalyi, M. (1990). *Flow: The Psychology of Optimal Experience*. Harper & Row.

11. Kotler, S. (2014). *The Rise of Superman: Decoding the Science of Ultimate Human Perfor-mance*. Houghton Mifflin Harcourt.

12. Tang, Y. Y., Hölzel, B. K., & Posner, M. I. (2015). The neuroscience of mindfulness med-itation. *Nature Reviews Neuroscience*, 16(4), 213-225.

13. Dietrich, A. (2004). Neurocognitive mechanisms underlying the experience of flow. *Con-sciousness and Cognition*, 13(4), 746-761.

14. Lutz, A., Slagter, H. A., Dunne, J. D., & Davidson, R. J. (2008). Attention regulation and monitoring in meditation. *Trends in Cognitive Sciences*, 12(4), 163-169.

15. Draganski, B., et al. (2004). Neuroplasticity: Changes in grey matter induced by long-term learning. *Nature*, 427(6972), 311-312.

16. Kaplan, R., & Kaplan, S. (1989). *The Experience of Nature: A Psychological Perspective*. Cambridge University Press.

17. 1. Mehta, R., Zhu, R., & Cheema, A. (2012). Is noise always bad? Exploring the effects of ambient noise on creative cognition. *Journal of Consumer Research*, 39(4), 784-799.

References

Adams, J. L. (2001). *Conceptual blockbusting: A guide to better ideas* (4th ed.). Perseus Books.

Arnsten, A. F. T. (2009). Stress signalling pathways that impair prefrontal cortex structure and function. *Nature Reviews Neuroscience, 10*(6), 410-422.

Ashford, S. J., Blatt, R., & Walle, D. V. (2003). Reflections on the looking glass: A review of research on feedback-seeking behavior in organizations. *Journal of Management, 29*(6).

Baumeister, R. F., & Tierney, J. (2011). *Willpower: Rediscovering the greatest human strength*. Penguin Press.

Beaty, R. E., Benedek, M., Silvia, P. J., & Schacter, D. L. (2016). Creative cognition and brain network dynamics. *Trends in Cognitive Sciences, 20*(2), 87-95. https:// doi. org/10.1016/j.tics.2015.10.004

Beaty, R. E., et al. (2015). Creativity and the default network: A functional connectivity analysis of the creative brain at rest. *Neuropsychologia*, 64, 92-98.

Beilock, S. L., & Carr, T. H. (2001). On the fragility of skilled performance: What governs choking under pressure? *Journal of Experimental Psychology: General, 130*(4), 701-725.

Bergson, H. (1910). *Time and free will: An essay on the immediate data of consciousness.* George Allen & Unwin.

Berka, C., Levendowski, D. J., et al. (2007). EEG correlates of task engagement and mental workload in vigilance, learning, and memory tasks. *Aviation, Space, and Environmental Medicine, 78*(5), B231-B244.

Bhikkhu, T. (1996). *The wings to awakening: An anthology from the Pali Canon.* Dhamma Dana Publications.

Bonanno, G. A. (2005). Resilience in the face of potential trauma. *Current Directions in Psychological Science, 14*(3), 135-138.

Botvinick, M. M., Cohen, J. D., & Carter, C. S. (2004). Conflict monitoring and anterior cingulate cortex: An update. *Trends in Cognitive Sciences, 8*(12), 539-546.

Brewer, J. A., et al. (2011). Meditation experience is associated with differences in default mode network activity and connectivity. *Proceedings of the National Academy of Sciences, 108*(50), 20254-20259.

Brown, R. P., & Gerbarg, P. L. (2005). Sudarshan Kriya yogic breathing in the treatment of stress, anxiety, and depression. *Journal of Alternative & Complementary Medicine, 11*(4), 711-717.

Brown, R. P., & Gerbarg, P. L. (2012). *The healing power of the breath: Simple techniques to reduce stress and anxiety, enhance concentration, and balance your emotions.* Shambhala Publications.

Bryant, E. (2009). *The Yoga Sūtras of Patañjali.* North Point Press.

Cain, S. (2012). *Quiet: The power of introverts in a world that can't stop talking.* Crown.

Christakis, N. A., & Fowler, J. H. (2009). *Connected: The surprising power of our social networks.* Little, Brown.

Clark, A. (2008). *Supersizing the mind: Embodiment, action, and cognitive extension.* Oxford University Press.

Clark, A. (2016). *Surfing uncertainty: Prediction, action, and the embodied mind.* Oxford University Press.

Critchley, H. D., & Garfinkel, S. N. (2017). Interoception and emotion. *Current Opinion in Psychology, 17,* 7-14.

Csikszentmihalyi, M. (1990). *Flow: The psychology of optimal experience.* Harper & Row.

Csikszentmihalyi, M. (1996). *Creativity: Flow and the psychology of discovery and invention.* HarperCollins.

Csikszentmihalyi, M. (1997). *Finding flow: The psychology of engagement with everyday life.* Basic Books.

Csikszentmihalyi, M. (2003). *Good business: Leadership, flow, and the making of meaning.* Viking.

Csikszentmihalyi, M., & LeFevre, J. (1989). Optimal experience in work and leisure. *Journal of Personality and Social Psychology, 56*(5), 815-822.

Damasio, A. R. (1994). *Descartes' error: Emotion, reason, and the human brain.* G.P. Putnam.

Damasio, A. (1999). *The feeling of what happens: Body and emotion in the making of consciousness.* Harcourt Brace.

Decety, J. (1996). The neurophysiological basis of motor imagery. *Behavioural Brain Research, 77*(1-2), 45-52.

Deloria Jr., V. (1994). God is red: *A native view of religion.* Fulcrum Publishing.

Devrix. (2024, September 18). User attention span: The biggest challenge for marketers [2025]. Devrix.

Dietrich, A. (2004). Neurocognitive mechanisms underlying the experience of flow. *Consciousness and Cognition, 13*(4), 746-761. https://doi.org/10.1016/j.concog.2004.07.002

Duckworth, A. (2016). *Grit: The power of passion and perseverance.* Scribner.

Dupuy, O., et al. (2018). An evidence-based approach for choosing post-exercise recovery techniques to reduce markers of muscle damage, soreness, fatigue, and inflammation. *Frontiers in Physiology, 9,* 403.

Elliott, S., & Edmonson, D. (2005). *The new science of breath*. Coherence Press.

Ericsson, K. A., Krampe, R. T., & Tesch-Römer, C. (1993). The role of deliberate practice in the acquisition of expert performance. *Psychological Review, 100*(3), 363- 406.

Farb, N., Daubenmier, J., Price, C. J., Gard, T., Kerr, C., et al. (2015). *Interoception, contemplative practice, and health. Frontiers in Psychology*, 6, 763.

Feuerstein, G. (2001). *The Yoga tradition: Its history, literature, philosophy and practice*. Hohm Press.

Feuerstein, G. (2008). *The Yoga tradition: Its history, literature, philosophy and practice*. Hohm Press.

Flowly. (n.d.). Relaxing in flow state: How flow can regulate your nervous system. Flowly.

Forbes. (2025, February 8). Job burnout at 66% in 2025, new study shows. *Forbes*.

Fox, K. C. R., Spreng, R. N., Ellamil, M., Andrews-Hanna, J. R., & Christoff, K. (2015). The human default network: A review and synthesis. *NeuroImage, 102*(Pt 2), 1–15. https://doi.org/10.1016/j.neuroimage.2013.05.060

Fredrickson, B. L. (2004). The broaden-and-build theory of positive emotions. *Philosophical Transactions of the Royal Society B: Biological Sciences, 359*(1449), 1367–1377. https://doi.org/10.1098/rstb.2004.1512

Freelancers Union, & Upwork. (2020). *Freelancing in America: 2020*. Upwork.

Frontiers in Integrative Neuroscience. (n.d.). *Polyvagal theory: A science of safety*. Frontiers Media.

Gallese, V., & Lakoff, G. (2005). The brain's concepts: The role of the sensory-motor system in conceptual knowledge. *Cognitive Neuropsychology, 22*(3–4), 455–479. https://doi.org/10.1080/02643290442000310

Gethin, R. (1992). *The Buddhist path to awakening*. Brill Academic Publishers.

Ginwright, S. (2018, May 31). The future of healing: Shifting from trauma informed care to healing centered engagement. *Medium*.

Golden Steps ABA. (2025, March 4). Average human attention span (statistics). Golden Steps ABA.

Gollwitzer, P. M., & Sheeran, P. (2006). Implementation intentions and goal achievement: A meta-analysis of effects and processes. *Advances in Experimental Social Psychology*, 38, 69-119.

Gottman, J. M., & Silver, N. (2015). *The seven principles for making marriage work*. Harmony.

Goyal, M., et al. (2014). Meditation programs for psychological stress and well- being: A systematic review and meta-analysis. *JAMA Internal Medicine, 174*(3), 357- 368.

Grant, A. M. (2014). The solution-focused advice trap. *Psychology Today*.

Grant, A. (2021). *Think again: The power of knowing what you don't know*. Viking.

Han, B.-C. (2015). *The burnout society*. Stanford University Press.

Harmat, L., de Manzano, Ö., Theorell, T., & Ullén, F. (2015). Physiological correlates of the flow experience during computer game playing. International Journal of Psychophysiology, 97(1), 1-7.

Harris, R. J., O'Boyle, M. W., & Sutton, K. C. (2017). The neural basis of flow experience. *Neuroscience and Biobehavioral Reviews*, 75, 559-568. https://doi. org/ 10.1016/j.neubiorev.2017.01.025

Hasson, U., et al. (2012). Brain-to-brain coupling: A mechanism for creating and sharing a social world. *Trends in Cognitive Sciences, 16*(2).

Hawkins, D. R. (2002). *Power vs. force: The hidden determinants of human behavior*. Hay House.

Hebb, D. O. (1949). *The organization of behavior: A neuropsychological theory*. Wiley.

Helm, J. L., et al. (2012). Assessing cross-partner associations in physiological responses via coupled oscillator models. *Emotion, 12*(4), 748-762.

Herman, J. (1992). *Trauma and recovery: The aftermath of violence*. Basic Books.

Hohwy, J. (2013). *The predictive mind*. Oxford University Press.

Hölzel, B. K., Carmody, J., Vangel, M., et al. (2011). Mindfulness practice leads to increases in regional brain gray matter density. *Psychiatry Research: Neuroimaging, 191*(1), 36-43.

Huberman, A. (2022). How to optimize your work and rest cycles. *Huberman Lab Podcast*.

Huberman, Andrew. "Using Light for Health." *Huberman Lab Newsletter*, February 2025. https://www.hubermanlab.com/newsletter/using-light-for-health.

Iacoboni, M. (2008). *Mirroring people: The science of empathy and how we connect with others*. Farrar, Straus and Giroux.

Jerath, R., Edry, J. W., Barnes, V. A., & Jerath, V. (2006). Physiology of long pranayamic breathing: Neural respiratory elements may provide a mechanism that explains how slow deep breathing shifts the autonomic nervous system. *Medical Hypotheses, 67*(3), 566-571.

Jung, C. G. (1959). *The archetypes and the collective unconscious*. Routledge.

Kahneman, D. (1973). *Attention and effort*. Prentice Hall.

Kaplan, S. (1995). The restorative benefits of nature. *Journal of Environmental Psychology*, 15, 169-182.

Kaufman, S. B. (2013). *Ungifted: Intelligence redefined*. Basic Books.

Kaufman, S. B., & Gregoire, C. (2016). *Wired to create: Unraveling the mysteries of the creative mind*. Perigee Books.

Kegan, R. (1994). *In over our heads: The mental demands of modern life*. Harvard University Press.

Keysers, C., & Gazzola, V. (2010). Social neuroscience: Mirror neurons recorded in humans. *Current Biology, 20*(8), R353-R354.

Kleitman, N. (1963). *Sleep and wakefulness.* University of Chicago Press.

Kleitman, N. (1982). Basic rest-activity cycle—22 years later. *Sleep, 5*(4), 311-317.

Kosslyn, S. M., et al. (2001). Neural foundations of imagery. *Nature Reviews Neuroscience, 2*(9), 635-642.

Kotler, S. (2014). *The rise of Superman: Decoding the science of ultimate human performance.* Houghton Mifflin Harcourt.

Kotler, S., & Wheal, J. (2017). *Stealing fire: How Silicon Valley, the Navy SEALs, and maverick scientists are revolutionizing the way we live and work.* Dey Street Books.

Kounios, J., & Beeman, M. (2015). *The eureka factor: Aha moments, creative insight, and the brain.* Random House.

Lally, P., et al. (2010). How are habits formed: Modelling habit formation in the real world. *European Journal of Social Psychology, 40*(6), 998-1009.

Landhäußer, A., & Keller, J. (2012). Flow and its affective, cognitive, and performance-related consequences. In S. Engeser (Ed.), *Advances in flow research* (pp. 65-85). Springer.

LAOP Center. (2025, May 20). *Anxiety statistics in the United States in 2025.* LAOP Center.

Laozi. (1997). *Tao Te Ching* (D. C. Lau, Trans.). Penguin Classics. (Original work published ca. 6th century BCE).

Lazar, S. W., et al. (2005). Meditation experience is associated with increased cortical thickness. *NeuroReport, 16*(17), 1893-1897.

LeDoux, J. (1996). *The emotional brain: The mysterious underpinnings of emotional life.* Simon & Schuster.

Lehrer, J. (2012). *Imagine: How creativity works.* Houghton Mifflin Harcourt.

Lehrer, P. M., Vaschillo, E., & Vaschillo, B. (2000). Resonant frequency biofeedback training to increase cardiac variability: Rationale and manual for training. *Applied Psychophysiology and Biofeedback, 25*(3), 177-191.

Levenson, R. W., & Gottman, J. M. (1983). Marital interaction: Physiological linkage and affective exchange. *Journal of Personality and Social Psychology, 45*(3).

Malesic, J. (2022). *The end of burnout: Why work drains us and how to build better lives.* University of California Press.

Maquet, P., Smith, C., & Stickgold, R. (2005). *Sleep and brain plasticity.* Oxford University Press.

Mark, G. (2023). *Attention span: A groundbreaking way to restore balance, happiness and productivity.* Hanover Square Press.

Mark, G., Gudith, D., & Klocke, U. (2008). The cost of interrupted work: More speed and stress. *Proceedings of the SIGCHI Conference on Human Factors in Computing Systems*, 107-110.

Maslach, C., Leiter, M., & Schaufeli, W. (2001). Measuring burnout. *Annual Review of Psychology, 52,* 397-422.

Maslow, A. H. (1943). A theory of human motivation. *Psychological Review, 50*(4), 370-396.

Mauri, M., et al. (2011). Why is Facebook so successful? Psychophysiological measures describe a core flow state while using Facebook. *Cyberpsychology, Behavior, and Social Networking, 14*(10), 577-583. https://doi.org/10.1089/cyber.2010.0250

McCraty, R. (2003). *The energetic heart: Bioelectromagnetic interactions within and between people.* HeartMath Research Center Publication, No. 03-015, 1-22.

McCraty, R., & Childre, D. (2010). Coherence: Bridging personal, social, and global health. *Alternative Therapies in Health and Medicine, 16*(4), 10-24.

McGaugh, J. L. (2004). The amygdala modulates the consolidation of memories of emotionally arousing experiences. *Annual Review of Neuroscience, 27,* 1-28.

McKinsey Global Institute. (2012). *The social economy: Unlocking value and productivity through social technologies.* McKinsey & Company.

McNeill, W. H. (1996). *The pursuit of power: Technology, armed force, and society since A.D. 1000.* University of Chicago Press.

Microsoft. (2025, June 17). *New Microsoft study reveals the rise of the 'infinite workday'.* Microsoft.

Mindful Ecotourism. (n.d.). *Deep embodiment and the flow of embodied awareness.* Mindful Ecotourism.

Moneta, G. B., & Csikszentmihalyi, M. (1996). The effect of perceived challenges and skills on the quality of subjective experience. *Journal of Personality, 64*(2), 275-310.

Mullainathan, S., & Shafir, E. (2013). *Scarcity: Why having too little means so much.* Times Books.

Nakamura, J., & Csikszentmihalyi, M. (2002). The concept of flow. In C. R. Snyder & S. J. Lopez (Eds.), *Handbook of positive psychology* (pp. 89-105). Oxford University Press.

Nakamura, J., & Csikszentmihalyi, M. (2009). Flow theory and research. In C. R. Snyder & S. J. Lopez (Eds.), *Oxford handbook of positive psychology* (pp. 195-206). Oxford University Press.

Nakamura, J., & Csikszentmihalyi, M. (2014). The concept of flow. In M. Csikszentmihalyi (Ed.), *Flow and the foundations of positive psychology* (pp. 239-263). Springer.

Nature. (n.d.). Enhancing interoceptive sensibility through exteroceptive techniques. *Nature.*

Neff, K. (2003). Self-compassion: An alternative conceptualization of a healthy attitude toward oneself. *Self and Identity, 2*(2), 85-101.

New York Post. (2025, May 17). Attention spans are dropping, research shows: How to focus. *New York Post.*

Newport, C. (2016). *Deep work: Rules for focused success in a distracted world.* Grand Central Publishing.

Nickerson, R. S. (1998). Confirmation bias: A ubiquitous phenomenon in many guises. *Review of General Psychology, 2*(2).

Norway Cup. (n.d.). *About the Norway Cup.* Accessed July 16, 2025.

Okonek, K. (n.d.). Flow triggers: Deep embodiment.

Oppezzo, M., & Schwartz, D. L. (2014). Give your ideas some legs: The positive effect of walking on creative thinking. *Journal of Experimental Psychology: Learning, Memory, and Cognition, 40*(4), 1142-1152. https://doi.org/10.1037/a0036577

Patañjali. (circa 400 CE). *Yoga Sutras of Patañjali.* (Various translators).

Pentland, A. S. (2012). The new science of building great teams. *Harvard Business Review, 90*(4).

Polyvagal Institute. (n.d.). *What is polyvagal theory?* Polyvagal Institute.

Porges, S. W. (2011). *The polyvagal theory: Neurophysiological foundations of emotions, attachment, communication, and self-regulation.* W.W. Norton & Company.

Rama, S. (1982). *Choosing a path.* Himalayan Institute Press.

Rein, G., et al. (1995). Effects of coherent heart rhythms on long-term DNA winding. *Journal of Biological Physics, 21*(3), 151-160.

Rheinberg, F., Engeser, S., & Vollmeyer, R. (2022). A scoping review of flow research. *Frontiers in Psychology, 13*, Article 815665. https://doi.org/10.3389/fpsyg.2022.815665

Rilke, R. M. (2001). *Letters to a young poet* (S. Mitchell, Trans.). Modern Library.

Robinson, B. (2025, February 8). Job burnout at 66% in 2025, new study shows. *Forbes.*

Rosen, D., Kounios, J., & Beaty, R. E. (2024). Creative flow as optimized processing: Evidence from brain network dynamics. *Neuropsychologia, 190*, Article 108582. https://doi.org/10.1016/j.neuropsychologia.2024.108582

Rossi, E. (1991). *Ultradian rhythms in life processes: An introduction to chronobiology.* Springer.

Rubinstein, J. S., Meyer, D. E., & Evans, J. E. (2001). Executive control of cognitive processes in task switching. *Journal of Experimental Psychology: Human Perception and Performance, 27*(4), 763-797.

Salanova, M., et al. (2006). Perceived collective efficacy, subjective well-being and task performance among electronic work groups. *Small Group Research, 37*(3), 299-330.

Samba Recovery. (2025, June 25). *Average human attention span statistics & facts [2024]*. Samba Recovery.

Sawyer, R. K. (2007). *Group genius: The creative power of collaboration*. Basic Books.

Sawyer, K. (2017). *Group genius: The creative power of collaboration* (2nd ed.). Basic Books.

Schaffer, O. (2013). *Crafting fun user experiences: A method to facilitate flow*. Human Factors International White Paper.

Schimmel, A. (1975). *Mystical dimensions of Islam*. University of North Carolina Press.

Schippers, M. C., Homan, A. C., & van Knippenberg, D. (2020). To reflect or not to reflect: Prior team performance as a boundary condition of the effects of reflexivity on learning and final team performance. *European Journal of Work and Organizational Psychology, 29*(2), 218-234.

Seligman, M. E. P. (2006). *Learned optimism: How to change your mind and your life*. Vintage Books.

Shafran, R., Cooper, Z., & Fairburn, C. G. (2002). Clinical perfectionism: A cognitive-behavioural analysis. *Behaviour Research and Therapy, 40*(7), 773-791.

Siegel, D. J. (2012). *The developing mind: How relationships and the brain interact to shape who we are*. Guilford Press.

SingleCare. (2025, January 24). *Anxiety statistics 2025*. SingleCare.

Steger, M. F., Frazier, P., Oishi, S., & Kaler, M. (2006). The Meaning in Life Questionnaire: Assessing the presence of and search for meaning in life. *Journal of Counseling Psychology, 53*(1), 80-93.

Stokes, P. D. (2006). Creativity from constraints. *Psychology of Aesthetics, Creativity, and the Arts, 2*(3), 167-172.

Superhuman Blog. (2025, June 11). *Executive burnout statistics 2025: A look into the leadership crisis*. Superhuman.

Suzuki, S. (1970). *Zen mind, beginner's mind*. Weatherhill.

Swann, C., Keegan, R. J., Piggott, D., & Schweickle, M. J. (2017). The zones: A systematic review of qualitative studies on flow and clutch states in sport. *Sport, Exercise, and Performance Psychology, 6*(4), 372-392.

Tang, Y. Y., Hölzel, B. K., & Posner, M. I. (2015). The neuroscience of mindfulness meditation. *Nature Reviews Neuroscience, 16*(4), 213-225.

Tang, Y. Y., Ma, Y., Wang, J., Fan, Y., Feng, S., Lu, Q., & Posner, M. I. (2007). Short-term meditation training improves attention and self-regulation. *Proceedings of the National Academy of Sciences, 104*(43), 17152-17156.

Taylor, J. (1995). A conceptual model for integrating athletes' needs and sports psychology interventions. *The Sport Psychologist, 9*(3), 339-357.

Thaut, M. H. (2005). *Rhythm, music, and the brain: Scientific foundations and clinical applications.* Routledge.

Thayer, J. F., Hansen, A. L., Saus-Rose, E., & Johnsen, B. H. (2009). Heart rate variability, prefrontal neural function, and cognitive performance: The neurovisceral integration perspective on self-regulation, adaptation, and health. *Annals of Behavioral Medicine, 37*(2), 141-153.

The Rooted Way. (2025, April 8). *Executive burnout in 2025: A comprehensive analysis.* The Rooted Way.

TherapyRoute.com. (2025, June 27). *Anxiety: 2025 statistics.* TherapyRoute.com

Ulrich, M., Keller, J., & Grön, G. (2020). Go with the flow: A neuroscientific view on being fully engaged. *Psychological Research, 85*(6), 1471-1487. https://doi.org/10.1007/s00426-020-01359-8

Van der Kolk, B. (2014). *The body keeps the score: Brain, mind, and body in the healing of trauma.* Viking.

Van der Linden, D., et al. (2021). The neuroscience of the flow state: Involvement of the locus coeruleus-norepinephrine system. *Frontiers in Psychology, 12*, Article 645498. https://doi.org/10.3389/fpsyg.2021.645498

Varela, F. J., Thompson, E., & Rosch, E. (1991). *The embodied mind: Cognitive science and human experience.* MIT Press.

Villemure, C., & Bushnell, M. C. (2015). Neurophysiological and neurocognitive mechanisms underlying the effects of yoga-based practices: Towards a comprehensive theoretical framework. *Frontiers in Human Neuroscience, 9*, Article 235. https://doi.org/10.3389/fnhum.2015.00235

Walker, M. (2017). *Why we sleep: Unlocking the power of sleep and dreams.* Scribner.

Wallas, G. (1926). *The art of thought.* Harcourt, Brace and Company.

Ward, A. F., Duke, K., Gneezy, A., & Bos, M. W. (2017). Brain drain: The mere presence of one's own smartphone reduces available cognitive capacity. *Journal of the Association for Consumer Research, 2*(2).

Wilson, G. (2010). The infomania study. Commissioned by Hewlett-Packard. Wiltermuth, S. S., & Heath, C. (2009). Synchrony and cooperation. *Psychological Science, 20*(1): 1-5.

cloudHQ. (2025, April 22). *Workplace email statistics 2025: Usage, productivity, trends.* cloudHQ.

World Health Organization. (2022, March 2). *COVID-19 pandemic triggers 25% increase in prevalence of anxiety and depression worldwide.* World Health Organization.

Yogananda, P. (1946). *Autobiography of a yogi.* Self-Realization Fellowship.

Zeidan, F., et al. (2010). Mindfulness meditation improves cognition: Evidence of brief mental training. *Consciousness and Cognition, 19*(2), 597-605.

Further Reading

Core Flow Theory
Mihaly Csikszentmihalyi - Flow: The Psychology of Optimal Experience
Susan A. Jackson & Mihaly Csikszentmihalyi - Flow in Sports

Neuroscience & Peak Performance
Daniel Kahneman - Thinking, Fast and Slow
Steven Kotler - The Art of Impossible

Mindfulness & Practice
Jon Kabat-Zinn - Wherever You Go, There You Are
Thich Nhat Hanh - The Miracle of Mindfulness
W. Timothy Gallwey - The Inner Game of Tennis

Creativity & Innovation
Julia Cameron - The Artist's Way
Steven Pressfield - The War of Art

Deep Work & Productivity
Cal Newport - Deep Work
Daniel H. Pink - Drive

Trauma & Resilience
Bessel van der Kolk - The Body Keeps the Score
Kelly McGonigal - The Upside of Stress

Philosophy & Meaning
Viktor E. Frankl - Man's Search for Meaning
Alan Watts - The Way of Zen
Eckhart Tolle - The Power of Now

About the Author

Carolyn Bentley Wells is a published researcher, flow expert, and author of *The Transformative Flow*, endorsed by Harvard's Dr. Irene Pepperberg as offering "a clear path to achieve a life of harmonic flow."

Her journey into the science of optimal experience began in Dr. Pepperberg's animal cognition lab, where she worked directly with Alex, the world-renowned African Grey parrot whose intelligence reshaped our understanding of consciousness. Combined with field research in Cameroon's rainforests, this work revealed universal patterns of peak performance that transcend species.

Carolyn later applied these principles at Fortune 50 ALCOA, as a Health & Safety Manager, helping achieve a 70% reduction in injury rates while strengthening team performance—extending the transformational model documented in Harvard Business School's most-studied organizational change case.

From representing the USA in international soccer tournaments abroad to guiding clients into authentic flow states as a multicultural destination wedding photographer, Carolyn bridges athletic excellence, scientific research, corporate leadership, and ancient wisdom.

She holds degrees in Biochemistry and Environmental Science from The University of Arizona and formal training in yoga therapy and performance psychology. As founder of Our Green Moment LLC and creator of The Green Moment™ methodology, she helps individuals and organizations and individuals integrate neuroscience, seasonal wisdom, and practical flow principles for sustainable excellence.

Carolyn leads flow workshops and The 108 Event experiences from her base in Greater Phoenix, Arizona, where she continues to research and write at the intersection of peak performance, resilience, and conscious living.

Connect: carolynbentleywells.com

Thank You for Reading

The practice begins now.

Keep the Flow Alive

Discover your unique Flow Fingerprint and receive a personalized practice guide at: **thetransformativeflow.com/quiz**

Join monthly micro-challenges and connect with the community.

Share the Flow

If this book made a difference for you, one of the most meaningful ways to support it is to leave a short review on Amazon, Goodreads, BookBub, or your local bookstore's website. Even a single sentence helps other readers discover this work.

Return to Rhythm

thetransformativeflow.com

Return to rhythm.

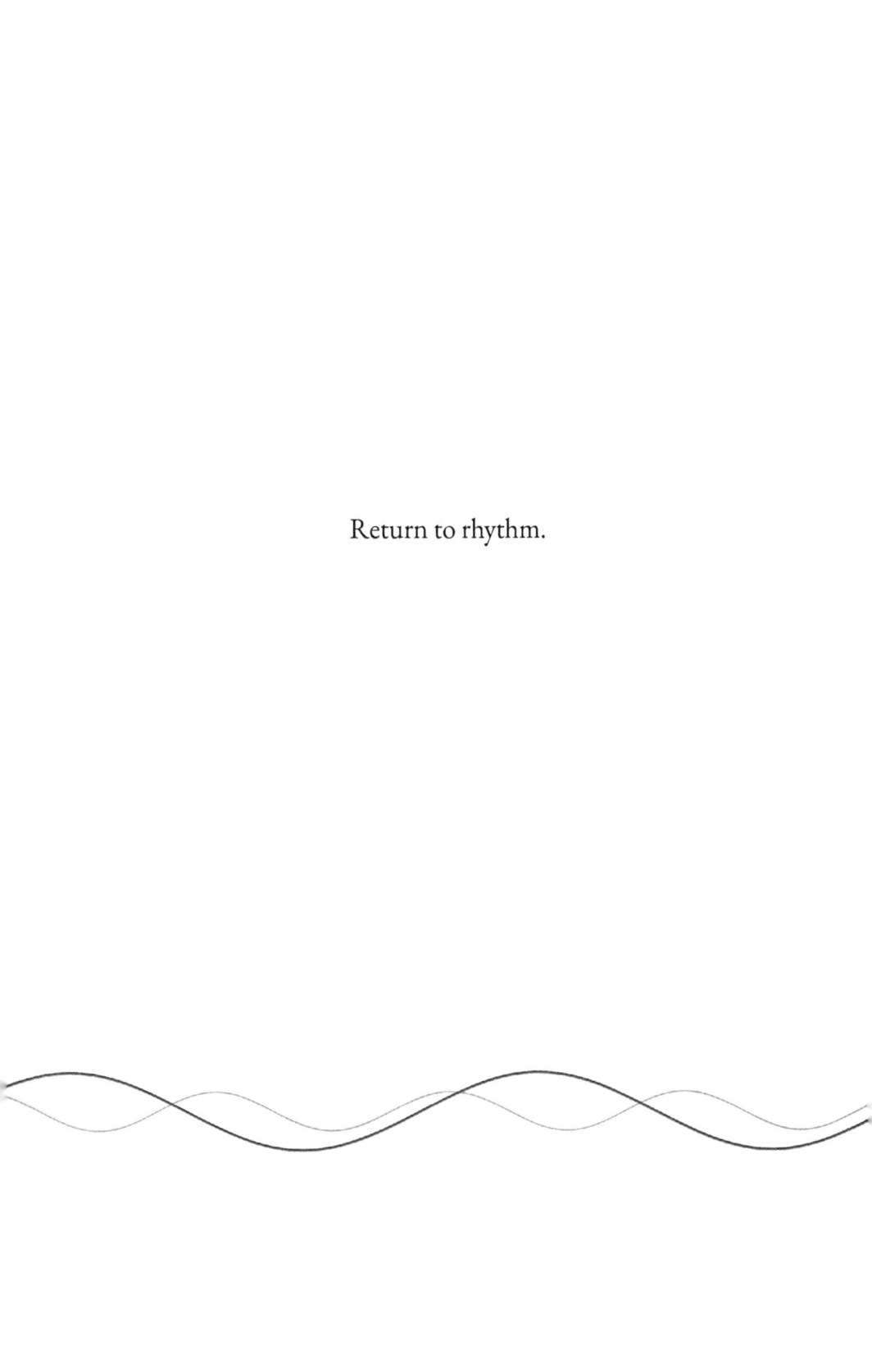